Claudio Baraldi, Giancarlo Corsi, Elena Esposito
Unlocking Luhmann

BiUP General

Claudio Baraldi published several works in international books and journals on communication systems. His research concerns interaction systems related to facilitation of children's participation, interlinguistic and intercultural mediation, conflict management.

Giancarlo Corsi worked and published intensely on the theory of social systems, public opinion and communication media, education, career and social inclusion. His current research deals with the relationship between public sphere, mass media, and new communication technologies.

Elena Esposito published many works on the theory of social systems, media theory, memory theory, and sociology of financial markets. Her current research on algorithmic prediction is supported by a five-year Advanced Grant from the European Research Council.

Claudio Baraldi, Giancarlo Corsi, Elena Esposito
Unlocking Luhmann
A Keyword Introduction to Systems Theory

Translation by Katherine Walker

[transcript]

Bibliographic information published by the Deutsche Nationalbibliothek
The Deutsche Nationalbibliothek lists this publication in the Deutsche Nationalbibliografie; detailed bibliographic data are available in the Internet at http://dnb.d-nb.de

This work is licensed under the Creative Commons Attribution-NoDerivatives 4.0 (BY-ND) license, which means that the text may be shared and redistributed, provided credit is given to the author, but may not be remixed, transformed or build upon. For details go to http://creativecommons.org/licenses/by-nd/4.0/
To create an adaptation, translation, or derivative of the original work, further permission is required and can be obtained by contacting rights@transcript-publishing.com
Creative Commons license terms for re-use do not apply to any content (such as graphs, figures, photos, excerpts, etc.) not original to the Open Access publication and further permission may be required from the rights holder. The obligation to research and clear permission lies solely with the party re-using the material.

© 2021 Bielefeld University Press
An Imprint of transcript Verlag
http://www.bielefeld-university-press.de

Cover layout: Maria Arndt, Bielefeld
Printed by Majuskel Medienproduktion GmbH, Wetzlar
Print-ISBN 978-3-8376-5674-9
PDF-ISBN 978-3-8394-5674-3
https://doi.org/10.14361/9783839456743

Printed on permanent acid-free text paper.

Contents

Preface to the English Edition
Claudio Baraldi, Giancarlo Corsi and Elena Esposito 9

Foreword to the Italian Edition
Niklas Luhmann 13

Introduction 17

Ways to Read this Book 21

Art System (*Kunstsystem*) 27

Asymmetrization (*Asymmetrisierung*) 31

Attribution (*Zurechnung*) 35

Autopoiesis 37

Code 41

Communication (*Kommunikation*) 45

Complexity (*Komplexität*) 49

Conflict (*Konflikt*) 53

Constructivism (*Konstruktivismus*) 57

Differentiation (*Differenzierung/Ausdifferenzierung*) 61

Differentiation of Society (*Differenzierung der Gesellschaft*) 65

Dissemination Media (*Verbreitungsmedien*) 71

Double Contingency (*Doppelte Kontingenz*) 75

Economic System (*Wirtschaftssystem*) 79

Education System (*Erziehungssystem*) 83

Event (*Ereignis*) 87

Evolution 91

Expectations (*Erwartungen*) 95

Functional Analysis (*Funktionale Analyse*) 99

Identity/Difference (*Identität/Differenz*) 101

Inclusion/Exclusion (*Inklusion/Exklusion*) 105

Information 109

Interaction (*Interaktion*) 111

Interpenetration and Structural Coupling (*Interpenetration und strukturelle Kopplung*) 115

Language (*Sprache*) 121

Legal System (*Rechtssystem*) 125

Love (*Liebe*) 129

Mass media (*Massenmedien*) 133

Meaning (*Sinn*) 137

Meaning Dimensions (*Sinndimensionen*) 141

Medical System (*Krankensystem*) 145

Medium/Form 149

Morality (*Moral*) 151

Negation 155

Operation/Observation (*Operation/Beobachtung*) 157

Organization (*Organisation*) 163

Paradox (*Paradoxie*) 167

Political System (*Politisches System*) 171

Power (*Macht*) 175

Process (*Prozess*) 179

Program (*Programm*) 181

Property/Money (*Eigentum/Geld*) 185

Protest 187

Psychic Systems (*Psychische Systeme*) 189

Rationality (*Rationalität*) 191

Redundancy/Variety (*Redundanz/Varietät*) 193

Re-entry 195

Religious System (*Religionssystem*) 197

Risk/Danger (*Risiko/Gefahr*) 201

Scientific System (*Wissenschaftssystem*) 205

Self-description (*Selbstbeschreibung*) 209

Self-Reference (*Selbstreferenz*) 213

Semantics (*Semantik*) 217

Social System (*Soziales System*) 221

Society (*Gesellschaft*) 223

Sociological Enlightenment (*Soziologische Aufklärung*) 225

Structure (*Struktur*) 227

Symbolically Generalized Media (*Symbolisch generalisierte Kommunikationsmedien*) 229

System/Environment (*System/Umwelt*) 235

System of Families (*System der Familien*) 239

Time (*Zeit*) 243

Truth (*Wahrheit*) 247

Values (*Werte*) 251

World (*Welt*) 253

World Society (*Weltgesellschaft*) 255

List of Luhmann's works 259

Preface to the English Edition

Claudio Baraldi, Giancarlo Corsi and Elena Esposito

The first edition of this book appeared in 1989 as a working tool for our students at the University of Urbino in Italy. In the reception of Niklas Luhmann's theory there is an interesting analogy between the situation in Italy in the 1980s and 1990s and the current situation of the English-speaking world: a growing interest in the theory and an increasing number of translations, powered by circles of enthusiastic scholars, but at the same time a widespread difficulty to familiarize with it, that has so far hindered a mainstream recognition.

The situation is certainly connected with the characteristics of the theory itself, which is very complex and articulated, built on a network of concepts mutually related and referring to each other. Moreover, the theory is developed in many books on topics that are often distant from each other (law and arts, mass media or economy, religion, politics, general systems theory, and more), yet always presupposing the entire theoretical construction and often referring to arguments presented in other texts. In Italy in those years, as in the English-speaking world today, there was an additional difficulty: not all books of Luhmann's large production had been translated into Italian (or now English), so even the best-intentioned scholar could not access all the notions she needed.

But the challenges of reading Luhmann's work are not limited to those caused by the lack of translations. All scholars who are entering the complex world of systems theory—inside and often also outside sociology—are confronted with them. In meeting these needs, the book has not only been translated into several languages (Spanish, Japanese, Portuguese and Korean) but has also become a much quoted classic in Germany itself.

It has been several years, but from a certain point of view the text is even more relevant today, in a context like that of the present English-speaking research, where there is widespread distrust and lack of patience for big theoretical constructs and often simply for long and complex books—and at the same time there is a resurgence of the need of general theory to address more and more extended and interconnected issues (just think of topics like new media, globalization or ecological challenges). In that context, today one writes and reads differently than three or four decades ago, when the majority of Luhmann's works were written. Sociology frequently bases its agenda on mainstream themes of public interest rather than on conceptual orientation, and in general there is little willingness to engage with a theory that reveals its utility only after a quite high competence threshold—but then opens an incomparable space of stimuli, references and research opportunities.

Precisely because of its complexity, there are many introductions to Luhmann's theory. This book, however, has peculiar characteristics that distinguish it from alternative proposals. Using the form of a keyword introduction, i.e. a glossary, the text does not introduce the theory by simplifying it or offering shortcuts. The book is explicitly constructed as a working tool to make the theory more accessible while maintaining its complexity and does not aim at replacing the reading of Luhmann's work. The glossary provides support to deal more productively with it, without being obstructed by knowledge gaps or by the reference to concepts presented elsewhere—but also without doing violence to the complexity and the careful articulation of the theory of social systems.

In his introduction to the Italian edition (also included in this book) Luhmann himself points to these features of our glossary. Current sociology, he argues, requires a theoretical frame constructed in a heterarchical and reticular way, with a complex network of references between concepts that get transformed in the very connection.

The reticular structure of the theory is preserved in the glossary by a series of internal cross-references between the various items, with the effect that the book appears as a different text at each reading, according to the selected references and the resulting connections. To facilitate the understanding of the links between items, moreover, the text has been integrated with seven "Ways to Read this Book" that indicate privileged connections between concepts and groups of concepts, according with thematic affinities or structural reasons.

After so many years, the meaning of this glossary can be extended to not only encourage working *with* systems theory, but also working *on* sociological theory. Luhmann himself presented his systems theory as a proposal in search of competitors, inviting scholars to develop and compare alternatives.

Showing the ambitious conceptual structure of his theory could be useful to stimulate experimentations starting with different distinctions.

The English version of the glossary differs slightly from the Italian and German editions. We introduced some concepts that have become increasingly important in the recent discourse (such as protest and mass media) and changed the content of some other entries, more linked to the debate of the 1980s.

We would like to thank the Niklas Luhmann-Archiv at Bielefeld University, in particular Johannes Schmidt, for his support in our search for the English translations of Luhmann's texts and for his work on a systematization of Luhmann's publications and of the research about his theory.

Modena and Reggio Emilia, June 2020

Foreword to the Italian Edition

Niklas Luhmann

As the current century draws to a close, sociology finds itself confronted with tasks of a new kind. The society that we observe is no longer that of Marx, of Weber, of Durkheim. Still less is it that of the Enlightenment or the French Revolution. More than ever before, the past has lost its authority—even in terms of the value criteria that were once fundamental to the pursuit of rationality. And more than ever before, perhaps for exactly this reason, it has become uncertain what kind of future awaits us. Matters are little changed by the application of specific scientific methods, of explanation and prognosis. However, it should be a least possible to appropriately describe what we face.

In many respects, we are and remain beholden to the methods that generated the problems. One cannot simply abandon economic growth or the regulatory state, long-term education in schools or ever more successful scientific research, technologies or therapies of various types when one perceives how many resulting problems arise from them. At the same time, confidence is waning in the solutions on offer. Planners bemoan the complexity of the situation and the improbability of achieving successful control. Others complain the multiplicity in postmodern discourse, the unavoidable relativity of all perspectives, the new lack of transparency. However, if one takes these complaints literally, one might also discover new opportunities. If now the world can be described only as polycontextural and if the methods of the description of science, as well as those of art, determine what can be made visible or invisible, then right now it is possible to insist, according to the method of description each time chosen, on theoretical rigor, on precision and on elaborate awareness of one's construction. Right a new accuracy and a new responsibility for theoretical tools are possible. One can easily give up the attitude to see the world correctly and thereby the temptation to teach one's truth to others. There is neither a non-controversial location for such a representation of society within society, nor a single correct method of description. But it is for exactly this reason that one must be mindful of making the methods of description, the construction of theory, transparent: in order that others can observe how to observe the world when it is observed in this way. A theory that offers a description of society must, for its part, be exposed to observation and description, and supply what is necessary for this.

The leads neither to a form of decisionism, nor to an "anything goes" approach. Even when one could arbitrarily select a starting point, the demands of theory construction would very soon restrict the space for pursuing alternative possibilities. As soon as everything is only a matter of choice, considering other choices very quickly reduces convenience. The construction is fixed in place. One may make changes at any point, since there is neither nature nor necessity, but each variation has consequences in the system; in principle it should be possible to control such consequences, and this can be illustrated by a work of art, but also by the pragmatics of juridical argumentation.

An overview of the state of the discipline shows that sociology is currently not ready for such a task. From the methodological point of view, the problem does not lie in the domain of empirical research. What is crucial is not the collection of new data but rather a new way of dealing with what one already knows. Empiricism may work out a program to fill in the gaps, but this is not the primary concern. Even the classics, recognizable by the vultures circling above their carcasses, offer little help. To be sure, the theoretical program of the sociological classics is, as ever, exemplary and has not been matched yet; however, the methods are hardly adequate for today's tasks. One would need to do similar things in a completely different way.

However, against the background of the past isolation of the discipline, one can focus more on the new developments of interdisciplinary theoretical elaboration. One might also speak of transdisciplinary fields and refer, for instance, to system theory, cybernetics, biological epistemology, evolutionary theory, or communication theory. Here, truly fascinating theoretical developments are currently taking place and sociology should try them out for itself. Yet this cannot occur neither as metaphorical discourses, nor through analogical deductions. In sociology, external theories do not prove anything. What is involved, though, is a kind of circular learning, a selective acquisition of experiences that are based on approaches to theory building, already exploited and already present in sociology. Currently, the best point of departure is offered, in my opinion, by the differentiation of system and environment, and it is exactly this difference which is also particularly relevant to the ecological issues in contemporary society.

The difficulties of such an undertaking arise from many sources. On the one hand, they stem from the level of abstraction of the concepts and, on the other, from the interdisciplinary nature of the resources. Above all, however, they stem from the architecture of the theory itself, which is not constructed hierarchically, but heterarchically; it cannot be viewed from a single point, but is connected in the form of a network. There are neither *a priori* certainties, nor a founding principle; rather, all concepts can be explained only as moments of differences, as the marking of differences and as points of departure for the opening and preforming of further options.

This theoretical architecture cannot be adequately made explicit in writing books as monographs, since they lack the necessary linearity that the text would demand. All the more meritorious, then, is the attempt by Claudio Baraldi, Giancarlo Corsi and Elena Esposito to represent the central decisions of the theory in the form of a glossary. In so doing, it may be that the often difficult and sometimes inadequate translations from German into Italian can be, if not resolved, then at least made visible. Above all, however, the form of the glossary, which at first appears simply as a list of keywords and usable as a dictionary, is a remarkable technique for representing theory. Since it is exactly the breaking down of the theory into individual concepts that brings into focus the problem of recombination—as if something that grew more or less naturally were brought to a genetic laboratory and should there be tested for the range of possible new combinations. The care with which the texts have been developed for the keywords means that the glossary should find ample opportunities for productive application, and as such consideration of the "original intent" (as it is called in US constitutional law) should not be the sole decisive perspective.

Bielefeld, November 1989.

Introduction

This book is designed as a tool. The rather unusual idea of writing a companion text to a theory at the center of current intellectual debate resulted from the authors' impression that certain circumstances were getting in the way of properly engaging with the theory. These circumstances are linked to its specific characteristics and career, and make it more difficult to approach the theory. This glossary attempts to make the initial approach easier.

The difficulties in the theoretical discussion can be primarily traced back to the internal structuring of Niklas Luhmann's theory. Above all, this theory is characterized by a very high level of complexity, which, on the one hand, is expressed in a large number of concepts that must be mastered in order to engage in the interplay of their differences. On the other hand—and this is the theoretically interesting aspect—the complexity is also expressed in a multitude of relations and mutual dependencies between the concepts. Every key concept in Luhmann's theory can only be defined in reference to other concepts: the concept of meaning, for example, cannot be sufficiently grasped without taking the concept of complexity into account, which is linked to the concepts of selection and contingency. In turn, these concepts presuppose the concept of meaning, but meaning cannot be defined independently of the concept of system, which contains implicit reference to an environment, which is distinguished from the system through a difference in the relative degree of complexity, and so on. The theory works with an invariably internal reference structure, in which each additional concept specifies and uses the initial concept. This circularity of construction is explained and justified within the theory; it is one of the reasons for its effectiveness, but at the same time makes the first encounter with its categories more difficult. This is because, in principle, the mastery of one category presupposes knowledge of all the others, while the others, in an infinite circle of references, also demand knowledge of the initial category.

This intrinsic difficulty in the theory is made yet more complicated by a second network of references: the references between Luhmann's different works. Apart from a small number of relatively self-contained works, each of his books contains certain particular differences with a view to explaining a particular problem, whilst presupposing the entirety of the theory and therefore also the differences introduced in earlier works. It is thus impossible to fully grasp the scope of Luhmann's discussion of a particular problem without knowledge of the general theoretical structure of references. However, this knowledge cannot be expected of those who come from a specific area of interest and concern themselves with one of the many domains touched upon in Luhmann's reflections. After all, he wrote from a sociological perspective about law, education, epistemology, political theory, historical semantics, the economy, religion, art, the theory of risk and many other topics, and, in each of these domains, it would be interesting to engage with experts on each topic. That said, it is somewhat unrealistic to expect those experts to possess sufficient knowledge of Luhmann's theory to be able to grasp and use its advantages within their respective fields of interest.

It is the purpose of this glossary to at least partly overcome these difficulties. Even through this book cannot replace a direct reading of Luhmann's books, it should (as a tool) make it easier to approach the general theory of social systems and (provisionally!) remove the obstacles to a fruitful engagement. The first way in which the glossary can be used is to understand it as supporting companion literature to Luhmann's books: should you, in the course of the text, stumble upon a concept that can only be understood in conjunction with another part of the theory or other books, looking this up in the glossary should provide enough information to be able to continue reading. For those who are not concerned with theoretical sociology, it should then be easier to recognize the advantages and specifics of Luhmann's theory in treating certain problems. Furthermore, the glossary should make it easier for sociologists to engage with Luhmann's systems theory. In this case in particular, the information in the glossary must be supplemented by a selective study of Luhmann's texts. For this reason, we have given a number of bibliographical references at the end of each keyword for further reading. Although in some cases a multitude of references would be possible, we have limited ourselves to a maximum of three entries per concept, in order not to overly weigh down the text.

Due to the above, it is understandable that the organization of the glossary—i.e., the arrangement of the keywords—is problematic in the face of the circularity of the theory. If it is already difficult to define a concept individually, then it is even more difficult to present the individual concepts independently of their place within the theory. In many cases, a distinction or a theoretical decision could be justified in being introduced under one concept or many others, and each choice is equally arbitrary. Repeating the discussion of the relevant categories for each key concept would clearly have led to an intolerable redundancy—and ultimately also (due to the circularity of the theory) to an infinite reflection of the book within itself.

Instead, we have decided on a compromise. In this glossary, we use a system of selective references: within each keyword, we indicate the concepts that we believe are required in order to be able to understand the respective keyword. An arrow → with italics references another keyword in the glossary.

We have supplemented the references with "Ways to Read This Book," which indicate privileged connections between the concepts and provide links between the presentation of the individual concepts and the glossary as a whole. The purpose of these ways of reading are, first, to emphasize the close interdependencies between certain concepts and thereby to counter, at least in part, the artificiality of splitting the book into individual keywords. Each way of reading runs through a group of keywords that are tightly linked together; if read in a sequence, they offer a relatively complete picture of the internal dependencies within a certain topic, such as the question of self-reference or the differentiation of society.

At the same time, the ways of reading serve the second purpose of the glossary: to be an autonomous text. This book can also be used as a kind of introduction to Luhmann's systems theory, which is divided into particular problem areas according to the structure of the ways of reading. In this case, the ways of reading correspond rather to the chapters of a book, with the difference that (although they are naturally linked to one another) they form relatively independent units and do not necessarily need to be read in sequence. They allow to take a modular approach to the theory, in the sense that it can be considered according to the particular perspective of a certain problem and, starting from there, the other components can be combined into a whole framework.

As an autonomous text, too, this book presents all the features of a glossary: a certain fragmentariness, a rather artificial isolation of the topics and, above all, a principally uncritical treatment. The purpose of the book is to make the central concepts in Luhmann's theory as clear as possible, and not to discuss the personal considerations of the authors, or their objections or suggestions for improvement. Even if this is clearly never entirely possible in practice, the authors should keep to the background at all times and serve only to provide a neutral representation of the theory.

However, we have already seen above that the authors' decisions become important when it comes to the organization of the concepts and the internal references. There were also decisions to be made concerning putting the book together and the selection of topics. We decided to limit ourselves to treating the Luhmannian version of systems theory, and not to engage fully with the basic concepts of systems theory that do not diverge significantly in Luhmann's version compared with traditional systems theory, and which require no essential amendments. For example, the glossary contains no independent keywords for concepts such as homeostasis or entropy. In the same way, there are no keywords for the classical concepts in the sociological tradition that Luhmann did not amend, or which no longer have the significance of deep, underlying, essential concepts, such as action, individual, integration, socialization, etc.

This book should simply provide an interpretive framework that, concerning the obstacles mentioned above, makes it easier to get a complete picture of the state of Luhmann's reflections. It is our impression that the debate surrounding the theory of social systems could and should be more fruitful; a less fragmentary reference framework than the one to be drawn from Luhmann's labyrinthine output could contribute to weakening some of the less substantive polemics and, in their place, to facilitate more well-informed and appropriate criticism.

Ways to Read this Book

It is not easy to define ways of reading for this glossary, since, as mentioned, Luhmann's theory eludes a linear logic: he himself once defined the theory as a type of labyrinth in which one sooner or later finds oneself back at the beginning or somewhere in the middle. More has been discovered about the labyrinth, but not a direct way through it as yet. Nor is it possible, as in the case of putting a puzzle together, to simply add the individual ways to read the book to one another. Reading according to the following ways therefore allows no more than excerpt-like observation of the respective topics. Additionally, the references in each of the keywords draw attention to the necessity of diverging from a certain way and following a different way of reading this book. The ways to read this book are a kind of integration of the references that one comes across also through a selective reading.

Despite this obvious limitation, we have persisted with the idea of ways of reading because they offer an additional point of orientation to the reader approaching Luhmann's theory for the first time. The differentiation of the ways of reading primarily serves the purpose of showing how abstract and concrete arguments from Luhmann's theory can be consistently organized and linked to each other. The organization of the different ways of reading reveals a particular logic, which, however, need not be adhered to by readers with their own perspectives and interests. More important is to respect the sequence within the individual ways of reading, since this sequence ensures a certain unity in the line of reasoning despite the fragmentation of the theory's line of reasoning into keywords.

Fundamentally, we have tried to avoid redundancy within the keywords in the ways of reading. In some cases, however, we have considered it necessary to repeat the same keyword in multiple ways of reading. In this way, specialized readings are made easier.

The first way of reading begins with the phenomenological concept of meaning and follows its development in the theory of social systems. Luhmann often referred to the relevance of the concept of meaning in his theory, which aims to achieve an integration of a human and a technical approach. This way of reading follows the former approach, explaining the use of concepts taken from philosophy and their integration in systems theory. In the most recent texts from Luhmann, the relevance of these components is naturally presupposed: it is therefore even more important to gain complete clarity about this background. The concepts in the first way of reading are:

- Meaning
- Complexity
- World
- Meaning Dimensions
- Attribution
- Negation

The second way of reading presents the basic concepts of Luhmann's variant of systems theory; as such, it is complementary to the first. We have not tried to reconstruct the history of the concept of system in Luhmann's theory, but instead refer to the latest formulation of the most abstract aspects of the theory. For Luhmann, insights in systems theory are decisive for the development of sociology—especially in allowing the discipline to gain independence from classical modes of thinking. In this way, Luhmann does not want to negate the relevance of the classics for sociology; his intention is much more to make sociology a scientific discipline, which, like other disciplines, is able to rapidly produce new insights without always having to reference what was said earlier. Accordingly, theoretical research should attain the same status in sociology as empirical research based on data processing: systems theory serves this purpose. The keywords in the second way of reading are:

- System/Environment
- Autopoiesis
- Operation/Observation
- Self-Reference
- Paradox
- Asymmetrization
- Redundancy/Variation

- Structure
- Process

The third way of reading describes the foundation of the theory from its "technological" side. Once again, it concerns Luhmann's epistemology and, in particular, how he grounds his theoretical and epistemological program. This way of reading primarily concerns the meaning and consequences of the observation of the environment through the system's own operations. In this respect, Luhmann employs a "constructivist" approach (also called "second-order cybernetics"), which spread quickly into other disciplines (biology, neuroscience, psychology). Contributions to the formulation of constructivism have been made by both logicians (such as Gotthard Günter and George Spencer Brown) and natural scientists (such as Heinz von Foerster, Humberto Maturana, Francisco Varela, Henri Atlan and others). Luhmann demands the use of this epistemology on social systems and therefore offers a solid foundation for the development of sociology. This means that sociology can learn from other disciplines without having to forego its autonomy: by abstracting and re-specifying the concepts with reference to their own problems. This way of reading ends with the representation of the outlines of Luhmann's theoretical and sociological program. The keywords are:

- Science
- Constructivism
- Operation/Observation
- Identity/Difference
- Information
- Re-entry
- Reflection
- Rationality
- Sociological Enlightenment
- Functional Analysis

The fourth way of reading concerns a group of concepts that refer in a narrow sense to sociological questions of the theory of social systems. Here, it becomes clear which changes result in the classic conceptual repository of sociology when one allows system-theoretical and sociological concepts to meet. Luhmann's theory includes all the basic concepts of sociology: society, interaction and organization, construction and maintenance of social structures, conflict, communication, action, the relations between society and individuals, socio-cultural evolution. We cannot comprehensively acknowledge Luhmann's full treatment of these topics. Instead, we have tried to deliver a guiding thread through which these questions can be approached. The keywords in this way of reading are:

- Double Contingency
- Expectations
- Communication
- Social System
- Society
- Differentiation of Society
- Semantics
- Interaction
- Organization
- Conflict
- Interpenetration and Structural Coupling
- Psychic Systems
- Inclusion/Exclusion

The fifth way of reading focuses on one of the particularities of modern society emphasized by Luhmann: functional differentiation. First, the idea of the differentiation of society in general is presented along with the previous historical forms of society. Next, Luhmann's explanation of the structural changes and the complexity of today's society are analyzed. This topic is at the center of Luhmann's whole project of social theory. For several years, he has been writing monographs about the different subsystems of the functionally differentiated society. This way of reading ends with the question of risk, which is today gaining more and more significance in the sociological analysis of modern society. The keywords in this way of reading are:

- Differentiation
- Differentiation of Society
- Code
- Program
- Education System
- Art System
- Medical System

- Political System
- Legal System
- Religious System
- System of Families
- Economic System
- Scientific System
- Risk/Danger

The sixth way of reading is a further deepening of sociological questions and a second direction of development within Luhmann's general theory of society. Here, the questions of the improbability of communication and the means of transforming this improbability into probability are treated. The topic of the structures of modern society is treated once again. The fifth and sixth ways of reading are therefore complementary, in that they describe the characteristics of the functionally differentiated society. This way of reading also presents concrete sociological consequences of constructivism, and therefore links up to the third way of reading. In this case, too, we have tried to signal the outlines of the topics that are comprehensively treated in monographs. The keywords in this way of reading are:

- Communication
- Medium/Form
- Code
- Language
- Dissemination Media
- Symbolically Generalized Media
- Property/Money
- Art
- Love
- Power
- Truth
- Values
- Morality

The seventh and final way of reading highlights a particularly important dimension within Luhmann's theory that is not always dealt with explicitly in sociology: the temporal dimension. This way of reading may appear somewhat redundant, because it includes keywords that also appear in the other ways of reading. The meaning of the temporal dimension (which the theory of evolution also refers to), however, warrants particular attention. The level of abstraction in these keywords is remarkable, but the structure of the references can make it easier to locate connections with the concrete questions presented in the other ways of reading. It is exactly this degree of abstraction that allows this way of reading to more precisely pose the questions that deal with complexity of social systems and communication. The keywords in this way of reading are:

- Meaning Dimensions
- Time
- Event
- Structure
- Process
- Evolution

Art System (*Kunstsystem*)

The operations of the art system are observations oriented to works of art. The communication of art requires objects produced specifically for that purpose. While everyday objects are (or can be) observed simply as what they are, objects observed as artworks are perceived as artificial objects, which were produced by somebody and must be observed in reference to the observations of the creator. Both the observer and the artist realize second-order observations [→*Operation/Observation*]. The artist must observe the artwork to be produced in reference to the way in which others will observe it; she must try to guide and surprise the expectations of the observer through the artwork. The observer, for her part, must decode the structure of distinctions in the artwork and recognize that they were produced in order to bind observations. Through the directions given in the artwork, the observer connects herself with the (coordinated or uncoordinated) observations of others.

The function of art is to establish in a reality of its own in the world, i.e. an imaginary or fictional reality. The work of art brings about a duplication of the real in a real and an imaginary reality and gives it meaning by combining removed or unrealized possibilities. Art can do this by exploiting the difference between perception and communication: perception, unlike thoughts and communication, can produce astonishment and recognition at the same time. It can describe the world as a re-entry of the difference between perception and communication into communication.

Art shows how, in this fictional domain—in this domain of unrealized possibilities—, an order can be found: beginning from an arbitrary starting point, the simple sequence of mutually limiting operations produces an order that appears necessary. The real reality is set against a domain of alternative possibilities in which another order is valid, which nevertheless is non-arbitrary. Within its specific (fictional) domain of reality, art can experiment with different forms; it can imitate reality with reference to an ideal of perfection which has never been realized as such; it can criticize reality; it can appeal to the observer as an individual and lead her to observe in a different way than she does in her everyday context (as is the case of a novel). In other words, the function of art is to offer the world a possibility to observe itself—to let the world appear in the world. Therein also lies the specific paradox of art, which it generates and resolves at the same time: the paradox of the observability of the unobservable (or of the necessity of what is only possible).

In order to fulfill this function, art requires a →*symbolically generalized medium*, which (like money) corresponds to a constellation of attributions in which alter's action is experienced by ego. The artist acts, and the spectator experiences. The situation becomes problematic when it gets difficult for ego to accept as meaningful what alter produces as action, i.e., when the artwork is presented as an object produced by someone without a recognizable purpose.

The question of the purpose of the artwork becomes particularly relevant when art is differentiated as an autonomous function system [→*Differentiation of Society*] and therefore rejects external motivation and support. The purpose of art is thus no longer to refer to something that is directly accessible or to imitate nature, but rather to experiment with new combinations of forms. Unlike other artificial objects, artworks have no external use. They are ends in themselves.

The communication medium of art serves to make an improbability more probable, i.e., the improbability that certain objects are observed according to differences located exclusively within the artwork itself. Art strives to reactivate precluded possibilities. It refers to those possibilities that, due to the realization of certain things, have been reduced to mere possibilities, and attempts to show how an order with its own necessity is possible in this domain. We must observe how, in a non-arbitrary, combinatory game, the distinctions within the artwork lead to other distinctions and thereby generate an order that cannot be attributed to an external order. Every decision made by the artist in producing the artwork (a brushstroke, the selection of a tone, the beginning of a novel) limits the possibilities available for further steps. However, this is not due to the material properties of the medium used, but exclusively to autonomous internal limitations.

The observation of art is based on a specific code, which in traditional aesthetics is expressed according to the difference beautiful/ugly. Today, this difference is reinterpreted as the alternative fits/does not fit. Within the work of art, each new form must be compared with the previous forms to determine whether the new form fits or does not with the previous ones, whether or not it produces connectivity within the artwork. Once this has been achieved, the artwork generates its own order with its own necessity. We are dealing here with communication, because this order contains information that is disseminated and must be understood.

When what is demanded of artworks is novelty and not simply the correct application of certain rules, art needs specific programs that allow each difference to be determined in terms of whether it fits or not. We can speak of self-programming: each artwork programs itself in the sense that the necessity of the order produced by this programming results from the decisions made within the artwork itself. The rules followed by the artwork in the selection of its forms are generated by this selection, which gradually binds itself. Therefore, the ties do not come from external laws, but from the way the artist began the work of art. The program is the result of operations that themselves perform the programming.

Although each work programs itself, one does not need to start from the beginning each time. Styles create connections between different works of art. They make it possible to connect artworks to one another and to establish art as a system. In attributing a style to a work of art, its belonging to the art system becomes recognizable; what cannot be subsumed under any style loses its meaning as an artwork and cannot be observed as art. Style, however, is not a meta-program, since it delivers no exact instructions regarding the differences to be drawn. It is not enough to follow a style in order to generate a work of art that presents itself as new; rather, what is demanded is self-programming and the genesis of new combinations of forms. Style thus protects the autonomy of the artwork, but delivers no general instructions that may or may not be followed. Moreover, the existence of a social system of art demands that individual works of art are placed within an autopoietically reproducing network, so that every artwork is realized within the recursive connection to other works of art, and within a written or orally disseminated communication about art.

In this sense, the autonomy of art is always operative autonomy, therefore self-limitation of the work of art. At the same time, however, autonomy is also the object of the reflection of the art system [→*Self-reference*]. With Romanticism, reflection manifests itself as artistic criticism and gives the theory of art the status of self-description of the system. Criticism is not a program for creating works of art. It is a program for second order observation that formulates the autonomy of art as a constant negation of art itself, as a necessary and impossible transcending of imagination.

In order to allow the recognition of art as art, specific institutions become necessary, where works of art are presented as such. This is the function of exhibitions, museums, theatres, galleries, public debates with art experts and so on. However, this does not change the fact that it is the work of art that must prove to be concrete and unique. [E.E.]

> The Work of Art and the Self-Reproduction of Art (1985); Weltkunst (1990); Art as a Social System (2000).

Asymmetrization (*Asymmetrisierung*)

→*Meaning*-constituting systems are self-referential systems, since each element therein refers only to other elements in the system, and through them refers back to itself [→*Self-Reference*]. This circularity becomes a problem if it takes a pure, tautological form, as in the case of "A is A". In this form, the operations cannot find any identifiable connection, because they occur with no informational content and without any anchor point. Meaning-constituting systems interrupt pure self-reference by selecting reference points in the operations, and introduce an asymmetry in the circularity of the references. For instance, in the case of "A is A only when...", the condition "only when..." makes the statement informative, offering connections for (possible) future operations. Connectivity is the condition for the operational capacity of the system, and it therefore constitutes the necessary condition for its autopoietic reproduction [→*Autopoiesis*].

The introduction of asymmetries does not change the fact that systems are self-referential. Meaning-constituting systems presents the problem of tautology, since they can operate only on the basis of self-reference. Social systems can only communicate and psychic systems can only think: every communication can connect only to other communications, and every thought only to other thoughts. For this reason, social and psychic systems are forced to constantly create conditions that avoid the short circuit of self-reference: they must de-tautologize themselves and unfold their self-reference. Tautology does not disappear in asymmetrization; it remains as a condition for self-reference, and both tautology and self-reference remain the prerequisites for the existence of the system. The introduction of asymmetries solves the problem of the unproductive purely tautological circulation. The system must be capable of inserting additional meaning, which determines the direction in which the system can operate informatively.

Asymmetry can be introduced through the structure of language. Here, the language- and communication-based differentiation of subject and predicate creates the impression that the projected objects are responsible for their own properties, independently of communication.

The most general forms of asymmetrization can be observed and differentiated by referring to three →*meaning dimensions*:

(a) In the temporal dimension, the irreversibility of time permits the introduction of asymmetry. This arises through the differentiation of, on the one hand, the past, which is from this moment onwards lost and irretrievable, and, on the other hand, the contingent, uncertain future. The past provides the opportunity to accept and legitimize the situation in the present; whereas the open, foreseeable future makes it possible to set goals and finalize decisions regarding what we have, in a specific instance, attempted to achieve or imagined as probable. Situations and events are revealed in the passage of time, and, in the present, we must act in order to bring about or avoid future situations or events. The immutability of the past and the uncertainty of the future create an asymmetry in the temporal dimension, an asymmetry that can only be introduced in the present: past and future are imaginary constructs of a system that exists only in its present.

(b) In the fact dimension, the asymmetry is introduced in the differentiation of system and environment [→*System/Environment*], which guides the operations of the system. The system structures itself in relation to an environment upon which it makes itself reliant, and in which it monitors controllable and uncontrollable variables. Tautology would be re-introduced if the system assumed that its relationships to the environment would be different if the structures were different. No system would be able to operate according to the idea that everything that happens is dependent upon it, and that reality is therefore merely its own projection.

(c) In the social dimension, asymmetrization means that many observers are differentiated, each of which observes according to their own, differing perspectives. In modern society, this form of asymmetrization is expressed in the recognition of the individual as point of reference and final decision-maker regarding personal behavior: each person is different from all other persons and is recognized as such in this asymmetrical relationship. This applies to the functionally differentiated society, whereas stratified societies construct an equivalent asymmetrization in that they structure the social dimension hierarchically. Recognition of the individual and hierarchy are functional equivalents that solve the same problem: the tautological basis of the social dimension. Both these forms of conditioning reveal that, for every individual (ego), other individuals can be observed only as alter ego, that is a projection of the ego in another person.

All forms of asymmetrization are "created" for, and in view of, a specific function. This demands that the semantic forms in which asymmetrizations are processed are made plausible at the social level. The operating system that uses these asymmetries treats them as given, as natural, as unavoidable or necessary, despite being introduced self-referentially in the system by the system. Usually, these points of reference can only fulfill their function if and when the system accepts them as necessary without having to consider that these are system-internal constructs that require specific operations. *[G.C.]*

Selbstreferentielle Systeme (1988); The Paradox of Form (1999[1993]); Sthenography (1990[(1987/88)].

Attribution (*Zurechnung*)

Attribution is a technique for localizing selections [→*Meaning*]: the observed selections are ascribed to someone or something. Attributing selections, a system can determine everything in the world. Attribution is thus a prerequisite of observation [→*Operation/Observation*]. Attribution is determined in the three dimensions of meaning [→*Meaning Dimension*] and therefore it is based on their different schematizations.

In the temporal dimension of meaning, the basic schematization of attribution is constant/variable: we can attribute to anything either constancy (objects and situations) or variability (events). In the social dimension of meaning, the schematization is ego/alter: we can attribute anything either to ego's selection or to alter's selection. In the fact dimension of meaning, the schematization is internal/external: the selections are attributed here to either action or experience. Thus, the observer ascribes selections either to a system (action) or to its environment (experience). In both cases, however, the observing system ascribes the selection to the observed system: in the first case as action and in the second case as experiencing environmental selections. The difference is between experienced meaning taken as externally constructed (in the environment of the observed system), and meaning of action taken as →*complexity* reduction carried out by the observed system itself. This attribution demands the constant dual presence of both sides of the differentiation of experience/action: experience and action can only be understood in relation to each other and are functionally equivalent modes of selection.

There is an important difference between the attribution of action and of experience. The attribution of actions permits the observation of the reproduction of a system: a system can only be observed through the attribution of actions [→*Communication*]. This does not mean that the system reproduces itself through the attribution of actions; the attribution is a product of observation that reflects the view of the observer, rather than the →*autopoiesis* of the observed system. The attribution of experience, on the other hand, allows the observation of the reproduction of meaning. Meaning can only be created and reproduced through experience since every observation is the experience of something. The possibility to ascribe action to a system is much more limited than the possibility to ascribe experience: everything that is not action is experienced.

Attribution renews →*self-reference*, both the self-reference of the system (through the attribution of action) and the self-reference of meaning (through the attribution of experience). Attribution is a condition for the self-reference of the system because it allows the →*asymmetrization* of →*double contingency*. When ego can attribute a selection (uttering something) to alter, communication arises: ego can ascribe to alter an action (alter utters what she has decided) or an experience (alter utters what she knew). Thus, the production of communication requires the possibility to ascribe an utterance to alter, which can show both alter's action and alter's experience. Since it depends on observation, the modality of attribution is contingent. What is attributed in a certain way (for instance, as experience) can be attributed differently (as action) at other moments, under different conditions, or from a different point of view. The formation of a social system requires attribution rules, as well as the possibility to coordinate experience and action. Only in this way can expectations of any kind stabilize.

In the course of societal evolution, the contingency of attributing experience and action grows and coordination problems increase. As the complexity of social systems increases, so too does the scope of attributing action, because higher complexity means more possibilities to attribute action. A more complex social system can attribute itself more selections. Law is no longer attributed to nature, but is set down by the legal system. Power is no longer attributed to God's will, but rather to the decisions of political systems. Nature is no longer viewed as an unchangeable reality, but rather as being constituted by the scientific system. In this perspective, the change in the scientific system is the most relevant: causality and deduction are regarded as attributed by an observer able to construct some determinacy. In a sociological perspective, the functional method [→*Functional Analysis*] allows the view of attribution as a form of asymmetrization that makes the system capable of operation. [C.B.]

Social Systems (1995: 83-86; 165-166); Meaning as Sociology's Basic Concept (1990).

Autopoiesis

The term "autopoiesis" was coined by Chilean biologist Humberto Maturana as part of an attempt to develop a definition of the organisation of living organisms. Maturana states that a living system is characterized by the ability of its constituent elements to produce and re-produce themselves, and in so doing to define its unity: every cell is the result of the network-internal operations [→*Operation/Observation*] of the system to which it belongs—it is not the result of any external intervention.

The theory of social systems adopts the term autopoiesis and broadens its frame of reference. While it is applied in a biological setting exclusively to living systems, Luhmann's view is that we may speak of an autopoietic system in all cases in which it is possible to determine a specific mode of operation that is found only in that system. Thus two further references of the configuration of autopoietic systems are defined, each characterized by its specific operations: social systems and psychic systems. The operations of a →*social system* consist of communications that reproduce based on other communications and thus establish the unity of the system; outside social systems, communications do not exist. The operations of →*psychic systems* are thoughts, and no thoughts exist outside consciousness.

All autopoietic systems are therefore characterized by an operational closure. This term is used to indicate that the operations leading to the production of new elements in the system are reliant on earlier operations of the same system and are at the same time prerequisites for later operations [→*Self-Reference*]. This closure is the basis for the autonomy of the system and enables it to be differentiated from its environment. In the case of a living system, the transformations that lead to the production of a new cell are exclusively internal transformations: even though the reproduction of the organism's elements uses material external to the cell (the organic molecules to be processed), no cell production takes place outside of a living organism. The same is true of the other autopoietic systems: the operations of a social system—communications—are the result of earlier communications and themselves trigger further communications. The unity of a social system is based entirely on the recursive interconnection of communications and not, for instance, on the psychic processes of either the systems of consciousness or the organisms involved. Only social systems can communicate. Likewise, the operations of a psychic system—thoughts—perpetually reproduce themselves as a result of other thoughts and are a direct reflection of neither organic nor communication processes. Only consciousness is capable of thought, as it cannot transfer its thoughts to another consciousness; for this, it must resort to communication. Life, consciousness and communication are separate levels of autopoiesis, each with its own distinct autonomy.

The term operative closure is the result of the assumption that no system can operate beyond its boundaries. It goes without saying that every system has an environment and is dependent on being compatible with it [→*Interpenetration and Structural Coupling*]: if, for instance, the systems of consciousness ceased to participate, a social system would no longer be able to reproduce itself. At the level of the constitution of its elements, however, the system operates exclusively in "self-contact"—it refers, therefore, exclusively to the network of its own operations and can only "survive" as long as it can maintain the condition of closure. The moment an external instance dictates the workings of the system operations and interferes in the constitution of its elements, the autonomy of the system is lost and its end is inevitable. In the case of a living system, such an end to the existence of the system means death: an organism can live only so long as it is able to reproduce cells by virtue of its own cells. A social system, too, that is incapable of generating new communications is, as a system, determined to disappear—even though the systems of consciousness still think of contents linked with past communications, without expressing them and thus without being understood by others. The existence of a system depends on its ability to maintain a boundary separating it from the environment. At the same time, the autopoietic reproduction of operations generates the unity of the elements, the unity of the system to which they belong, and the boundary between them and the environment. Against this background, the idea of a "relative autonomy" is ruled out: a system is either autopoietic or it is not (in which case one cannot refer to a "system" at all).

Within a social system, further autopoietic systems may develop, each reproducing a specific type of operation—i.e., mode of communication—that appears only in this system. Through this, a further boundary is drawn between the system and the environment, this time within the system itself. In modern society, there are, for instance, various functional systems [→*Differentiation of Society*] seen as distinct on account of their communications, being oriented towards their specific →*codes*.

With the exclusion of any direct contact with the exterior, the term "of the system" takes on a radical meaning. Entities are not imported or exported either from the inside to the outside or vice versa. Communications can, for instance, refer only indirectly to what is given in the environment if and when this is the subject of communication, and only in the system-specific forms. Further, the interests and motivations of the systems of consciousness participating in communication can appear only in the form of a topic of communication (if communication refers to interests and motivations). It follows, thus, that no system can connect to its environment through its operations, and neither can it use these operations to adapt to the environment. A system is—as far as it exists and operates—already adapted to the environment.

Emphasizing the closure of the system is not to deny the relevance of the environment for the system: the now classic comparison of open and closed systems is overcome with the premise that closure is the condition for the opening of the system. Only under the condition of autonomy is a system in the position to separate and differentiate itself from the environment. A system can only process external materials for the construction of its elements by demarcating an area in which specific conditions are valid and in which no direct adaption to the conditions of the world is needed; only in this way can it (in its own form) react to irritations from the environment [→*System/Environment*]. In this way, a system can introduce its own distinctions [→*Identity/Difference*] and deal with the states and events of the environment using these distinctions, which themselves generate →*information*.

At the level of autopoiesis, the system confines itself to the reproduction of its operations. The differentiation of system and environment requires an observer to link the internal processes with the outside world [→*Operation/Observation*]. Thus, only the observer can attest to the existence of causal relationships between environment and system. Everything that can be said about an autopoietic system—including ideas of time, function, adaptation, evolution—is voiced by an observer and does not concern the workings of the operations. At a certain level of complexity, the system itself can be the observer of its own autopoiesis.

The theoretical decision for the concept of autopoiesis leads to substantial revisions in terms of the theory of cognition and epistemology in general

[→*Constructivism*]. The introduction of the concept of "autopoiesis" constitutes an important advance with regard to the concept of self-organization. While the concept of self-organization regards the ability of the system to construct and modify its own structures, the concept of autopoiesis stresses that the system also operates autonomously in the constitution of its own elements; therefore, everything in the system (elements, processes, structures and the system itself) is generated internally.

In the social sciences, and especially in Luhmann's theory, the introduction of the term autopoiesis is not simply a direct transfer of a biological concept. The fact that that it has proved useful in research on living organisms tells us nothing about its explanatory power in the domain of sociology. The precondition for the relevance of autopoiesis in this domain is that the observation of analogies with living systems is of sociological interest, and this implies the revision and extension of the original term. The most important innovation in Luhmann's version of autopoiesis is the emphasis on the "→*event* character" of the final elements of the social and psychic systems. Communications and thoughts are events, i.e. they have no duration and disappear in the same moment in which they appear. Social and psychic systems exist only moment-to-moment, and every prolongation of →*time* is the result of an observation based on the distinction between before and after, which is itself a system operation. *[E.E.]*

The Autopoiesis of Social Systems (1986); Autopoiesis als soziologischer Begriff (1987); Die Wissenschaft der Gesellschaft (1990: 28 ff., 128 ff.); Theory of Society (2012: 32-35).

Code

The term code indicates a "duplication rule" which allows the correlation of every entity within its area of observation with a corresponding entity within the system. This applies in the first instance to the code of →*language* which allows the correlation of every positive formulation with a corresponding negative formulation. That is, the positive statement "it will rain today" can be understood as the negation of the negative statement "it will not rain today." With language at their base, this also holds for the codes of different functional systems [→*Differentiation of Society*], which are always based on a binary schematization.

Binary schematizations are particular forms of distinctions [→*Identity/Difference*] characterized by a rigid binarity that excludes third values. This binarity is expressed in logic through the principle of excluded middle (tertium non datur): a scientific communication is either true or false, and no other option exists; an organism is either alive or not, and cannot be "only a little bit alive." Binarity implies a drastic reduction, restricting the infinite range of possibilities to just two options connected through a negation. Distinctions that fulfill this condition are called "technicized," where technique signifies the simplification in the information processing that results from not taking into account all implied meaning references.

Binarity offers specific advantages. It facilitates the transition from one value of the distinction to the countervalue. Once third values are excluded, one negation is sufficient to move from one side of the distinction to the other: to get to the illegal, it is enough to negate the legal; to get to the untrue, to negate the true. The connection to the countervalue is more direct than that to the values of other distinctions. Thus, the true is connected more directly with the untrue than it is with the legal, the beautiful, or anything else.

In this way, the completeness of the code is secured, meaning its ability to identify for each entity a correlating entity—one negation suffices. Binary distinctions are universally valid in their field of application: they are responsible for every possible communication. For instance, communication can be defined as true or untrue. At the same time, contingency [→*Double Contingency*] is generalized because every communication based on the code refers unavoidably to the possibility of being different (i.e., to the countervalue): what is true is not untrue. Truth cannot be posited without alternatives; it emerges in relation to the discarded possibility of untruth.

Thus, the capacity for gathering →*information* is also generalized. Information is generated within the system as a distinction that produces further distinctions. Reducing every communication to the form of a distinction between a negative and a positive value, the code allows the system to process every communication as a distinction (i.e., as information).

However, binary schematizations also create specific difficulties; above all, the artificial exclusion of third values brings with it the ineradicable presence of latent or non-latent →*paradoxes*. A code always generates a paradox when it is applied to itself: with the code true/untrue, it is impossible to decide whether the distinction between true and untrue is itself true or untrue (thereby leading to Epimenides' paradox: is the utterance "I'm lying" true or untrue?). Equally, it is not possible to use the distinction between legal and illegal to discern whether the distinction itself is on the side of the legal or the illegal. The code only has two values and must assign one of them to every communication: the code true/untrue cannot maintain its binarity and claim that the utterance "I'm lying" is meaningless ("meaningless" would be a third value).

When operative closure [→*Autopoiesis*] is added to binarity, it can lead to the differentiation of an autopoietic system. In the case of the scientific system, for instance, this is expressed in the condition of limitationality [→*Science*]. Limitationality means that the field of possible options is reduced in such a way that a code-related definition restricts the area of what is possible: the discovery of a falsehood is not only a negative fact that would yield no information in a further search for truths; it is, at the same time, positive information about the range of truths that are still possible. Under these conditions, every code-oriented operation contributes to define the boundaries of the system with the outside, and to specify its internal connections. Thus, a network of interconnected communications is created that develops a form of independence from the remaining parts of society. Scientific communication differentiates itself in society, for instance, through its orientation towards the code true/untrue. It constitutes an autopoietic system, whose operations refer to earlier operations oriented to the code true/untrue (because these define the conditions and possibilities of further truths) and to later communications (because these, in the same way, specify the area of future operations).

Codes, therefore, are distinctions through which a system observes its own operations; they determine the unity of the system. They allow the system to recognize which operations contribute to its reproduction and which do not. For instance, all and only those communications oriented to the code true/untrue belong to the system of science; only those oriented to the code legal/illegal belong to the legal system. Every system processes all its communications exclusively through the values of its code: the legal judgment or the aesthetic beauty of a communication is irrelevant for its scientific truth and vice versa. Every operation oriented to a code draws a boundary between inside and outside (thereby the distinction between self-reference and other-reference). This yields the differentiation of coding problems and reference problems [→*Constructivism*].

A functional system processes every possible object through its code, including the communications that belong to other functional systems. A legal communication oriented to the code legal/illegal is, for instance, processed by science according to the distinction true/untrue. Using an expression proposed by Gotthard Günther, Luhmann claims that the code of every functional system operates as a *rejection value* towards the binarity that orients another system. Thus through the rejection value, it is possible to refuse the binary schematization of that communication and to deal with it from another perspective. Society as a whole is thus defined as polycontextural, this mean that it includes many "contextures," each oriented to a different distinction.

Binarity is essential for the functioning of the code, which must process its values symmetrically: an institutionalized preference for positive values (e.g., the beautiful or the legal or the true) would make the reversibility between positive and negative values more difficult and partially destroy the benefits of binarity. The code itself produces no criteria for action and sets no preferences. However, within operations oriented to the code, choosing one value over the other has different consequences. True, legal, ownership (the positive values) represent the connection capability of the operations and their compactness (different truths confirm each other), while the negative side of the codes stand for reflective values (an untruth leads to the revision of earlier truths). The form of asymmetry thereby introduced in the strict symmetry of the code leads to the issue of →*programs*, which translate codes into directions for action. [E.E.]

Distinctions directrices. Über Codierung von Semantiken und Systemen (1986); Die Codierung des Rechtssystems (1986); Die Wissenschaft der Gesellschaft (1990: 173 ff., 194 ff.).

Communication (*Kommunikation*)

Communication is the basic element and operation of social systems. It consists of the unity of the difference among three selections: utterance (*Mitteilung*), information, and understanding (*Verstehen*) of the difference between utterance and information.

Communication is achieved if information (e.g., today it is raining) and the participant's responsibility for uttering it (saying that today it is raining) are understood as different selections. Without such an understanding, there is no communication. This means that communication cannot be reduced to perception; for instance, to one participant's sight of another participant or hearing her voice, since perception does not include understanding the responsibility for producing an utterance; we can perceive that our stomach grumbles, but we cannot attribute any responsibility for selecting an utterance to our stomach.

Information, utterance and understanding are selections. Information is a selection because the choice of a topic excludes other topics. In other words, information (today it is raining) draws a distinction between what is said and what is not said (e.g., today is beautiful day). In communication, information is uttered by a participant and understood by at least another participant. Therefore, in communication information is produced, rather than transmitted: information is not lost by someone and gained by someone else, but is uttered by someone and understood by someone else.

Since it is designed in a unique way, an utterance of information is a selection. Utterance of information shows intentions, motives, reasons and knowledge. It shows responsibility for speaking and for the reasons for speaking (e.g., by saying that it is raining, the speaker is answering a question, or is trying to make it clear that she would like to stay at home). However, utterance of information is not communication in itself, as understanding is the selection that realizes communication. Understanding draws a distinction between information (today it is raining) and utterance (the reason why the interlocutor says that today it is raining). The realization of communication requires the understanding of this difference, between information and (responsibility for) its utterance. Understanding does not concern objective pieces of information or authentic reasons for uttering; rather, it concerns the →*attribution* of selections as information and (reasons for) utterance.Thus, understanding is achieved even if the uttered information or reasons for utterance are misunderstood or deceptive, and any kind of understanding realizes communication.

Through understanding, communication can stress who has uttered what. Therefore, understanding makes it possible for further communication to refer to either previous utterances (someone's motives or intentions) or uttered information (what), thus generating communication →*processes*. Understanding, rather than for thinking, is important for the reproduction of communication, although thinking is related to communication [→*Interpenetration and Structural Coupling*].

Utterance, information and understanding can be separated for analytical purposes, but they are a unity in communication, which cannot be decomposed. This unity does not last, since understanding, utterance and information are realized simultaneously. Communication is an →*event*, which immediately disappears. Since each communication disappears immediately, each communication is new. Going beyond specific communicative events, communication processes require that each communication is followed by another communication connecting to it through understanding. Thus, each communication is produced by a recursive network of communications which defines the unity of a →*social system*, and communication may be seen as the specific operation that produces a social system. In other words, social systems use communication as a specific operation for autopoietic reproduction [→*Autopoiesis*], and the continuation of communication achieves the autopoiesis of a social system. Social systems have communication as their basic operation and include only communication. An important consequence is that individuals, as →*psychic systems*, are not included in social systems; rather, they are systems in the environment of social systems.

Since all communications are included in social systems, there is no communication between a social system and its environment. Social systems are closed systems that produce information through communication; they do not receive information from their environments. However, social systems are also open to their environments, as they can observe [→*Operation/Observa-*

tion] it in the form of information produced in communication: what is not communication (e.g., conscience, biological life, physical machines, chemical elements) can be observed in communication as information. Communication allows the differentiation of the attribution of selections to the system (as utterance) and to its environment (as information). This also means that communication allows the distinction and recombination of the reference to the system and reference to the environment [→*Self-Reference*].

The process of communication can be observed as decomposed in actions, since reproduction of communication requires attribution of action. Action is not an operation of social systems, but a way of making this operation visible in the system. Firstly, attribution of action makes it possible to observe if understanding, and therefore communication, has been achieved. Secondly, attribution of action refers to previous utterance or information and makes it possible to attribute responsibilities, intentions and motives for it. Thus, by attributing action, participants can know whom they are addressing. Attribution of action enables the observation that someone has said something, and thus the observation of the difference between utterance and information. This observation allows the self-referential connection between communications, making it possible to establish the communication process as a series of observable events. Thus, through attribution of action, the communication process can observe itself: the following communication can refer to what has been said, by answering, questioning, refusing, and so on. Attribution of action is a simplification of communication, as it does not include observation of connections between communications and autopoiesis. It is a necessary simplification that allows a social system constitute its operations with reference to its operations. The attribution of action is necessary for the autopoiesis of social systems, as it provides the possibility for self-reference. However, the attribution of action also presupposes the autopoiesis of communication, as action can be attributed only if it is understood.

There are no social systems without communication. Nevertheless, communication is an improbable event. First, at the most basic level, understanding, and thus achievement of communication, is improbable. Second, in more complex situations, reaching interlocutors through utterance is improbable. Third, in the most complex situations, acceptance of communication is improbable. An important sociological problem is understanding how improbable communication can become probable. Some media [→*Medium/Form*] are used in society to make communication probable: →*language* makes understanding probable, media of communication diffusion make reaching interlocutors probable [→*Dissemination Media; Mass Media*], and →*symbolically generalized media* of communication make acceptance probable. [C.B.]

> Social Systems (1995: Ch. 4); Theory of Society (2012: 35-49); The Autopoiesis of Social Systems (1986); What is Communication? (1992).

Complexity (*Komplexität*)

Complexity is a specific condition of a collection of interconnected elements: the elements cannot be connected to one another at the same time. Therefore, complexity means that a selection is necessary in order to create relations between the elements. Consequently, the distinction between element and relation is fundamental to this definition of complexity, which requires selective connectivity between the elements. To observe complexity, we must distinguish a situation of selective connectivity from one that is not selective. Complexity can thus be defined as a form, the two sides of which are the selective connectivity and the complete connectivity of the elements.

Complexity can be observed in a system or from the point of view of a system if it is observed in the system environment [→*System/Environment*], as well as in the →*world*. Only the complexity of a system is organized complexity. It consists of the selective connectivity of the elements of the system; it is the selective organization of →*autopoiesis*.

The number of abstractly possible relations between the elements of a system increases exponentially with the increase in the number of elements: two elements form four relations, three elements nine, and so on. When the number of elements in a system is very large, the number of relations reaches orders of magnitude that cannot be directly controlled by the system itself. This implies that, within the system, not everything can be actualized and simultaneously connected to everything else; each of the system operations refers to a further domain of potentialities.

Complexity describes the fact that there are more possibilities than can be actualized, i.e., more communication in social systems and more thought in psychic systems. For what concerns →*social systems*, a specific communication ("What do you think about that?" or "the exchange rate has gone up") can only connect directly to a limited number of further communications. Since every actualized communication refers to a domain of alternative possibilities, every connection must choose between numerous possibilities: for instance, the answer to the question "what do you think about that?" is only one of many possible answers, the comment on the news that the exchange rate has changed is only one of many possible comments. Here we observe a compulsion to selection: something is realized as a datum and the rest remains in the background as a domain of possible references. Selection constitutes the temporal dynamic of complexity [→*Time*]; the basis of selection is the fact that actualizations occur sequentially since no system can actualize everything at the same time.

The observation of complexity emerges alongside →*meaning*. A meaning-constituting system observes the complexity of the world from its own point of view. Since the world is conceived as a unity of the difference between system and environment, complexity is also relative to this differenceand is dependent on the observation of this difference through meaning-constituting systems. Complexity (including that of the environment) exists only when it is observed by a system. The relevance of observation for the construction of complexity is particularly emphasized in the concept of hypercomplexity, which means that complexity also includes the consequences of its observation. Hypercomplexity is the result of a second-order observation [→*Operation/Observation*], i.e., the result of including the observing system in the observation: a society, for instance, is hypercomplex if it observes the consequences of its observations on its environment.

A system observation does not determine the complexity of that system environment. The complexity of the environment is constituted independently of the system, since the system can only grasp it through observational operations, which can irritate the system itself. This is the paradox of the system which is unable to control environmental complexity, even if this complexity only exists as observed by the system.

The difference between system and environment marks a difference in the level of complexity: the environment is always more complex than the system, because the system draws a boundary which limits the domain of the possible within the system itself. The difference in level of complexity between system and environment appears as relating of relations, whereby the abstractly possible relations between the elements in the system (system complexity) are limited from compatibility with its environment (environmental complexity). In a (social) system, it is not possible to actualize everything in the operations (in the communication) at the same time, for the reason that complexity is structured according to a perspective of compatibility with the environment.

In such a system, reductions are necessary to realize and maintain an internal complexity that renders the system compatible with the environment. Reduction of complexity means that the abstract possibility of relations between elements is structured into a specialized system including a limited number of possible relations.

Complexity reduction means selectively maintaining a domain of possibilities based on structures. The →*structures* determine how much internal complexity a system can generate and tolerate. Complexity is only realized and maintained in a system through reduction: reduction and maintenance of complexity do not contradict one another, but are rather mutual conditions. The maintenance and reduction of complexity depend on structures which preselect the possibilities available to connect the elements to one another.

The complexity level of a system changes with the change of the selectivity of the relations made possible by the system structure. A system can increase its complexity in connection with an increase in the complexity of its environment—not because it conforms to the environmental complexity, but because it operates autonomously on the basis of its own structures. The increase in complexity in a system triggers an increase in complexity in the systems observing it, because their environments become more complex. Under these conditions, an evolution of the system is possible; however, this evolution is not a simple increase in complexity, but rather a change in structure.

The concept of complexity must be distinguished from that of →*differentiation*. Differentiation refers to the distinction system/environment and not to the distinction element/relation. An increase in complexity does not mean an increase in differentiation; whilst complexity varies continuously, differentiation varies discontinuously (as in the case of change in the form of society differentiation).

However, the concepts of complexity and differentiation can be linked together. The increase in complexity—i.e., in the relations between the elements—entails limits to the widening of the system: no system can withstand an arbitrary and undefined increase in its complexity. Thus, limits are drawn within the system, which generate subsystems. The form of differentiation among subsystems determines the limits of complexity that can be attained in the system. The changes in the level of complexity can trigger changes in the system form of differentiation. Changing the system differentiation criteria has decisive consequences for the level of complexity that the system can tolerate. This is particularly important for the system of society; today's society, for instance, generates far greater complexity than earlier societies due to its forms of differentiation [→*Differentiation of Society*]. [C.B.]

Social Systems (1995: 23-28); Theory of Society (2012: Ch. 1.9); Temporalization of Complexity (1978); Introduction to Systems Theory (2012: Ch. II.8).

Conflict (*Konflikt*)

Conflict is a parasite social system that requires the communication of a contradiction, and tends to absorb the resources of the system in which it develops. This is where the danger lies for the host system. The system, which hosts to the parasitic conflict, is thus faced with the necessity to keep it within acceptable boundaries.

This demarcation of the conflict is one of the conditions under which the evolution of society is possible. On the one hand, →*evolution* requires the contradiction, which means the possibility to negate social contents and expectations and thereby produce evolutionary variations. The ability of society to facilitate and tolerate conflict is by all accounts an essential requirement of its evolution. On the other hand, conflicts rapidly grow to escape the control of the host social system, creating problems and interrupting communication, the consequences of which may not be positive. In older societies based on interaction [→*Differentiation of Society*], it was therefore necessary to suppress conflict. To do so, certain roles were differentiated for the purpose—for instance, notable citizens were given the responsibility of resolving disagreements. The stratification of society permitted instead the strengthening of particular differences drawn from the conflict. This role was played predominantly by the differentiation of a higher social layer, which, thanks to its innate moral quality, was able to concentrate resources without having to give account to lower layers or fulfill their demands. Moreover, the possibility arose to accept conflict and to eliminate it through social control and the influence that third parties have on the resolution of a disagreement. The results run from a differentiation of purpose-made dispute settlement procedures, through to the stabilization of a communicative legal domain.

Every conflict implies a contradiction. This term describes the case in which, within a social system, a possibility is exploited to communicate the rejection of a previous communication. The concept does not have, therefore, the meaning of a logical error to be avoided in constructing theory, but rather it describes a particularly unstable situation that can arise in communication. This is primarily possible thanks to the capacity of →*negation* possessed by →*meaning* and, with its code yes/no, →*language*.

In social systems, contradictions provide a moment of self-reference of communication and require particular operations. When a rejection is communicated, the problem for the social system is that it must react to the resulting situation of insecurity; the pre-programmed options (the offer of communication and its rejection) mutually exclude one another. One observes that they cannot exist simultaneously, and no reality corresponds to them. This impossibility of co-existence concerns the structures of →*expectations* of the social system, since these structures dissolve as a result of their contradictory characteristic. The connectivity of communication can only be secured by the contradiction itself, which provides the foundations for a particular social system: the conflict system. Conflict arises from the contradiction and is founded on the possibilities that it contains; namely, negation. Here, →*double contingency* takes on the form of a double negation: "I won't do what you want, if you don't do what I want." Communication can continue because it reacts to the contradiction as a contradiction.

Contradictions represent problems of undecidability for those observing the communication. The observer (which can be the social system within which the contradiction arose) lacks structural points of reference to guide the observation, and the situation thus appears to the observer to be undecidable. But even if the observation is blocked, operations within the system that generated the contradiction can still continue to be produced [→*Operation/Observation*]. Despite the insecurity of the expectation, the system can react operatively: it can react without cognition of the contradictory factor. The system does not react to the rejection (to the *no* generated by the contradiction) to maintain the endangered structures. Instead, it reacts to the inadequateness of these structures for the environment. It is therefore not a "conservative" reaction that resolves the source of disturbance for the benefit of the status quo; rather, the rejection that leads to the contradiction—and in some cases to the conflict—forces the system to suspend the connectivity of the structures and to rely on the new situation. The system protects only its own autopoiesis and not the given structures. In their place, the contradiction guides communication.

Contradictions fulfill a warning and alarm function in that they signal an inappropriateness of the system structures. They are regarded as an immune system that functions to protect the autopoietic reproduction of social systems. They warn the system that it could disappear due to internal disturbances triggered by the environment, whilst the conflict-generating *no* allows the system's reaction even without complete knowledge of the environment and the factors endangering the system itself. Against this background, the legal system functions as an immune system for society, creating contradictions and conflicts that protect the autopoiesis of communication. *[G.C.]*

Theory of Society (2012: 278-282]; Social Systems (1995: Ch. 9); Konfliktpotentiale in sozialen Systemen (1975).

Constructivism (*Konstruktivismus*)

Constructivism is the term used to describe a somewhat heterogeneous group of theoretical approaches from various disciplines (e.g., biology, neurophysiology, cybernetics, psychology). They share the assumption that knowledge does not rest on a correspondence with the external reality, but exclusively on the "constructions" of an observer. Knowledge is the discovery (Entdeckung) of reality—not in the sense of a progressive revelation of pre-existing objects, but in the sense of "inventing" (Erfindung) external data.

A crucial landmark for constructivism is Heinz von Foerster's research, which highlighted the relevance of some results of neurophysiology for the theory of knowledge. One is the so-called principle of undifferentiated encoding, according to which nerve cells encode only the intensity and not the nature of a perceptual stimulus. The brain uses the same operations (electrical stimuli) in order to see, hear, smell, taste and touch, and creates internally the corresponding qualitative differences. Differentiated perceptions according to different senses are based on an internal interpretation of undifferentiated external stimuli. The world as we perceive it —with all its variety and diversity—is the result of internal processes.

A further central element of constructivism has been formulated by Humberto Maturana as the principle of →*autopoiesis*. According to this principle, at the level of organization, every living system operates under conditions of closure without any input from the environment. The system never comes into direct contact with the environment and knows only its own internal states.

From these and other considerations, constructivists conclude that all knowledge is an internal construct of a system. At the same time, however, they refuse to describe their position as idealistic and assign to reality a critical role in the regulation of the operations of systems. Constructivists do not negate the existence of reality, but claim that there is nothing in it that corresponds to the categories of knowledge. There are no negative and no modalized objects (possible or necessary objects) and there are, in general, no distinctions. The reality is simply what it is: actual and positive. However, knowledge, based on observations [→*Operation/Observation*], can only grasp reality in the form of distinctions that have no direct correlates in reality. Thus the observer knows only her own categories and not primary data.

Although reality has no positive role in directing knowledge, it has a negative role in discriminating acceptable knowledge. Even if we cannot know what reality *is*, we can, according to Ernst von Glasersfeld, know what it is *not* on the basis of relations of compatibility. For instance, a key fitting a lock delivers no positive description of the lock (of what it is), but not fitting leads to disposing of the wrong key (knowing what it is not). In constructivism, negating the necessity of a correspondence with the external reality does not mean that any hypothesis can be accepted, leading to a form of relativism. Not every claim is allowed, and exact criteria discriminate between acceptable knowledge (termed "viable") and incorrect knowledge.

Arbitrariness of knowledge is also prevented by the recursive connection of operations within an autopoietic system. Due to the lack of a final point of reference that discriminates between correct and false hypotheses, we never arrive at definitive knowledge. All knowledge is but an observation and is relative to the categories of a specific observer. It must be traced back to this observer as her operation. Every operation is, however, bound to other operations in the same system, which determine its connections; every operation processes the results of previous operations and prepares the conditions for the next—and this also holds for the operation of observation.

The recursive application of an operation to the results of previous operations can also (as also shown in mathematical research) lead to the crystallization of relatively stable states (Heinz von Foerster's "Eigenstates"). These become conditions for the operations that follow and limit their freedom of movement. Even without an initial ordering principle, an order can emerge from the connections between operations (the idea of "order from noise"), selecting the acceptable operations that are compatible with the system.

Constructivism attributes each datum to an observation. Therefore, the task of the theory of knowledge is to observe observations. This is undertaken within the framework of a second-order observation, which does not refer to the observed "what", but rather to the "how" of first-order observation. Hence, it observes how the observed observer observes. The "classic" subject/object distinction, which assumes that objects are constant for different subjects, is replaced in this approach with the distinction operation/observation, which attributes each datum to the concrete operations of an autopoietic system. In order to emphasize that the critical innovation is the reference to operations, Luhmann's terminology prefers the phrase "operative constructivism" to the more widely used "radical constructivism."

Each observation can be observed in reference to its condition of possibility, as formulated in the principle of the blind spot, another of Von Foerster's contributions. This principle takes a discovery made in the study of ocular vision and applies it to every form of observation: one area of the retina has no photoreceptor cells, so our field of vision is incomplete. We cannot see what falls within this zone, and we cannot see that we cannot see, since we are unaware of this deficit. This principle is abstracted and applied to every type of observation. Observations are never able to observe the distinction that they themselves use [→*Paradox*]. When an observation orients itself, for instance, to the distinction true/untrue, it cannot observe whether the distinction itself is true or untrue: this is its blind spot. A second-order observation—which observes this observation based on a different distinction—can see what the observation itself cannot see, and also that it does not see it. However, it will also have its own blind spot associated with its observational schema and this blindness can also be observed (by another observation).

These considerations are valid for all binary distinctions guiding observations, including the →*codes* of functional systems, for instance true/untrue, legal/illegal, payment/non-payment. Every functional system observes its objects exclusively through its own specific distinction, and as such exhibits a form of undifferentiated encoding. For instance, in the economic system everything is grasped in reference to payments (i.e., with the code payment/non-payment) and the same goes for other systems. Moreover, every system operates under the condition of closure [→*Autopoiesis*] and never comes into direct contact with the environment. In science, for instance, objects such as neutrins only started to exist when scientific categories allowed their observation. What is observed results from the way in which the categories of science construct the objects, and not from the objects as originary given. In fact, every functional system has a blind spot because, due to its code, it cannot observe the code itself. Each functional system can ultimately be observed by a second-order observer with the capacity to see these limitations.

Once we reject the notion that the relation to a ultimate reality guarantees the stability and adequacy of knowledge, we cannot attain a new fixed point that permits definitive claims. There is no final observer who knows the truth. Thus constructivism leads to a recursive network of observations of observations. These do not reflect reality, but are nevertheless founded upon extremely selective conditions that self-regulate and produce ordered states that are compatible with reality. In a constructivist approach, however, the loss of an independent reference is not associated with any negative connotations, and does not coincide with the idea of a loss of realism. Both the objects and the operations that constitute them are real. What is important is to keep the different distinctions apart. The central point is the ability to distinguish distinctions. In outlining the distinction between operation and observation, one must separate coding problems from reference problems. Every observation uses its distinction as a code in order to observe its own objects, but at the same time—as an operation—it produces a boundary between inside and outside (and also the difference between self-reference and other-reference). For instance, based on the code true/untrue, the →*scientific system* can observe both itself and external objects, and both self-referential and other-referential observations can be true or false. The distinctions true/false and self-reference/other-reference stand in an "orthogonal relation" to one another, in the sense that there is no coincidence on their positive and negative values. This excludes any relativistic approach and corresponds to the form of differentiation of modern society [→*Differentiation of Society*], according to which every functional system is oriented to its own reality. [E.E.]

Erkenntnis als Konstruktion (1988); Die Wissenschaft der Gesellschaft (1990: 699 ff.); The Cognitive Program of Constructivism and a Reality that Remains Unknown (1990[1990]).

Differentiation
(*Differenzierung/Ausdifferenzierung*)

Differentiation (outdifferentiation) means that a system differentiates itself from the environment and draws a boundary between them. The differentiated system can also observe differentiation in its environment: in the environment of society, there are, for instance, psychic systems and living systems (organisms). The differentiation of the environment is not dependent on the system; nevertheless, it takes particular forms depending on the distinctions made according to the observation of the system. Every system can observe that other systems are present in its environment, and that they also differentiate themselves from their own environments. However, the system can observe these other systems in its environment only in accordance with its own distinctions: for instance, the systems in the environment can be observed as homogenous or heterogeneous, friend or foe, near or distant. Each differentiated system in its environment comes across other system references that introduce it to external perspectives of observation, beyond its control. This means that the environment of a system is always differentiated according to the system/environment perspective.

Differentiation is not only observed in the differentiation (outdifferentiation) between system and environment against the indeterminate background of the →*world*. Differentiation can also be observed within a system. System differentiation means that differentiation is applied to itself: the system repeats the difference between system and environment within the system itself.

Internal differentiation of a system is a product of the →*autopoiesis* of the system. Not only is the system differentiated from its environment, but there are also system/environment differences within the system: operationally closed subsystems can emerge within the overall system. In particular, social systems can include differences between subsystems and their environments:

in modern society, for instance, the political system and its environment, the economic system and its environment [→*Differentiation of Society*]. Every subsystem is differentiated from an environment that is not the same as that of other subsystems, because it includes these subsystems. For instance, the environment of the political system includes the economic system and the environment of the economic system includes the political system. The overall system (e.g. society) belongs to the environment of each subsystem.

System differentiation means differentiating between system/environment differences based on the autopoiesis of the subsystems, and not differentiating complementary parts of a whole through distribution or decomposition, thus the overall system cannot be observed as a whole divided into interlinking parts.

Internal differentiation increases the observational capacity of a system, which is its ability to reduce and maintain →*complexity*. The result of this differentiation is twofold. On the one hand, the environment of the overall system is observed differently by each subsystem: for instance, the political system deals with the problem of air pollution differently than the economic system. On the other hand, the internal environment of the overall system varies depending on the subsystem that observes it, for instance the political system or the economic system. Thus, internal differentiation leads to the increase in specific versions of the identity of the overall system. Every subsystem stabilizes a view that reproduces the view of the overall system: for instance, reality can be observed from a political, economic or scientific perspective. Internal differentiation also increases the selectivity of the overall system, since the internal environment constructs an area of reduced complexity that facilitates easier selections. The overall system defines the external boundaries and the internal environment, in which the subsystems can autopoietically construct and reproduce themselves. This reduction in the level of freedom available to the subsystems is defined as system integration. Thus, the term "integration" thus does not define a unified normativity of the system by which the subsystems must be governed.

The way in which a system is internally differentiated varies with the evolution of the system itself. The most important example is the primary differentiation of society in subsystems, the form of which changes through evolution. In the course of the evolution of society, the predominant change is not in the level (increase or decrease) of differentiation that occurs; rather, it is the form of primary differentiation that changes. Different forms of primary differentiation correlate with different levels of complexity: although differentiation does not mean an increase in complexity in itself, it does trigger an increase in internal complexity.

The differentiation of society does not only occur in the form of primary differentiation of subsystems, but also in the form of an internal differentiation of multiple further social systems that may or may not be connected to the primary subsystems. This additional differentiation results from situations of →*double contingency* within a society that is already structured. Thus, many small social systems emerge and they are constantly dissolved and reformed: →*interactions*. Moreover, in modern society, specific organized systems [→*Organization*] form in connection with the primary subsystems. *[C.B.]*

Social Systems (1995: Ch. 5.IV); Theory of Society (2013: Ch. 4.1); Einführung in die Theorie der Gesellschaft (2005: Ch. IV).

Differentiation of Society (*Differenzierung der Gesellschaft*)

The primary →*differentiation* of society is the formation of subsystems and system/environment relationships. The form of the primary differentiation is the →*structure* of society.

The form of the differentiation determines the way in which relationships between the subsystems are realized in the overall system: it concerns the difference between systems that belong to each other's environments. The form of differentiation creates the structure of society because it determines an ordering of the relationships between the subsystems that preselects the possibilities of communication. In this way, it determines the limits of the →*complexity* that society can reach. If complexity exceeds these limits, society continues to reproduce only once the form of the differentiation changes. The form of the primary differentiation is thus subject to evolutionary variation when exposed to the pressure of increasing complexity. With each new form of differentiation, a new maximum level of complexity is determined.

The forms of differentiation of society can themselves be differentiated according to how the boundaries are drawn between the subsystems and their environments. They result from the combination of two distinctions: (a) the distinction system/environment, and (b) the distinction similarity/dissimilarity regarding the relations between the subsystems. During the evolution of society, four forms of differentiation have served as structures: the differentiation into similar subsystems (segmentation); the differentiation of center/periphery; the hierarchical differentiation into strata; and functional differentiation.

Segmentary differentiation is the form that arose in archaic societies following an initial phase of differentiation according to sex and age. The subsystems in a segmentary society are similar according to the principle of differentiation: this principle is descent (subsystems are tribes, clans or families) or residence (subsystems are households or villages). In addition, the segmentation can be repeated within the primarily differentiated subsystems (families in tribes, households in villages).

In a segmentally differentiated society, complexity cannot reach particularly high levels: each subsystem can only observe other equal systems in the environment internal to society, and society overall has only limited selectivity. In this society, the observation of the world is always based on the difference familiar/unfamiliar, with the systematic need to ascribe everything to familiarity. All communication takes place as face to face interactions, because no medium exists through which absent addressees can be reached [→*Dissemination Media*]. The conceptual heritage of society [→*Semantics*] is transmitted orally. The norm of reciprocity fulfills the function of maintaining internal relations whereas magic fulfils the function of maintaining external relations.

The change in the structure of society begins with a collapse of the norm of reciprocity. Through contact between different groups and internal changes, differences in wealth and rank between families emerge, so that reciprocity is no longer possible.

The societies formed as a result of this process, combine the principles of kinship (from descent) and territorial control (from residence). This combination is based on the priority of one of the two principles formed in the previous form of differentiation. The principle of territoriality leads to the differentiation of center and periphery. The principle of kinship leads to the hierarchical differentiation into social strata. In both of these new forms of differentiation, the subsystems are dissimilar with regard to the formative principle (territory or kinship). The structural change is mitigated by the simultaneous maintenance of segmentary differentiation outside the center or the higher stratum.

The center/periphery differentiation has a hierarchical form based on the distinction civilized/uncivilized. Communication originating in the civilized center is dominant throughout the territory occupied by society. Inequality is based on the different residence, either in the center or in the periphery. Both the ancient cities and the large empires that emerged from segmentation show this form of differentiation, as power and bureaucracy are located in the center. The problem with this form of differentiation is the lack of contacts between center and periphery. The exercise of centralized power is therefore very limited. The center is a kind of island in society.

In the center, a new form of differentiation can also develop and become dominant: stratification based on the dominion of an upper stratum, i.e. aristocracy. An important example regards Europe between the late Middle Ages and the seventeenth century. This new form of differentiation is based on stratification in the center, while segmentation continues to be reproduced in the periphery. Stratification is the clearest example of the hierarchy principle, according to which the subsystems of society have unequal rank. Inequality arises with the closure of the upper level (the aristocracy) through endogamy, i.e. forbidding marriage outside of the stratum. Stratification means unequal distribution of resources and opportunities for communication between the upper stratum (aristocracy) and the lower stratum (common people).

Within the hierarchy principle, in stratified societies relations between subsystems always refer to rank. The upper level determines the internal order of society through inequality. Equality, on the other hand, regulates communication within the strata, for instance in the form of equality between aristocratic families. Stratification means, therefore, equality within a framework of inequality. The internal equality within the upper level of society, which does not necessarily mean cooperation, ensures limited access to the available resources: equality is limited to the few, because only a small number of families can benefit from the resources. The internal equality within the upper stratum, however, is also limited, as further differentiation can develop within the strata.

Since the upper level of society accumulates the capacity for selection, stratification allows the emergence of higher complexity, if compared with earlier structures. The important conceptual heritage is produced in the upper level of society, as the ability to write is exclusive to this level, while the lower level is occupied with the day-to-day problems of survival. It is, thus, the upper level that produces the →*self-description* of society.

Stratification produces a clear and overt order that makes further evolutionary changes probable. It is therefore no coincidence that in Europe in the eighteenth century, when complexity became too great for the stratification, a new structural change gets under way. Differentiation by autopoietic subsystems oriented to a single function appears. It breaks down the hierarchical order of stratification and is today characteristic of →*world society*.

In this functionally differentiated society, the subsystems are dissimilar from the perspective of the function fulfilled by each one. Each subsystem is differentiated according to its specific function in society: the primary differentiated subsystems are the political system, the economic system, the legal system, the scientific system, the education system, mass-media, the system of families, the system of religion, the medical system and the art system.

The most important communication in society is structured according to the functions of these systems.

Every function is fulfilled autonomously by a subsystem. Every subsystem hypostatizes the primacy of its own function. Thus, every subsystem observes society from the perspective of its own function. Each subsystem is guided by a binary distinction [→*Code*] that tolerates no interference in the fulfillment of the function from outside. In each subsystem, the code rejects the distinctions of other subsystems, but also accepting their relevance to the overall society. In the economic system, for instance, the orientation to scientific truth is rejected, but the relevance of science for society is accepted. Using a concept introduced by logician Gotthard Günther, the functionally differentiated society can be defined as polycontextural: many codes are valid at the same time, although they all mutually reject one another.

The relationships between the functions are not ordered hierarchically at the level of society as a whole; the dissimilarity between the systems is, therefore, no longer based on hierarchy. Despite the dissimilarity between the functions and each system hypostatizing its own function, society has no center and no top. All functions must be fulfilled, as they are essential for society; therefore, no function can have primacy over the others. An additional consequence of this is that self-description of society from a single perspective (the center or the top) is impossible.

In the functionally differentiated society, the subsystems observe the world neither uniformly (as in the segmentary society) nor dogmatically (as in the stratified society). The differentiation system/environment has a different meaning depending on the observing subsystem. Every functional system is operationally closed [→*Operation/Observation*] and produces selections according to its own distinctions. Every subsystem tolerates a very complex environment on the condition that the other functions are also fulfilled. Compared with earlier societies, redundancy is reduced and variety is increased [→*Redundancy/Variety*]. The problems of society as a whole are processed in every subsystem, each of which produces its own typologies and solutions. Thus, in the different functional systems, the most important problems of society are processed simultaneously. Facts, events and problems are generalized through their specification in the operationally closed subsystems. The increase in complexity compared with earlier societies emerges from this priority-free versatility of observation.

Each subsystem can observe not only society, but also other subsystems. In this case, we talk about performance. Even though it primarily refers to its function for society, every functional system must provide performance for the other subsystems. For instance, in the political system, laws for the economy are enacted; in the economic system, scientific research is funded; in the education system, training is given for the purpose of work. This means that the functional systems not only necessarily operate autonomously, but they are also highly interdependent. Interdependencies have different meanings in different systems. For instance, the education system observes the political system differently than the legal system does; for the political system, these different perspectives are an environmental differentiation that is absent from the environments of the education system or the legal system.

Communicative events can also be identified by different subsystems as simultaneous operations [→*Interpenetration and Structural Coupling*]; for instance, entering into marriage is both a legal communication and a communication within the family (and perhaps a religious communication). However, the operational closure of the functional systems involved is never broken and in fact determines the continuation of internal communication: following the marriage ceremony, communication in the family is not oriented to laws, whilst the legal status of the spouse is not oriented to the question of love.

Apart from society and the other subsystems, a functional system can also observe itself through reflection [→*Self-Reference*], which enhances self-observation. The political system can describe itself, for instance, with the help of political theory, just as the education system can with the help of pedagogy. Every system, by drawing on reflection, accesses the possibility of observing itself as differentiated from the environment, i.e., of referring to other systems (society or other subsystems).

In order to be able to reproduce itself, every functional system must be able to differentiate and combine its function (for society), its performances (for other subsystems) and its reflection (of itself).

The functionally differentiated society is the first example of a world society: it includes all communications produced in the world without being limited by territorial discontinuity. In the pre-modern period, each society was defined in terms of territorial boundaries, beyond which other conditions for communication were valid. Today, however, the different functional systems (e.g., the economic system, the political system, the education system, the system of science) are not fulfilled only within territorial boundaries, but simultaneously throughout the whole world. The unity of society can no longer be defined through these territorial boundaries; the differences between the geographical regions can only be observed in relation to the overarching functionally differentiated society, with the help of the distinction between developed and underdeveloped regions.

In the functionally differentiated society, stratification and segmentation do not disappear as patterns of differentiation. They are, however, no longer the primary forms of differentiation and therefore take on new meaning. Even when stratification is no longer a basic premise in society, it is constantly reproduced through the effects of functional differentiation, and actually strengthened as the differentiation in more or less overt social classes. Concerning segmentation, this reproduces itself in organizational forms [→*Organization*] that are dependent on functions: for instance, as the differentiation of nation states in the political system, companies in the economic system or schools in the education system.

Differentiation according to function widens and differentiates the horizon of possibilities available to each functional system, enriches the relationship between subsystems autonomy and interdependence, provokes variation in society, and raises the requirements for selectivity compared with earlier forms of differentiation. This implies both benefits and problems, because it causes very high levels of complexity in social and psychic systems. [C.B.]

Theory of Society (2013: Ch. 4.2-4.8]; Gesellschaftsstruktur und Semantik I (1980: Ch. 1); Einführung in die Theorie der Gesellschaft (2005: Ch. IV); Differentiation of Society (1982: 229-254, 390-394).

Dissemination Media (*Verbreitungsmedien*)

Dissemination media handle the improbability of a communication reaching the addressee. It is improbable that communication reaches people who are not physically present [→*Interaction*]. To disseminate communication beyond the boundaries of an interaction requires a particular technology that makes dissemination media available. Dissemination media desynchronise utterance and information on the one hand and understanding on the other, so that understanding can take place later than utterance. Thus, dissemination media amplify the possibility to generate a social memory [→*Time*]. They also amplify the possibility of rejecting communication [→*Symbolically Generalized Media*], as they overcome the constraints of physical presence and reach a much greater number of participants. They have two important effects on society: (1) they are important presuppositions for internal structural change, and (2) they transform the nature of communication.

Historically, the first medium of dissemination was writing. It enabled communication to overcome the boundaries of oral communication and brought about important changes in society in general. While oral communication occurs in the medium of acoustic perception, written communication introduces a symbolization in the medium of visual perception: it implies new operations (writing and reading) in which the distinction between sign and sound is replaced by the distinction between syllable combinations and meaning. With the invention of writing, the distinction emerges between two forms of speech perception: on one side, the written form guarantees that many addressees will be reached; on the other side, oral communication takes on new relevance due to the availability of written texts.

An important effect of writing is the spatial and temporal separation between utterance and understanding [→*Communication*], which opens up a great many possibilities for recombining (e.g., many people can read what has been written) and reorganizing communication sequences. Writing establishes a social memory, independent from the memory of individuals. Writing also creates the illusion of simultaneity in the case of the non-simultaneous and allows, in the present, the combination of many presents that, for each other, are the past or the future. In what is written and what is read, it is possible to describe a present that is in fact in the past for the current present (of the reader), or a future with respect to which the present is in the past. Ultimately, writing makes second-order observation [→*Operation/Observation*] and reflexivity (writing about writing) [→*Self-Reference*] easier: since written texts are available for reading and re-reading, communication more readily becomes the object of further communication. Communication sequences no longer require a strict reciprocity between the participants: the writer is alone and has the time and the opportunity to process her suggestions selectively and to take into account the communication partner's need for comprehensibility. This leads to important transformations of →*semantics* in society.

The advent of writing triggered a differentiation in society, was the starting point of the evolution of ideas, and increased the possibility of the communication being rejected. Many centuries later, these effects were strengthened enormously with the invention of the printing press. The printing press allowed the wider dissemination of written texts, promoting the standardization of language in large geographical areas (national languages). This led to the emergence of the requirement for reaching unlimited numbers of addressees.

The enormous increase in the number of readers radically changed communication. Before the invention of the printing press, writing served only as the social memory of pre-existing knowledge and oral communication remained essential. With the introduction of printing, the processes started by writing increased enormously the reach of written communication, the possibilities of spatial and temporal differentiation of communication, the probability of the communication being rejected, and the changes of semantics in society. The function of the printed book is not to store knowledge, but to broaden it and to produce new, original knowledge. The printing press makes the existing semantics observable and places this above the necessity to dispose of outdated knowledge that has been superseded. The printing press means that writers can no longer observe individuals in an audience, so that they must orient themselves exclusively to the interest and relevance of the text in society. However, printing also enhanced individualized participation in communication, introducing the importance of dealing with individual ignorance (not knowing what is printed) and individual dissent and interpretation (about what is printed).

Like the reader, the narrator also becomes invisible as an individual and the text becomes more and more autonomous. Triggered by the printing press, society made the transition from a hierarchical to a heterarchical order—from a stratified to a functionally differentiated society [→*Differentiation of Society*]. In the functionally differentiated society, the dissemination media developed further, which again supported the change towards a heterarchy.

The dissemination media that emerged in the functionally differentiated society are above all telecommunications: from radio, to cinema and television, to telephone and telefax. The evolution of telecommunications emphasizes the medium of visual perception and tend to remove the spatial and temporal limits on communication. In addition, communicating in moving images means that every reality can be reproduced with a guarantee of faithfulness to the original. Media such as the cinema and television combine visual and acoustic perception so that the world can be communicated as a whole. When the images and sounds of the world are directly communicable, we need not (and cannot) continue to differentiate between utterance and information—and when information and utterance are no longer differentiated, communication (which nevertheless takes place) becomes invisible. Thus the question arises of what can still be distinguished as communication.

A further important effect of telecommunication (excluding the telephone) is the establishment of one-sidedness in communication (the person speaking does not listen; the person listening does not speak). The utterance is no longer a selection within communication, but rather a selection for communication: whoever produces the utterance chooses the themes, forms and times for a one-sided communication. The situation is similar for understanding: the person listening and watching chooses what to hear and see. As such, selection is no longer based on the coordination of utterance and understanding: these are becoming more and more separate. With this separation, comes the loss of the self-correction mechanism of "traditional" communication: a participant listens to what another participant says and answers, then the other participant must take this answer into account, and so on.

The newest technological development is the computer as a medium. This medium allows the differentiation of, on the one hand, entering data into the communication and, on the other hand, requesting information. As in the case of writing, there is no unity between utterance (here, data entry) and understanding. Unlike for writing, however, the unity of information is also missing: the person producing the utterance does not know how the computer will process the data entered. This technological development intensifies and accelerates communication in the →*world society*, both amplifying communication (i.e., enhancing its unpredictable forms) and restricting it (i.e. making its source, the invisible machine, inaccessible).

The new dissemination media have radically broadened communication possibilities. Today, there is nothing that can be left out of communication. The influence of dissemination media on society is very important. First, the evolution of dissemination media creates a progressive societal change, from hierarchical organisation based on direct contacts, to heterarchical organisation, in which the public opinion is important (in the press and above all on television) and the authority attributed to "experts" is undermined (on the internet). Second, this evolution determines a growing discrepancy between actual and potential communication and a stronger compulsion to select. The dissemination media go on to develop their own selectivity, which affects the content of communication and communication possibilities: the topics of communication must be adapted to the selection of whatever can be communicated "well" by the technologies of the media. Finally, with the evolution of dissemination media, society becomes more and more dependent on technology, which determines the structural coupling [→*Interpenetration and Structural Coupling*] with its environment, with increasing risks of failure and costs for safeguards against failures. [C.B.]

The Form of Writing (1992); The Reality of the Mass Media (2000); Theory of Society (2012: Ch. 2.2-2.8).

Double Contingency (*Doppelte Kontingenz*)

The term double contingency (or social contingency), originally from the theory of the famous American sociologist Talcott Parsons, describes the fact that both ego and alter [→*Meaning Dimensions*] reciprocally observe their selections as contingent.

In logic, contingency means the exclusion of both necessity and impossibility. The term contingency determines a datum in reference to the possible alternatives: it describes the situation in which what is current (i.e., not impossible) could also be different (i.e., not necessary). Therefore, contingency describes the possibility that a datum is different than it is. A datum is contingent when it is observed as a selection from an area of background possibilities: the datum derives from a selection that determines its non-being as the being of other possibilities.

The selectivity of →*meaning*-constituting systems is always contingent, i.e., the operations [→*Operation/Observation*] of these systems are not clearly determined in advance. Contingency is the fundamental problem for the coordination of selectivity in social and psychic systems, since possibilities for communication and thought are indeed only possibilities: they may be realized differently than expected [→*Expectations*]. Thus, contingency means the potential for disappointment and the necessity of risk-taking. In the social dimension, this problem appears as double contingency: every selection is dependent on both ego and alter, and both are meaning-constituting systems.

For every ego, alter is an alter ego whose behavior is unpredictable and capable of variation. Both ego and alter determine their own behavior self-referentially within their own boundaries [→*Self-Reference*]. Each is a black box for the other, because their selection criteria cannot be observed from the outside. The only thing visible to ego is the selectivity resulting from alter's operational closure: everyone observes everyone else as a system in an environment, and can observe only the input and output from and to the environment and not the self-referential operations themselves. Every system shows the others the indeterminacy of its own self-reference, along with the determinacy of its own selections.

Due to these conditions, double contingency does not mean single contingency twice, but rather a specific social quality of contingency: it means that the construction of the social world comes about through a doubled perspective horizon (the perspectives of ego and alter). Ego can observe a datum from the perspective of the possibilities actualized by alter, thereby becoming also ego's possibilities. Ego cannot experience alter's experiences, but can observe alter's perspectives and adopt them as her own as necessary. Thus, with these restrictions, alter's world is made available to ego (and vice versa): the world becomes socially contingent. Both ego and alter experience double contingency; they each include in their own perspectives the perspectives of the other and must then take them into account.

Both partners observe double contingency and the resultant indeterminacy of behavior. This leads to the emergence of a tautological circularity dependent on neither ego nor alter, in which ego constantly refers to alter and vice versa, according to the general pattern: "I'll do what you want, if you do what I want."

This circularity is interrupted by a new systemic order and becomes asymmetrical [→*Asymmetrization*]. The new order originates from the reciprocal observation of ego and alter, and from the information this observation creates. This new order is an operationally closed social system that autopoietically reproduces through the coordination of alter's and ego's contingent selections. Double contingency is thus the foundation for the autocatalysis of social systems.

Double contingency constantly dissolves because its emergence triggers a process that leads to the solution to the problem. In its "pure" form, therefore, double contingency does not exist; it is a constant problem that is included in social systems as a fundamental part of their own reproduction.

A social system emerges because there is no certainty in a situation of double contingency. Social systems control the uncertainty by structuring communication possibilities based on the indeterminacy of ego's selectivity for alter and alter's selectivity for ego. The structures of expectations fulfill the function of managing uncertainty, ensuring the potential for coordinating selections, and structuring social systems. [C.B.]

Social Systems (1995: Ch. 3); Generalized Media and the Problem of Contingency (1976); The Differentiation of Advances in Knowledge (1984).

Economic System (*Wirtschaftssystem*)

The operations of the economic system are payments; all operations concerning money must be attributed to the economic system. The communication medium of money [→*Property/Money*] is essential for the possibility of differentiating an autonomous economic system, because the definition of the operations themselves requires the monetization of the economy.

The problem in the economy is the scarcity of goods, i.e., the fact that certain goods are only available in a limited quantity. Thus, one person accessing these goods precludes the possibility for others to access them. The problem intensifies in long-term perspectives, because both alter and ego try to secure in the present what they might need in the future. Scarcity is the basis for specific →*paradoxes* in the economy: attempting to resolve scarcity through gaining access to goods creates the problem of scarcity. When alter secures goods for himself, thereby resolving his problem of scarcity, it creates scarcity for ego. Therefore, at the level of society, decreasing scarcity leads to an increase in scarcity.

The paradox is unfolded by the property code (which rests upon the distinction ownership/non-ownership) and can then become operative. For all goods that can be owned, participants in the economy have two alternatives: to be either the owner or the non-owner, to have them or not to have them. The circularity of the paradox is transformed into a distinction where ego's scarcity is not alter's scarcity, since one person's ownership is unavoidably the non-ownership of all others. From this, the possibility emerges for the exchange and circulation of goods.

In its pre-monetary form, however, property remained an extremely improbable disposition: it is improbable that everyone accepts being excluded from the enjoyment of a good. For the same reason, non-monetary economies could not be sufficiently differentiated, primarily in relation to politics because economy was too closely connected to it. The situation changed with the secondary coding of the economy through money, which subordinates the distinction ownership/non-ownership to the distinction payment/non-payment. The code now refers to the distinction between ownership and non-ownership of particular sums of money. Only those who own a given amount of money (i.e., can have non-ownership of it) can pay, and the payment is the transformation from ownership into non-ownership. This means a doubling of scarcity: next to the scarcity of goods, there is now also the scarcity of money.

Every use of money under these conditions is at the same time its transfer to others, i.e., the circulation of property. This results in the "double circulation" of the economic system. Every payment simultaneously generates the ability to pay in the receiver of the payment and the inability to pay in the giver of the payment, who must take care to restore her ability to pay through further operations in the economy. This forces the system into a remarkable dynamic. Ability and inability to pay must be constantly transferred and circulated.

Every payment requires justifications that ultimately go back to the satisfaction of particular needs, because needs are the other-reference of the system. The code (in this as in every case) gives no indication about the acceptability and unacceptability of payments. For this, we need →*programs*, which in the economy are founded on prices. The motivation to complete a payment cannot be derived directly from a need (which, as an environmental condition, cannot be processed within the system), but rather requires an orientation to a price. The price allows a rapid judgment about whether a payment is correct or not: we pay when the price is right. Thus, it is possible to produce constraints to payment processes based on the internal criteria of the economic system. Environmental conditionings appear in the economy only in the form of prices and price changes: problems appear as costs, and the decision of whether or not to complete the respective payment is subject to economic calculations.

In the modern, functionally differentiated society, there is no system-external (moral- or natural-law-based) regulation of prices. The "right price" is determined in the economic process in a self-regulated way, i.e., within the dynamic of the market. The market is the "internal environment" of the economic system, the place in which the economic system, referring to its own activities, presents itself as if it were the environment. In observing the market, participants in the economic system observe how others observe the system operations, and observe the observations of the other participants.

Through observation of price changes, the participants can obtain specific economic information about the tendencies of the system and the payments that can be expected. When, for instance, producers observe the market, they observe both themselves and other producers, and thereby obtain information for their own production and investment plans. *[E.E.]*

Die Wirtschaft der Gesellschaft (1988); Limits of Steering (1997[1988]); The Economy as a Social System (1982[1970]).

Education System (*Erziehungssystem*)

The education system is a subsystem of modern society [→*Differentiation of Society*] whose function is to trigger changes in individual →*psychic systems*. This is so that psychic systems can also take part in more improbable communication, which society produces and occurs in other functional systems.

The particularity of the education system is therefore the fact that its primary function is not oriented towards processing communication or generating communicative consensus, but rather towards transforming the psychic environment of society. The results of education are manifested outside of society, appearing in the skills and knowledge of the individual, i.e., in the individual's ability to take part in communication. In this sense, the individual has been observed as a potential on whom it is possible to intervene. The pupil has therefore been observed as a medium in which education can give forms [→*Medium/Form*], even if she remains an autonomous and non-transparent psychic system. However, since contemporary education extends not only to childhood or youth, but to the whole life of the individual, the potential for educational intervention has shifted from the pupil to the life course, which today may be considered as the medium of the education system.

Due to this particularity, education lacks a →*code* in the strict sense, since it is impossible to code what occurs outside of society. For the same reason, there is no →*symbolically generalized medium* to make educational communication more probably. This is because not even these media can operate in the environment of society: there is no way to motivate individuals requiring education to accept the educational intention of the teacher and to orient their behavior according to the teacher's expectations. Nevertheless, education develops a specific code that distinguishes between conveyable and unconveyable contents, i.e., between what can be taught and what is not suitable as educational material.

A further notable feature of education is the fact that it only functions when interactions between teachers and pupils can be organized regularly in the classroom. Interaction in schools is a functional equivalent of the absent symbolically generalized medium. This is because it creates situations in which socialization [→*Interpenetration and Structural Coupling*] is forced in a very improbable way, and this improbability enables education to plan and, where possible, to trigger targeted effects in the conscious systems of the pupils.

However, teachers can never be sure of the effects of their pedagogical behavior; they can only observe how the pupils behave and assess deviation or non-deviation from their expectations. In this sense, education entails the possibility of selection, which means producing assessments based on the difference between improvement and deterioration of the pupils' achievements. The selection therefore has a code, the two values of which are the tendencies towards improvement or deterioration. The code of the selection refers not to the act of educating itself, but rather to the building of school and university careers. The only way to enable society to process learning in the education system is take the comparison, assessment and judgment of a pupil's behavior up to the point of establishing a career and process these as forms of longer and more complex selection sequences. Selection has the function of secondary code of the education system, as in itself the primary code conveyable/non-conveyable does not guide the assessment of results.

This complex combination of different codes must be based on programs, for instance in the form of curricula. Such programs specify goals that determine which changes in the psychic states of the pupils should be generated through communication in the classroom. At the same time, the intention to educate means that results must be evaluated. Evaluation is carried out in the form of programming by conditions (selections); for instance, through reports, certificates, titles, qualifications, which can be awarded for commensurate achievement.

Education becomes necessary in society when socialization alone no longer suffices to secure appropriate behavior. Alongside normal socialization, which takes places continuously and simultaneously through simply participating in communication, a particular, intentional and therefore educational socialization develops: education happens when, assuming pedagogical intent, a behavior is presented as correct. Socialization and education are not the same thing, even though socialization is clearly a precondition for education—only those who are already socialized can be educated.

Pedagogy in the education system fulfills the function of a theory of reflection[→*Self-Reference*] and is concerned with the educational conditions of the education. In other words, it delivers a theory of education that is usable within the system. Its classic topics include: (1) the question of autonomy in education compared with other societal domains; (2) the relationship between, on the one hand, the function of education being to unfold individual human possibilities, and, on the other hand, its achievements in terms of training and applicability of skills learned; (3) the planning of the curricula; (4) the problem of lacking a technology that can guarantee the success of education; (5) the tendency to treat the constant reform of school and university facilities as a condition for improving education. *[G.C.]*

Problems of Reflection in the System of Education (2000[1979]); Das Erziehungssystem der Gesellschaft (2002); Schriften zur Pädagogik (2004); System und Absicht der Erziehung, in Zwischen Absicht und Person (1992: 102-24).

Event (*Ereignis*)

The concept of event expresses the temporal quality of elements in meaning-constituting systems. Communication in social systems and thoughts in psychic systems are not permanent states, but events without duration. The →*autopoiesis* of these systems is forced to constantly reproduce elements that disappear in the moment they occur. Moreover, every event (communication or thought) does not simply occur; it also establishes the difference between before and after. With this difference, referential horizons for other possibilities (of communication in social systems and of thoughts in psychic systems) are also established. That is to say, other things are possible after the event, and this difference (as a difference) gives the elements of the system, despite their lack of duration, a certain operative connectivity.

The relationship between continuity and discontinuity, i.e., between the system structure and its final elements, is one of the most important consequences of introducing the concept of event into systems theory. On the one hand, elements have no temporal duration and must be constantly produced: the system must select them anew in each moment. On the other hand, despite the discontinuity at the level of the elements, the →*structures*, which allow the production of elements, guarantee a certain continuity: they must remain available beyond the moment in which a communication or thought occurs. The relationships allowed by the structures do not coincide with the relationships between elements. For instance, the structures of →*expectations* in social systems represent an initial selection of what can happen, while communications (the operations) require a further selection in order to occur. If the relations between the elements (as events) were to coincide with the relations allowed by the structures, the structure and the system itself would disappear along with the event. On the other hand, elements as permanent states result in a stark reduction of the internal variability of a system. This is the case for organic systems, which reproduce themselves on the basis of long-lasting cells. The structural variability of organisms is highly restricted: a human organism, upon finding itself in the desert, does not suddenly transform into a camel.

The →*complexity* of social and psychic systems is a temporalized complexity, and it must be constructed and structured in the temporal dimension. Thus, the complexity that a system can reach depends not only on the relationships between its constitutive elements, but also on the variability of those states in temporal succession.

The potential to exploit temporal succession of events leads to higher levels of complexity: the relationships between elements can change from one moment to the next, and the system has a wide variety of possible connections at its disposal, allowing its assumption of different states depending on the environmental situation.

Introducing the concept of event has a further consequence, which concerns the concept of relationships of interpenetration [→*Interpenetration and Structural Coupling*] in social and psychic systems. Since communication and thoughts occur only as events, social systems can make use of the complexity of consciousness without having to represent psychic-structural features internally, and vice versa. Though every single event functions as an element of both consciousness and communication, it disappears immediately, and this leads to constructing differing meaning connections in each system. What is produced as a conscious operation only gains social and communicative relevance in moments without duration: every individual can begin to communicate or be the addressee of a communication, but communication disappears as soon as it occurs, and with it the coexistence of psychic and social events. In the next moment, a new communication must be started or not started, as the case may be. The coexistence of communicative and conscious operations is reduced to an event, which, as a communication, has a selectivity for the social system, and, as a thought, a different selectivity for the consciousness. Both types of system remain in the environment of the other and their boundaries remain intact: the momentariness of their coupling ensures that they do not merge with one another and that interpenetration is dissolved and created anew. If everything that was thought and said lasted, an uncontrollable chaos would very soon emerge.

The concept of event also concerns what is understood as "system change." At the operative level, meaning-constituting systems are very unstable, their basal →*self-reference* signaled by the constant destruction and production of elements. Elements as events can only be identified through the difference between before and after, i.e., elements cannot be changed. Only structures can change, because their identity remains relatively stable over time. For instance, a scientific discipline can change its paradigms upon the establishment of new distinctions that guide the development of research. However, in order for that to happen, communications must be produced that orient themselves to this new distinction. This means that social systems, at the level of its structures of expectations are capable of learning. This cannot happen at the level of communication, since communication flow is irreversible. The stability of systems with temporal complexity must therefore be attributed to their structures and not their autopoiesis, where they are instead constitutively unstable. From this perspective, memory [→Time] does not have the function of maintaining elements, but rather the function of maintaining their ability to generate structures. This is possible only due to the constant reproduction of disintegration and reintegration of elements.

Unlike objects, which manifest only their own state, identifying events requires distinguishing between two states: the state before and the state after. This gives the event a paradoxical character—it is neither the before, nor the after. Instead, it is the unity of this distinction: an event's identity is itself a distinction and both the before and the after are always present in every event. [G.C.]

Social Systems (1995: Ch. 8.III); The Autopoiesis of Social Systems (1986); Selbstreferentielle Systeme (1987).

Evolution

The theory of evolution describes how a structurally determined system can change its structures through its operations [→*System/Environment*]. Explanations of structural evolutionary changes are founded on the distinction of three mechanisms: (1) variation, (2) selection of variations and (3) retention or stabilization of the system.

We can speak of evolution when these three mechanisms can be distinguished, though the relationship between them is circular: the potential for variation demands selections that are already stabilized, just as stabilizing changes is only possible through mechanisms that secure a selection of the changes that are taking place.

In the classic theory of evolution applied to organisms, variation is attributed to endogenous causes (mutations) and selection is conceived as environmental pressure to make selections in order to adapt. In systems theory, however, it is claimed that self-referential autopoietic [→*Self-Reference, Autopoiesis*] systems can be irritated by disruptions in the environment, but cannot be forced to adapt to it. More precisely, every system is already adapted to its environment, at least for as long as it can continue to exist; hence, we cannot speak of better or worse adaptation. A fundamental property of the system is that it cannot be connected with the environment item by item: environmental →*complexity* can be understood by a system only in a reduced and limited form. This separation (and not adaptation) of system and environment must be viewed as the decisive element in explaining, for instance, the stability of life and the fact that organisms exist which remain entirely unchanged throughout evolution. Autopoietic system are equipped with structures that allow their reproduction, but this reproduction only takes place on the basis of the system elements and not in relation to the environment. The environment is a condition of the system's persistent existence; it can become incompatible with the autopoiesis of the system, in which case the system disappears.

Under these premises, the drive towards structural variation in social systems may not be traced back to their instability (as in the case of genetic mutations), but to disturbances from the environment, to which the system can only react in a way that is compatible with the continuation of its own autopoiesis. Which disturbances irritate the system and which can trigger structural change depends on the system structures. The system can be indifferent or sensitive, and this characteristic conditions its degree of irritability, and thus also its ability to change its structures. Variation always appears as deviation from existing structures, i.e., as a failure of communication that, to the observer, can seem an internal error, or a problem in the relationship between system and environment. The system reacts to this problem because communication is disrupted. In this sense, systems cannot evolve on their own: they evolve when the environment is unstable and this instability is not synchronized with that of the system. The discontinuity between system and environment guarantees that irritations are produced, and the system can react to them by increasing its indifference or by varying its structures.

Selection processes take place only within a system. Selections are based on the connectivity that the variation gains in autopoietic reproduction. In the scientific system, for instance, a new distinction is selected when sufficient connections are found in scientific communication, whereby it stimulates the production of research, experiments, tests, publications. In the case of social systems, we can therefore speak of the self-selection of communication.

Regarding the third evolutionary mechanism, the system stabilizes the selected variations when it can integrate the new elements into its internal structural features.

In the case of society, the mechanism of variation is →*language*, which sets no limits on the variation of communication. By using language, themes can be introduced in communication without any limitations. In addition, language offers the possibility to form both positive and negative statements: it is possible to trigger structural variation because →*negation* allows diversions from existing structures of expectations. The code of language allows communication variations to be generated, which can be selected in the functionally differentiated society by →*symbolically generalized media*. These communication media, such as money, power or truth, create conditions under which the probability to incorporate the suggested variation is relatively high, and determine the societal usefulness of communicative selections. Scientific communication represents, for instance, a kind of improbable and divergent communication, which in modern society requires a particular communication medium—scientific truth—in order to guarantee a certain degree of success: without this medium, scientific statements would be barely acceptable. In order for the selected variations to obtain stability at the structural level, society must also trigger the internal differentiation of subsystems. These secure the reproducibility of the selected variations even under changeable environmental conditions.

The difference in relative degree of →*complexity* between system and environment is decisive for the continuation of evolution. The evolution of social systems can be ascribed to the interpenetration [→*Interpenetration and Structural Coupling*] of psychic and social systems. Conscious systems can only contribute to the variation of social structures because they are structurally coupled with the communication. They can therefore irritate social structures through intentional communicative contributions. It is impossible to predict the content of these contributions and they can induce unexpected deviations from the social structures of expectations. The "contingency" (i.e., the unpredictability) introduced in communication through interpenetration is itself observed and judged, and either incorporated and stabilized or rejected.

The mechanisms of variation, selection and stabilization are not coordinated with one another, since the positive selection of variations or the stabilization of selections do not proceed automatically: the positive selection of a variation is a coincidence. This lack of coordination does not hinder the evolution and it even accelerates it, while the results of evolution contribute to differentiating the three mechanisms. [G.C.]

Theory of Society (2012: Ch. 3); The Direction of Evolution (1992); Einführung in die Theorie der Gesellschaft (2005: Ch. 3).

Expectations (*Erwartungen*)

Expectations are condensations of →*meaning* references that show how a certain situation is constituted and what lies ahead of it. Their function is to provide a relatively stable orientation to communication and thought, despite the complexity and contingency of the world. In this sense, expectations are the →*structures* of social and psychic systems, because they stabilize the selectivity of these systems and hold open a horizon of possibilities. Expectations of expectations (or reflexive expectations) serve as the structures of social systems.

Expectations form by selecting a limited number of possibilities that the system orients itself towards (we expect asphalt to be wet or dry, but not that it sinks). The selection is carried out by the condensation of meaning references, which forms an expectation. Condensation comes about through a generalization of meaning, which allows the upholding of identities (the asphalt, the sinking, the idea of solidity) independently of their respective specifications. Identities that condense expectations can be maintained in the system beyond the individual event or situation (we continue to expect that asphalt does not sink). The condensation of expectations has a dual function:

a) To select from a general domain of possibilities and then maintain complexity in a reduced form (we expect asphalt to sink only in an earthquake);
b) To use generalizations of meaning beyond the specific situation (anyone who has driven a car at least once expects the asphalt not to sink).

Through the unity of both functions, the condensation of expectations allows the structuration of complexity and the recognition of external reality without the possibility of direct access [→*Constructivism*]. A system observes the reality of its environment in the form of uncertain expectations. Anything in the external reality that is utterly indeterminable and unpredictable is transformed internally into something that the system can understand and use, i.e., the uncertainty of the expectation that becomes an orientation of the system.

Through their orienting function, expectations organize a system →*autopoiesis*, thus becoming structures of the system. They enable the operations of psychic and social systems to be reproduced and guarantee connectivity between their elements (thoughts or communications).

Expectations are constructed in relation to stable entities, such as objects, individuals, events, values, concepts and norms. Simple expectations are, for instance, that asphalt does not sink, that leaves are green in spring, and that children grow. Against this background, expectations are also constructed in relation to individuals, who are attributed with their own selectivity: ego expects that alter, unlike asphalt and leaves, can complete his own selections. Thus, ego must expect variability and unpredictability from alter, capable of making selections. Expectations of alter's contingent and unpredictable selections increase the risks of the world's contingency, which becomes →*double contingency*. Alter is free to vary; she can also be wrong or deceive ego.

Ego must thus construct expectations so that the variability and unpredictability of alter's actions can be predicated and expected. However, ego can also expect that alter (who is an alter ego) also orients herself to expectations. So that she can act when faced with alter, ego cannot orient herself only to the expectation of alter's actions, but also—and primarily—to the expectation of alter's expectations. →*Communication* is accomplished not simply through each participant expecting their partner's selectivity; rather, everyone must be able to expect what others expect from them. Only the expectation of each other's expectation enables ego and alter to introduce the orientation to each other's selectivity into their own orientation.

Through expectations of expectations, situations of double contingency can be organized: ego expects, that alter expects, that ego will act in a certain way. Ego is then able to understand alter's orientation and use it to orient her own action. Communication relies on this possibility of structuring expectations about expectations. If it were not possible to expect a partner's expectation, the possibility of orienting action and continuing communication would not exist, and there would be no social system. Hence the sociological relevance of the expectation of expectations: in social systems, the problem of double contingency becomes the problem of expecting expectations.

This means that expectations of expectations are structures in social systems. They are the only structures possible: the structures of social systems are constituted from expectations of expectations (or reflexive expectation:

expectations that refer to other expectations). This structure of reflexive expectations enables the participants' selectivity to be coordinated: since reflexive expectations allow communication, they also allow the autopoiesis of a social system. Reflexive expectations serve as structures in operationally closed social systems because they are required by every unit and every selection sequence in communication. The stabilization of reflexive expectation determines a domain of structured complexity within a social system.

Since a partner's selectivity in the communication is contingent and unpredictable, reflexive expectations can be disappointed. However, it is improbable that expectations in a concrete communication that is not particularly rich in prerequisites will be disappointed: for instance, the expectation that the communication partner will not respond to the question "what's the time?" with the answer "it's raining," or that she will not fall asleep in the middle of the conversation (expect in rare and justifiable circumstances). In such cases, expectations are taken to be secure. On the contrary, in situations with higher degrees of complexity, where the expectation pertains to something uncertain, we must expect disappointments. The disappointment of expectations has an important function, because it enables surprising events in the environment to be processed: a system can transform undefined complexity into disappointment and then confront itself with the different situations in its environment. Through disappointment, expectations can refer to the external reality, and the perturbative relevance of this reality can be grasped.

Since structures of expectations transform undefined complexity into the potential for disappointment, the problem of disappointment cannot be avoided: it is almost impossible not to react to a disappointment. It is therefore prudent to ascertain in advance what the reaction might be. We must also be able to expect how we will react to the disappointment of the expectation. As such, we require mechanisms to process disappointments: these mechanisms are the constituents of the structures themselves and define different modalitiesof expectation.

Society offers two different possibilities to react to disappointments of expectations—i.e., two modalities of expectations: (1) to change the expectation in order to match the disappointing reality, or (2) to cling to the expectation despite the disappointing reality. In the first case, we talk of cognitive expectations (cognition), in the second case of normative expectations (norms). Thus, in a system, there are two functionally equivalent strategies to react to situations of disappointment of expectations [→*Functional Analysis*]: the system can be ready to learn (cognitive expectations), or it can decide not to learn (normative expectations). Through these strategies, the risk of disappointment can be processed within the structure of expectations.

At specific levels, cognitive and normative expectations are blended together and cannot be clearly separated. In cases that are important in society, however, the conditions of stability of cognitive and normative expectations must be generalized separately. This generalization is performed by social structures such as law [→*Legal System*] for normative expectations and scientific →*truth* for cognitive expectations. Law generalizes a normative strategy of absorbing disappointments (a legal contravention as such in no way implies that the law will be changed) and scientific truth generalizes a cognitive strategy (new scientific discoveries imply that the theory will be changed).

In the case of normative expectations, the difference between fulfillment and disappointment corresponds to the distinction between conforming behavior according to the expectation and diverging behavior disappointing the expectation. In the case of cognitive expectations, the difference between fulfillment and disappointment corresponds to the distinction between knowing (which matches expectations) and not knowing (which disappoints expectations). In this way, the difference between fulfillment and disappointment is highlighted through the distinctions between conformity/non-conformity and knowing/not-knowing, which refer to the normative or cognitive modalities of expectation, respectively. *[C.B.]*

Social Systems (1995: 292-294); Law as a Social System (2004: 106ff); Die Wissenschaft der Gesellschaft (1990: Ch. 3.II).

Functional Analysis (*Funktionale Analyse*)

Functional analysis is the scientific method associated with the theory of social systems. It allows the understanding of every phenomenon and every datum as contingent and comparable with others. Knowledge is constructed through comparing the datum with alternative possibilities, the comparison being undertaken by an observer.

In functional analysis, every phenomenon becomes a problem that opens up different possibilities for connection. The analysis describes the relationship between the problems and their possible solutions: the data are the initial problems; the solutions offered are contingent and could also be different. The function is therefore to provide a schema of comparison for different solutions that, in relation to the function, are considered to be equivalent. The analysis achieves a situation in which functionally equivalent solutions are taken into account for the problem in question.

The relationship between the problem and its solution serves to steer research towards other functionally equivalent possibilities. By seeing data as problems, the method offers a way to connect them to various alternative solutions, i.e., numerous possibilities can be taken into account. We are able to find possible functional equivalents since we observe that only one of many possibilities is actualized that fulfills the function in question. This allows functional analysis to both widen and narrow the field of observation. Through the discovery of functional equivalents, functional analysis contradicts the ontological assumption that every actual being necessarily excludes the non-being (of other possibilities of being).

In the scientific system, problems and their solutions are specified with the help of relationships of cause and effect. Therefore, recourse to cause/effect hypotheses is a specification of functional analysis. However, the basic contribution of the functional method does not lie in ascertaining the connection between causes and effects, but rather in highlighting the comparison that this connection makes possible: between different causes of the same effect or between different effects of the same cause. The functional method allows a comparison of functional equivalents: different causes are functionally equivalent when they produce the same effect, and different effects are functionally equivalent when provoked by the same cause. The relationships between causes and effects are related to the problem of →*complexity*, i.e., to the reference to further functionally equivalent possibilities. Hence, functional analysis does not contradict the analysis of causal relationships, but includes it.

In sociology, functional analysis refers to the problems and solutions of →*meaning*-constituting systems. The functional method fulfills a dual observation of these systems: (1) it highlights distinctions that are not visible to the observed system, due to the function of latency [→*Sociological Enlightenment*], and (2) it includes what is known and familiar to the system (manifest structures and functions) in a domain of alternative possibilities, thus showing its contingency. The concepts of latency and contingency connect the functional method with systems theory.

This functional method differs from traditional functionalism because it is connected with a new version of systems theory. Traditional functionalism observes a social system as a whole consisting of parts that guarantee its continuation. Such an approach is called "structural functionalism", since the function is related to the maintenance of structures, of stability (or of dynamic equilibrium). Conforming to the paradigm shift in system theory, functionalism in Luhmann's theory no longer views the maintenance or non-maintenance of a system stability (or equilibrium) as the problem. Instead, the problem is the continuation or interruption of the reproduction of elements and operations of the system [→*Autopoiesis*], i.e., the maintenance of its operational closure. In relation to this problem, functional analysis is able to reveal actual solutions and functional equivalents. [C.B.]

Soziologische Aufklärung (1970: 9 ff.); Funktionale Methode und Systemtheorie (1964); Social Systems (1995: Ch. 1.IV); Die Wissenschaft der Gesellschaft (1990: Ch. 6.VIII).

Identity/Difference (*Identität/Differenz*)

Luhmann's systems theory is a constructivist [→*Constructivism*] approach based on differences. This means that it does not start from an identity, such as an object or a concept taken for granted, for instance the existence of individuals or the concept of "system". The point of departure is a distinction—the distinction →*system/environment*—to which further distinctions are connected, such as →*operation/observation*, identity/difference, actual/possible [→*Meaning*]. When understood in this way, the distinction is also described with the expression "two-sided form", i.e., a form as a distinction, a separation, or a difference.

The orientation towards distinctions (or towards forms) is the result of deciding to take observation as the basic concept, referring to George Spencer Brown's logic. According to this theory, observation is only possible when a continuum is interrupted drawing a distinction between what is observed and the background: we refer to something indicating it, and at the same time distinguish it from the background. The operation of observation always includes both moments of indication and distinction, which only ever appear together. When there is an indication there is also a distinction and vice versa, but their simultaneity should not lead to confounding the two. Observation is an articulation of their difference. What is processed is not the identity of indication and distinction, but rather their difference—the difference between that which remains fixed (identity) and that from which it is distinguished (difference).

The initial distinction guiding a system's operations determines what it can observe, as well as what it cannot see [→*Operation/Observation*]. This also applies to theories that are the expression of a "guiding difference" (*Leitdifferenz*), which directs the possibility to process information. In the case of the theory of social systems, the guiding difference is the distinction between system and environment. In the case of functional systems, the guiding difference is the respective →*code*. When the system observes the unity of its initial difference, the result is a →*re-entry*.

The orientation towards differences allows the explanation of →*information* processing, which relies on a distinction and proceeds according to the schema sketched by Spencer Brown. Many distinctions emerge from the starting one, until a complex network of connections (and distinctions) is produced. A distinction is always relative to the observer and is not given in the world independently of her categories; through the orientation to differences and the information processing that follows, a system withdraws from a one-to-one correspondence with the environment and builds its own complexity.

Starting with the initial distinction, an identity can be later "condensed" through repeatedly indicating one side of the distinction and thereby making it recognizable. If within the context of a distinction we refer many times to a particular side of the distinction, this side will gain its own contours and an identity that is partly independent of each actual context, which can possibly (but not necessarily) be denoted with a name. When, for instance, the distinction "chair/other objects" is used, the identity of the object "chair" builds a reference that collects and coordinates the numerous different impressions that refer to it. When we orient to the distinction system/environment, the system is understood as an entity that remains fixed against an environment from which it is distinguished. Instead of a stream of constantly changing experiences, meaning is articulated in relatively stable configurations, which can be recalled in other situations, at other points in times and with other communication partners.

An identity is a symbolic generalization in the stream of the experience of →*meaning*. It allows the reference of meaning to itself and the corresponding increase in complexity. Generalization deals with multiple references as a unity, and can be realized in all →*meaning dimensions*; one can generalize an identity (fact dimension: a chair is a chair, even when it is made of plastic) on a consensual basis (social dimension: the chair is also a chair for others) which assumes a certain duration (temporal dimension: the chair will be a chair also tomorrow).

Here identity does not mean a simple quality of the objects, but rather implies reference to an observer who establishes it. We always speak of the identity of something for someone based on a specific distinction. Identities are introduced, therefore, in order to organize the differences with which meaning functions. Identities are not primary givens, but rather they are negatively defined through their differences to something else; they combine a number of distinctions into a form that can be processed. The concept "chair" (the referred identity) is always a reduction of the wealth of meaning references of every real chair (its particular form, color, individual features). Both a stool and an armchair can be called a "chair" and their many differences set aside. The identity serves as a reference in order to organize the differences condensed therein, and, at the same time, the differences in the contexts in which it appears.

For both psychic and social systems, identities have the function to organize →*expectations* by referring to something that remains relatively stable. The domain of the experienceable is organized through identities, each of them connecting a range of differing expectations. We do not expect the same from a book as we do from a door—and even when we can expect both to be closable, we learn nothing about books when a door is closed. We can expect that a book, like a glass, will fall out of our hand, which cannot happen with a door.

In the social domain of expectations of expectations, it is necessary to construct more abstract ideas than those organizing the reference to things. We must take into account that the "object" we refer to has its own perspective of observation. Thus emerges a situation of →*double contingency*. The connections of the expectations are condensed on a scale of increasing abstraction according to four different modes of identity construction. First, there is the identity of →*persons*: something different is expected of each person and particular character traits, tastes and other characteristics are assigned to that person that characterize him or her. Second, there is the identity of roles that can be assumed by different people and only impact a limited segment of their behavior, for instance, the role of shop assistant, spouse or student. The identity of →*programs* can involve multiple individuals. Programs are defined as complexes of conditions of correct behavior that can include multiple roles at the same time, for instance, planning a surgical operation, building a new car motor or staging an opera. The most abstract points of reference that organize expectations are →*values*, which determine a very general orientation guiding the construction of preferences: someone is for freedom or against environmental pollution or for racial equality.

In reference to a system, unity and identity are distinguished; the unity of a system is generated through its operations [→*Autopoiesis*], which draw the boundary between system and environment but are not necessarily able to observe it. The unity of a system can only be observed as unity by an external observer. If, however, the observer is the system itself, we talk instead of identity. The identity of a system emerges, therefore, only when the system reflects [→*Self-Reference*] on its own unity. *[E.E.]*

Social Systems (1995: 9-11, Ch. 2.II., 2.VII, 8.XI); Identity—What or How? (2002); Die Wissenschaft der Gesellschaft (1990: Ch. 5.VI, 7.III); Theory of Society (2012: Ch. 1.3).

Inclusion/Exclusion (*Inklusion/Exklusion*)

The difference between inclusion and exclusion refers to the way in which a society permits individuals to be persons and therefore to participate in communication.

The concept of the person describes neither the consciousness nor the body of the individual, which are independent autopoietic systems. Rather, it is located at the level of communication: "person" is a social structure allowing society's finding of addressees for the continued production of →*communication*. As such, the reference to a person facilitates the attribution of communicative responsibility (for utterances) and the localization of possibilities of understanding. In this sense, persons are not systems in the way that conscious systems and bodies are, but rather artifacts of communication. They identify individual contexts that generate expectations of limited possibilities of behavior [→*Identity/Difference*], and in which each individual is faced with the alternative of confirming these expectations or surprising the communication with unexpected stimuli. The choice between confirming and surprising has a different meaning for the psychic and for the social system; it may have decisive consequences for the history of the consciousness, but remaining irrelevant for the history of communication.

Persons and their characteristics, which can be observed socially, emerge from the unstable circularity of →*double contingency*: ego and alter observe each other reciprocally, and this being observed leads to stabilizing the personal traits that can be expected both from the person herself and from other persons. Thus, the way in which we are observed determines the type of personality that can serve as the addressee of a communication.

Inclusion and exclusion are manifested in different forms depending on the structure of the society [→*Differentiation of Society*] in which persons are observed. In segmentary societies, inclusion consists in belonging to a segment, for instance to a tribe or to a village. Exclusion from a segment can occur through relocation to a different tribe or a different village, though it is practically impossible to survive outside all segments (which means outside society).

In the stratified society, belonging to society is organized by social layers, and belonging to a layer is determined primarily by ancestry. Exclusion is practiced predominantly through the endogamous closure of the social layer, which determines who is worthy of participating in layer-specific communication and who should be treated differently. Stratification is structured in households, or alternatively in corporations, armies, universities, convents and the like. Life outside a household, or its equivalents, is extremely difficult, although there are certain opportunities for survival, for instance, as a vagabond or, in a borderline case, as a pirate. In these cases, however, the normal reciprocity that secures the future and stabilizes expectations is interrupted; the relevance of situations and events is shifted away from a "normal" process of communication, and onto the critical alternative between salvation and damnation.

Functional differentiation means that the typical differences of stratificatory rank lose their primary relevance. A social structure emerges to take their place, which proceeds from the assumption that, in principle, everyone can participate in all forms of communication, and potential differences are not retained within this form of differentiation. Everyone can be economically active, can be educated, found a family or experience equal treatment in a court of law. In this sense, modern inclusion finds its semantic correlate in the postulates of freedom and equality: equality describes the conditions for social contacts—i.e., the lack of predetermined discrimination—whilst freedom describes the fact that establishing social contacts requires an individual decision. Differences in the use of this freedom can only be justified within each subsystem and not by society as a whole.

The postulates of freedom and equality are the semantic correlates of inclusion and have little to say about the structures that determine inclusion and exclusion. Compared with stratified societies, for instance, a structural change can be recognized chiefly by the fact that the person's quality and worth (*dignitas*) can no longer function as selection criteria. Having dissolved the typical hierarchical differences, modern society had to come up with an alternative and equivalent solution. This consists in observing persons on the basis of their biographies: the temporalization of the person is constructed as a career. Expectations relating to persons are primarily based on the biography-centered differentiation between past and future. Any anticipation of the future can only proceed from the expectations permitted by the past, while ascribed factors play only a very marginal role and are anyway—in principle—not acceptable as selection criteria for participation in communication. For instance, schooling for the whole population can be seen as generalized inclusion in the education system. Reorienting the criterion of inclusion towards the career leads directly to the early stages of biographies becoming imbued with significant meaning, since they constitute the past that will in future serve the career. However, because it concerns one of the most important career phases, the school career is constructed in such a way that it does not limit too strictly what can be done afterwards; everyone's individual school history allows a certain capitalization of the past, which is not determinative, but can be recombined according to the needs of each current situation.

In a certain sense, modern society simultaneously includes and excludes all persons; although everyone can participate in every communication, no-one can be fully integrated in a subsystem. There are no human beings who are only economic or only scientific. The difference between inclusion and exclusion is also addressed within the subsystems through formal →*organizations* of communication, which are needed in the subsystems. For instance, the economy can only reproduce itself when there are companies, and education could not exist without schools. Whilst each subsystem generally includes everyone, formal organizations include people only in a limited way: in a company, only members can make internal organizational decisions; in a school class, only pupils and a teacher are included. Though subsystems have no reason to exclude someone, formal organizations cannot make everyone a member; thus, this difference between subsystem and organization constitutes a modern version of the difference inclusion/exclusion.

Compared to older societies, modern society changes the criterion for inclusion above all in one respect: exclusion from one subsystem does not mean inclusion in another. If, in stratified societies, belonging to one social layer implied exclusion from the others, then in modern society the connections between the different subsystems are looser; a good education does not say much about a person's occupation in the economy or other domains. The modern form of inclusion implies a significant loosening of social integration, since inclusion in one subsystem says nothing about inclusion in another. The opposite phenomenon can be observed instead for exclusion, since exclusion from one subsystem sparks a kind of domino effect that can quickly make an individual as a person irrelevant to society. Should a person lose her job, it becomes difficult to keep a flat and health insurance, or vice versa; in extreme cases, it also becomes impossible to guarantee education for children in school. This close integration of exclusion can lead to observing individuals as being less and less valid as possible communication partners. In the case of slums or favelas, it goes as far as observing individuals only as bodies, which are subject to completely different conditions than persons are (e.g., problems of survival, violence, disease).

The difference between inclusion and exclusion is meaningful for the →*self-description* of society because it is the instrument through which the criteria for access to communication are determined: the inner side (inclusion) describes the conditions and possibilities for participating in communication and therefore demands care and attention; the outer side, exclusion, describes what remains and forces society to reflect. Today, this has become visible in the meaning taken on by, on the one hand, careers and an orientation towards success, and, on the other hand, by situations in which the opposite conditions are valid, such as, for instance, the ghetto, famine, overpopulation. [G.C.]

> Wie ist soziale Ordnung möglich? (1981: in Gesellschaftsstruktur und Semantik vol. 2: 195-285); Individuum, Individualität, Individualismus (1989: in Gesellschaftsstruktur und Semantik vol. 3: 149-258); Inklusion und Exklusion (1994); Theory of Society (2013: Ch. 4.3).

Information

Information is defined as an →*event* that selects the states of a system—an event, thus, that exerts a selective influence on the →*structures* of a system, triggering changes.

The capacity to process information depends on the capacity to orient towards distinctions [→*Identity/Difference*]: a message counts as information because there is a difference between what is received and what was expected. Information, therefore, is a difference. The information thus triggers further differences in the resulting inner restructuring: the difference between the system's actual and expected states forces numerous adjustments to be made in the structure of the system itself, which changes in order to take the information into account. Information therefore produces further differences within the system. For this reason, we also say—using Gregory Bateson's formulation—that information is a "difference which makes a difference". Information is oriented towards distinctions; this means that it is only produced in the structures of a system that changes its own states as a consequence of the changes in other points in the same system.

The environment's only function is of irritation and disturbance: what happens in the environment is only recorded in the system as "noise". Information is the result of irritations being processed by the system's own distinctions. Thus, information is not present as such in the environment, waiting to be grasped—in the words of Heinz von Foersters: "the environment contains no information; the environment is what it is."

In the case of a social system, whose structures are structures of →*expectations*, information arises when an unexpected event leads to changing what we later expect. For the economic system, the event of a change in the price of a product means restructuring the payment expectations; from that moment on, we are prepared to pay more (or less), or we decide to no longer buy that product (or to buy it for the first time).

An element of newness is required if we are to speak of information: a repeated news (for instance, a story read for a second time in a different newspaper without any additional content) no longer has any informative value, because it implies no restructuring of expectations. In this case, expectations have already been restructured in order to take the information into account. What counts as information for a particular system does not necessarily also count as information for another (other systems may, for instance, already know or not understand the content of the news). Thus, informativeness is always relative to the structures of the respective system.

Because information is always information *for* someone, it is inappropriate to define →*communication* as the transfer of information. Nothing is transferred, since the message giver does not lose the information, and the message receiver does not gain something. Instead, following a communicative stimulus, the receiver autonomously processes her structures according to her own forms.

The concept of information requires, therefore, a self-referential system [→*Self-Reference*], which changes its internal states based on its own internal states, even when the selection within the system is attributed to the environment and not to the system itself [→*Attribution*]. When the system learns, for instance, that quicksilver can be carcinogenic, it processes the datum as an environmental state. Still, it is only information because the system is able to process it.

We speak of information not when a change is determined from outside, but only in the case of a "determination to self-determination," i.e., when the system uses a stimulus attributed to the environment in order to change its own structures according to its own forms and in its own manner. It only ever concerns internal processes of self-referential systems.

This meaning of information, focused on the concept of difference, even allows something that it not given (such as a lack, a mistake, a disappointment) to have informative value, as well as allowing for the fact that the system can "self-inform" via comparison with its own past or with earlier states of its own structures. Everything that can be processed as a difference can function as information. [E.E.]

Social Systems (1995: 65-69, Ch. 4.II); Selbstorganisation und Information im politischen System (1991).

Interaction (*Interaktion*)

Interaction is a social system that requires the physical presence of the participants. Interactions form when communication is based on the perception of presence, which ensues from →*double contingency*.

Reflexive perception (the perception of perception) is the pre-social requirement of interaction. Communication demands the mutual perception of perception: the participants perceive that they themselves are perceived. If they perceive that they are perceived, and that their own perception is also perceived, the participants in communication can observe that their behavior is understood as information. This makes communication unavoidable, since even non-communication is observed as communication, i.e. as rejection of communication. Therefore, it is impossible not to communicate in interaction systems.

The selection principle and the only prerequisite for establishing the interaction system is presence based on perception. Since no absent person can contribute to interactive communication, the foundational distinction for observing interaction is the distinction between those present and those absent, although not everyone who is present must necessarily take part in communication (the bar tender does not necessarily participate in communication between customers at the bar). The distinction present/absent allows the formulation of a relatively simple definition of the boundary of communication: interaction is the simplest social system. Interaction is, however, still a complex social system because the number of possible communications makes a selection necessary [→*Complexity*].

The complexity of the interaction is processed by means of binary schemata [→*Code*]. Options for communication are pre-structured according to these schemata, which are thus the premises of communication. The schemata, which are the structures of interactions, correspond to the three →*meaning dimensions*: ego/alter (social dimension), constant/variable (temporal dimension), and internal/external (fact dimension). In every interaction, all three schemata operate simultaneously.

→*Attribution* of selections to ego or alter in the social dimension organizes interaction in terms of attributing responsibility and intentionality; we can know who said what and act accordingly. In the temporal dimension, the difference between constant characteristics and variable achievements allows the distinction between the conditions determined by what is constant, and the selection of what is variable. There is, on the one hand, structural conditioning and, on the other hand, there are contingent selection processes. In the fact dimension, the attribution to ego and alter can be internal or external; the internal attribution allows the understanding of intentions behind ego and alter's actions, while the external attribution allows the understanding of their experiences.

Interaction constitutes the minimum level of communication production: without interaction, a social system would not be possible. Interaction is, however, not equal to →*society*: interactions are episodes that contribute to the realization of society, whilst at the same time differentiating themselves within society. Society is simultaneously the condition for and the environment of interaction.

The difference between society and interaction is already present in the oldest segmentary societies, in which all communication is interactive and oral: no single interaction can include all communications, and not all partners can always be present at the same time. Later, the relationship between society and interaction evolves and varies in connection with the change in the structure of society [→*Differentiation of Society*] and new possibilities of reaching the addressee of the communication [→*Dissemination Media*].

In stratified societies, interaction is dependent on the hierarchical structure of society. At the same time, due to the invention of writing, it becomes possible to communicate regardless of whether the participants are present or not. Interaction upholds an important function within social strata and remains essential for the reproduction of society. For instance, interactions at court are particularly relevant for the upper stratum, and thus for society.

With functional differentiation, the invention of printing and, later, the new dissemination media, non-interactive communication becomes more and more frequent and continues to grow in importance in society. A significant share of the most improbable and societally relevant communication (e.g., payment, scientific discussion, political debates) no longer requires the physical presence of the participants and also includes people who are absent (through printing, TV and computers).

This situation reveals many structural limitations of interaction. It is reliant on physical presence; it necessitates the discussion of only one topic at a time; it dissolves easily when faced with conflict, unpleasant communication or attempts to impose hierarchies. Participants can easily withdraw. Overcoming these structural limitations becomes possible with the invention of media that increase the chance of success of non-interactive communication [→*Symbolically Generalized Media*].

Society determines globally the conditions for realizing specific interactions and creates (in the subsystems and in the organizations) a structured social environment to which interactions must adapt. Interactions themselves often concern problems that lie beyond their boundaries (e.g., parliamentary debates, office discussions, romantic rendezvous). In these cases, the interaction can take on a new meaning and importance. For instance, an interaction can ignore the role-based expectations of participants that are valid outside of the interaction (e.g. medical interactions ignore the political or economic roles of patients); or it can realize an intimacy that includes the participant as a whole person (in families). The interaction can be observed both within the functional systems (e.g., economic system, political system, scientific system, education system, system of families, medical system) and in function-free contexts (standing in line to buy theatre tickets, on the bus, in a bar).

Understood in this way, the distinction between society and interaction is incompatible with the traditional distinction between micro-sociology (analysis of interaction) and macro-sociology (analysis of complex social systems). This is because society and interaction are not different levels of the social, but are system references that are differentiated according to the type of boundary demarcation, to the structural rules of communication, and to the limit of admitted complexity. [C.B.]

Social Systems (1995: Ch. 10.III); Schematismen der Interaktion (1979); The Evolutionary Differentiation of Interaction and Society (1987); Theory of Society (2013: Ch. 4.13).

Interpenetration and Structural Coupling
(*Interpenetration und strukturelle Kopplung*)

The concepts of interpenetration and structural coupling explain the relationship between systems that are internally determined by their own operations and structures. These systems are in each other's environment and irritate each other, without having access to each other's operations. Each system is a source of irritation for the other, and it must continuously process these irritations. Irritations are not the result of transmitting information from one system to the other: they are self-produced within the system, as systems are operationally closed [→*Autopoiesis*]. Interpenetration and structural coupling are not based on a type of system project; they simply happen on the basis of the →*system/environment* differentiation.

What is interesting in social systems theory is the interpenetration and structural coupling between →*social systems* and →*psychic systems*. Social systems are closed →*meaning*-constituting systems based on the operation of →*communication*, and do not have access to the operation of thinking in psychic systems. Psychic systems are closed meaning-constituting systems based on the operation of consciousness, and cannot be included in social systems. Communication cannot observe [→*Operation/Observation*] what happens in participants' consciousness, although consciousness is always involved in communication. Consciousness cannot control or determine communication; independently of what participants think about utterances and information, understanding is used in social systems to continue communication. Understanding is followed by utterances, for instance by expressions of doubt about the sincerity of a previous utterance or surprise at unexpected information. Uttering information does not coincide with the content or intentions produced in participants' consciousness, therefore participants' thinking does not coincide with what is produced in the network of communication. Participants have their own individual intentions to buy an object, but these intentions do not determine either the economic value of the object or the consequences of the transaction. These are fixed in the communicative reproduction of payment that is generated when we understand that someone else is paying and how much they are paying. Researchers have their own intentions to present at a conference, but this does not decide the scientific relevance of their contributions, generated in a network of communications in which any presentation can find (or not find) connections. Summing up, social systems cannot result from individual intentions; they result only from the autopoiesis of communication.

Nevertheless, psychic systems are fundamental for the reproduction of social systems, as without consciousness communication is impossible. Psychic systems are the only source of environmental irritation for social systems, which have no direct access to physical, chemical or neurophysiological phenomena. Each external phenomenon needs to be filtered through consciousness to become the theme of communication and a source of self-irritation in social systems. Consciousness is therefore an essential environmental condition for communication. Social systems exist on the basis of the irritations that psychic systems create when they participate in communication. Psychic systems work as filters for any environmental irritation of social systems, thus allowing self-irritation of social systems.

The concept of interpenetration explains how systems within a system's environment contribute to system formation. Both social systems and psychic systems can exist only if they interpenetrate: communication is based on conscious thinking and conscious thinking is based on communication. Interpenetration allows mutual contribution to the selection of elements, communications and thoughts; however, communication and thought cannot coincide, as each of them is constituted in the autopoiesis of only one system. Although consciousness and communication cannot coincide, single selections can be produced simultaneously in both systems. Therefore, interpenetration does not mean mutual determination or fusion between the interpenetrating systems, since both psychic and social systems are operationally closed and can only create meaning internally. Interpenetration means that communication and thought are simultaneously produced in a specific event, as conscious thinking occurs at the same time as either understanding or uttering. However, communication and thoughts immediately separate as the event disappears: thinking immediately connects to other thinking, and communication immediately connects to other communication. As such, interpenetration ensures both the mutual condition of existence of the systems and the difference between the systems.

Through interpenetration each system makes its →*complexity* available for the operations of the other system. Psychic systems' complexity is available for the operational closure of social systems, and social systems' complexity is available for the operational closure of psychic systems. The penetrating system is co-determined by the penetrated system, which reacts to the structured complexity of the penetrating system. The penetrating system introduces disorder in the penetrated system, as its complexity is pre-structured, and the penetrated system creates order from this disorder, or order from noise [→*Constructivism*]. The co-evolution of these different types of systems is thus provided for by interpenetration. New conditions of communication stimulate changes in the participating psychic systems, and new ways of thinking stimulate changes in the social systems in which psychic systems participate. For instance, education transforms the conditions of self-irritation in psychic systems, and the development of individual expressions of need or knowledge transforms the conditions of self-irritation in social systems.

This implies that interpenetration means structural coupling. Structural coupling presupposes that the reproduction of each system is based on its own structures, and that each system can be irritated by another system structures. Continuous and specific self-irritations can trigger structural change in a system, in particular changes in the structures of reflexive →*expectations* in social systems. Structural coupling does not lead to durable structural connections between consciousness and communication; it does not produce operational coupling. Operational coupling means that specific elements are contingently shared by different systems. Structural coupling between social systems and psychic systems happens in single events, and the two types of systems immediately and continuously decouple. Structural coupling requires continuous decoupling: communications are connected to and find meaning in other communications; conscious thinking is connected to and finds meaning in other conscious thinking.

Structures of communication allow consciousness to take form. Social systems generate binary schematizations, distinguishing between two sides as forms of reduction of their internal complexity, which are thus made available for consciousness. Binary schematizations are used by both social systems and psychic systems in their operational closure. They are produced by a social system as reduced complexity and autonomously used by psychic systems, which can choose from the available options. Binary schematizations include, for instance, friendly/unfriendly, true/false, conforming/deviant, and attraction/aversion. These schematizations show that interpenetration means structural coupling, as it selects the structures that enable the reproduction of the interpenetrating systems. Binary schematizations are structural productions in social systems that are successful in providing self-irritations in psychic systems. Self-irritations arise from an internal comparison of events with the system's established structures.

Thus, structural coupling explains socialization, which is the process that forms the psychic system, as well as the bodily behavior of human beings that the psychic system can control. Socialization is based on individuals' participation in communication as experience of socially reduced complexity. This experience contributes to structuring the complexity of psychic systems. Binary schematizations are structural productions in social systems that are successful in causing self-irritations in psychic systems. Socialization means that the psychic system can use, in its self-reference, schematizations attributed to the social environment. Therefore, socialization is based both on the binary schematizations that are defined in communication, and self-socialization, which are meaningful operations produced by the psychic system. In socialization, it is the binary schematizations that are relevant, rather than the specific options that they offer: what counts is the distinction between attraction and aversion, not the choice of either attraction or aversion. Increased structured complexity in social systems changes the conditions of socialization, without denying the importance of self-socialization.

Structural coupling can also be observed between the subsystems of a functionally differentiated society [→*Differentiation of Society*]. Each functional system observes the other functional systems in its environment as relevant for its reproduction. This observation enhances interdependencies among the functional systems, which are based on structural coupling. For instance, the political system and the economic system are coupled through taxes and charges, in which both money and political power are involved; similarly, the legal system and the economic system are coupled through contracts and property, which are legally determined and economically relevant. These interdependencies are always observed from the perspective of specific functional systems, which in this way cause self-irritations. For instance, political taxation provokes self-irritations in the economic system. Any change or instability in a subsystem determines self-irritations in the others, with an ensuing intensification of irritations.

In a functionally differentiated society, structural coupling presupposes the operational closure of functional systems. However, structural coupling between functional systems is also operational coupling, because specific communications are contingently shared by different systems, although they are immediately connected to the internal autopoiesis of these systems (e.g., to the political system and the economic system or the legal system and the economic system). For instance, negotiating and signing a property contract is a communication which is contingently shared by the legal system and the economic system, and the government's reimbursement of tax is a communication which is contingently shared by the political system and the economic system. Operational coupling is possible in society because it involves the same type of operation (communication), but it is not possible between social systems and psychic systems, as communication and thought are different types of operation, ensuring the autopoiesis of different types of meaning-constituting systems.

Structural and operational coupling between functional systems show how functional differentiation determines the integration of society. This integration is necessary because the differentiation of functions also requires systematic interdependencies to reproduce society as a whole. However, the great quantity of structural and operational couplings between the subsystems exposes the functionally differentiated society to continuous and systematic self-irritations, which cannot be regulated at the level of the society itself. Therefore, in the functionally differentiated society, the combination of multiple forms of operational closure in functional systems, and the interdependencies that enhance continuous self-irritation in each functional system, create an exceptional level of complexity. [C.B.]

Interpenetration. Zum Verhältnis personaler und sozialer Systeme (1977); Interpenetration bei Parsons (1978); Social Systems (1995: Ch. 6); How Can the Mind Participate in Communication? (1994); Theory of Society (2012: Ch. 1.6); Theory of Society (2013: 4.9).

Language (*Sprache*)

Language is the medium that has the function to make understanding communication probable. Language makes it possible to go beyond the domain of what can be perceived and, with the help of symbolic generalizations in the form of signs, to communicate on something that is not present or is only possible.

A →*communication*—i.e., the understanding of the difference between information and utterance—does not necessarily have to take the form of language. It can also occur on the basis of perceptions: ego perceives alter's behavior (moving quickly and busily) and interprets it as an utterance intended to communicate a certain piece of information (alter does not want to stay and talk). Perception as such is not communication: we perceive sounds, images and stimuli without linking them to communication, processing them instead as information. To stay with the example above: through perception, we can conclude that alter is simply walking quickly. This perception becomes communication only if the distinction between a further piece of information and its utterance comes into play—only in the case that a communication is attributed to someone who utters it: alter communicates that she is currently not available.

At the level of perception, we can never be sure if it is really a question of communication, or whether it is simply behavior with a different purpose (alter was only moving quickly because she was running late): the distinction between information and utterance is never sharp and unequivocal. The situation changes when the utterance uses language: in this case, specific sounds are produced that are articulated in such an improbable and recognizable way that it is very difficult to deny the communicative intention of the utterance. Linguistic sounds are not produced by accident.

Spoken language has a specific form [→*Identity/Difference*]: the distinction between sound and meaning. The sound is not the meaning, but determines what the meaning is, that is being talked about. Meaning is not the sound, but determines which sound must be used in order to express the given meaning. The arbitrariness of language is based on this distinction: the connection between the linguistic sign and the signified content is not based on any similarity between them (a similarity between the object "table" and the sequence of sounds t-e-i-b-(ə)-l), and there is no internal reason for signifying a certain content with one particular sequence of sounds over another. For this reason, linguistic communication draws a strict distinction between the content and the forms that express them. It makes the distinction between information and utterance clear and generalizes it: we can produce a linguistic sign for any communication content regardless of whether the object concerned is present and can be perceived. As such, it is also possible to talk about "abstract objects," which can never be perceived: truth, justice, immortal people, objects that only exist in the communication, things that are absent or impossible and, above all, earlier communications.

Language, by allowing communication to treat every possible content as an object, also allows communication to take on reflective forms [→*Self-Reference*], i.e., to communicate about itself. Language makes the distinction between information and utterance clear and unequivocal enough to be able to be made into the object of further communication. We may ask, thus, why a certain piece of information was uttered in one way and not another, or check whether we have been understood. Linguistic communication is thus able to reach an extremely high level of complexity because, on the one hand, it refers to earlier communications recursively and can test their assumptions, and on the other hand, it can risk more and more improbable forms (we speak about things that are unknown to the communication partner or impossible). Misunderstanding can, if necessary, be clarified on a reflective level (i.e., with the help of communication about communication). The introduction of writing and, later, the printing press [→*Dissemination Media*] makes it possible to address someone who is not present, or even an unknown person, and thereby marks a further level of improbability of communication.

Using linguistic means, we can communicate a →*negation*, whilst there is no negative perception (the perception of a non-object). We can, for instance, speak about a non-given object as something that does not exist, but we cannot perceive this object. The capacity for negation derives from the specific →*code* of the medium of language: the code yes/no. Language correlates every positive statement ("yes" formulation) with a corresponding negative utterance ("no" formulation) in order that every linguistic communication unavoidably refers to the possible opposite statement. For every linguistic communication, a negating statement can be formulated and this possibility is always implicitly given alongside. Thus communication takes the form of the distinction between two opposing possibilities and can then—due to the distinction—be processed as →*information*. For this reason, language allows any content to be communicated informatively and is therefore the mechanism of variation for the →*evolution* of society.

Thanks to its particular characteristics, language also plays an essential role in the →*interpenetration* of psychic and social systems. Even though it is constituted of highly structured elements, language serves as a medium [→*Medium/Form*] for both communication and consciousness, which can impose their forms on it: language is suitable for expressing every thought and formulating every communication.

According to this understanding, and contrary to widely accepted linguistic theories, language as such is not a system but a medium, which is used by systems in order to structure their own operations—and in particular to gain reflexivity. Language has no specific operation: language exists only in the operations of psychic and social systems. Its internal systematicity must be traced back to the autopoiesis of the systems that use it and not to the operations of a system of language. Among the consequences that result from this view, it is particularly relevant that linguistic terms are not signs that represent an external referent, but are rather the expression of the autopoiesis of psychic and social systems. Under the condition of autopoietic closure, these operations do not refer to the external world, but rather to the internal operations of the system concerned. [E.E.]

Social Systems (1995: Ch. 4.V); How Can the Mind Participate in Communication? (1994); Die Wissenschaft der Gesellschaft (1990: Ch. 1.IV); Theory of Society (2012: 60-64, Ch. 2.3); Sign as Form (1999).

Legal System (*Rechtssystem*)

The legal system is a functionally differentiated subsystem in modern society [→*Differentiation of Society*], which functions to maintain stable →*expectations* even if they are disappointed. Such expectations are norms that remain stable regardless of their potential contravention.

The →*code* guiding the operations of the law distinguishes between who is right and who is wrong in case of a legal dispute. Communication encoded in terms of the law refers to cases of conflict in which rights are claimed and decisions must be made—in reference to valid norms—as to who is right and who is wrong. The legal system therefore resolves conflicts, but also generates them at the same time, because we can invoke the law whenever we do not want to succumb to pressure or obey commands.

The function of the legal system concerns the temporal dimension of communication and not the social dimension [→*Meaning Dimensions*]. While the law does not guarantee the integration of individuals or the social control of behavior, norms, guarantee that what can be expected over time is limited, and in this sense they limit freedom and discriminate decisively between what must and must not be expected. Through normativization, society attempts to bind and secure an inherently uncertain future. This is the sole basis for the social costs of such temporal binding, which predominantly consist of limiting an individual's future behavioral possibilities: law risks labeling people as deviant, even criminal, without knowing in advance the intentions or motives behind their possible deviant behavior.

The →*programs* that allow the code of the legal system to become operative are norms and procedures. These programs are always by conditioning and not by goals. Norms allow the allocation of the code values legal/illegal depending on the cases that arise: as programs, they assume the form "if..., then...", which are not specified in relation to a goal. Even when norms are introduced on an ad hoc basis, are therefore bound to certain situations and are defined according to a certain goal, it can still only occur within the scope of the general conditioning normativization. The programs of the legal system determine the conditions that must be fulfilled from the outset in order to be able to dispute; however, this does not preclude the fact that law is open to the future and has the capacity of cognition. Programming by conditioning allows the clare distinction in the legal system between →*self-reference* (formal relevance conditions emerging from experience gathered from handling legal cases and which can be stored as concepts) and other-reference (cases of harming interests, which allow substantial argumentation)—and therefore also the distinction between what is legally relevant and what is legally irrelevant. Programs that specify goals do not permit such discrimination because they are too closely related to each particular case: once the goal is reached, which norm should apply? Law therefore combines normativization and cognition such that both its stability (norms continue to be valid, even when they are disappointed) and its capacity to learn (in new kinds of disputes, new norms can be produced) are guaranteed.

In this respect, law is a social, evolutionary system [→*Evolution*]. Evolutionary variation lies in the communication of disappointed normative expectations: this occurs when behavior proves in hindsight to be a disappointment of expectations. The individual case reveals a norm that did not exist beforehand: *ex facto ius oritur*. This only occurs when a certain behavior is disputed and a conflict is generated as a result, because an observer, deciding between who is right and who is wrong, can only be differentiated when conflicts are communicated. Procedures facilitate the selection of the variations, and these procedures allow making decisions concerning who is right and who is wrong in such a way that they are repeatable and reusable and remain unchanged across many different situations. The procedures (such as a trial in court) are differentiated in order to come to a decision, and are therefore goal-driven episodes that "declare the law". Variation, thus, is concerned with the task of changing the law, whilst selection determines if the normative expectations that generated the conflict can be confirmed or rejected. In other words, the function of procedures is not to change the law, but simply to make the law clear and manifest. Legal knowledge is stabilized according to the experiences gathered from individual cases, in that old cases can be compared with new ones on the basis of conceptual classification, decision-making rules used before, and so on. Each new case must always be checked to see whether it is similar to others or not: if it is, then the case can be "subsumed"; if it is not, we must create new rules.

As it is now clear, modern law has eschewed establishing itself on external and necessary conditions: there is no natural law, only a positive law, i.e., a law in which no norm is indispensable. This implies difficulties for law's reflection on law, which stem, for instance, from the fact that without external references →*paradoxes* arise. Law cannot lay its own foundations, unless they are paradoxical: on the basis of which laws can law determine who is right and who is wrong? Law, of course, holds that such distinctions are made using law, just as moralizers hold that it is good to distinguish between good and bad. However, the paradoxical structure of law, like the one in every other system, allows it to remain sensitive to reality and therefore also to fulfill its function: if it were possible to justify law fully and finally, the meaning of any normativization would be lost. Alternatively, we should explain why nature or God allows people's transgression of universal norms, and this would only shift the paradox a bit.

The reference to "justice" as the highest value of the law also brings us no further. This reference remains a reference without an operative value, because it is impossible to translate it into programs. If only "just" norms were produced and if every individual decision were correspondingly "just", the system would rapidly lose any ability to reproduce itself. We must take into account the fact that law requires no consensus: we cannot demand that everyone agrees with all norms, since this would halt the evolution of the system. The procedures demand that only very few people (for instance, judges) see the validity of the norm as binding for all and decide accordingly. The value of justice is diffused in the system in the form of "equality" (equal treatment for the equal and unequal treatment for the unequal!) and no further justifications for legal practice are required.

The law appears to fulfill the function of an immune system for society [→*Conflict*], because it allows the reaction of society to unforeseen situations that lead to disruption (i.e., to contradiction and conflict), despite lacking complete knowledge of all the factors involved. On the other hand, disputes usually emerge from unclear facts and the law has no control over this production of disputes: law transforms the certainty that comes from expecting something as probable into the uncertainty that results from the possible disappointment of the norm. *[G.C.]*

A Sociological Theory of Law (1985); Law as a Social System (2004); Are There Still Indispensable Norms in Our Society? (2008).

Love (*Liebe*)

From a social systems perspective, love is observed as a →*symbolically generalized medium*, rather than as a feeling, which only concerns a →*psychic system*. Love facilitates the successful expression or negation of feelings, through which the corresponding expectations are produced and the acceptance of communication under particular conditions of improbability is made more probable.

In modern times (since the 17th century onwards), love has been differentiated on the basis of the semantic concept of individuality of the person. Love serves as the foundation for the differentiation between interpersonal and impersonal communication. At the same time, the reproduction of love depends on this differentiation [→*System of Families*].

Love concerns the particular improbability of intimate interpersonal communication. It is improbable that ego accepts alter's wish to talk about her/himself, then to listen to her/him, i.e., to accept her/his idiosyncrasies. Love makes interpersonal communication at higher levels more probable, whereby participants attempt to differentiate themselves from other individuals, to make themselves the topic of communication, to talk about themselves. Such communication is improbable because the interest and consensus of the listener diminishes with the increase in the idiosyncrasy of, and in the singularity of the point of view of the speaker. Demanding ego's consensus and support becomes improbable because alter's perspective is unique, specific and strictly personal. Something particular gains universal relevance: alter is relevant because s/he is how s/he is, and s/he demands that ego takes her/his perspective into account, supports it and confirms it. Love makes intimate personal communication probable because it can take the radical individualization of the person into account.

A particular constellation of attribution is linked with the medium of love: the experience of alter (who is loved) triggers the actions of ego (who loves).

Ego's orientation to the way in which alter experiences her/his actions is not specific of love: we often ask ourselves about the consequences of a certain action from the perspective of the observer. It is more important that this orientation is made concrete and alter's search for understanding, consensus and support becomes the basis of ego's worldview. Love addresses the problem of the improbability of ego accepting alter's experience as the basis for her/his own action; for instance, the improbability of ego watching a TV show s/he hates because alter likes it. Ego loves when alter's experience is the basis for how ego observes and acts. Love is therefore the medium for the construction of the world through the eyes of the other. Ego is incorporated into alter's world, observes herself/himself in this world and finds herself/himself confronted with the alternative of accepting or rejecting alter's egocentric projects.

In the semantics of functionally differentiated society [→*Differentiation of Society*], the medium of love was initially symbolized as passion: people who love suffer something that they can neither change nor explain. In the 20th century, however, the symbolization of love as understanding has prevailed: ego's observation includes alter's relationship to her/his environment.

In order to reach this understanding, love's orientation is to the person. Alter is a person because s/he is grasped in her/his relationship to herself/himself and to the environment. The orientation to the person, thus, permits ego to observe what serves as environment and what serves as structure for alter, in order to process information about this environment. Understanding also means forgoing communication: alter does not need to ask because her/his expectations trigger Ego's action in the most direct way possible. Love makes communication probable in that communication is avoided.

The medium of love must distinguish between what is included in intimacy and what is meant by lack of intimacy, not in the sense of what is alien to love, but of love's negation according to its own perspective (separation). It is the reference to the person which makes it possible to distinguish between love and not-love and to switch from one to the other.

The programs that determine the conditions of correct attribution of love mostly take the form of remembering shared histories, which limits the possibilities of allocating the code values ("that wonderful weekend we spent together"). The reflexivity of love is expressed in the fact that love can only be motivated by love, refers only to love, and only develops when it can connect with love. Love allows itself to be irritated by the physicality of the partner through symbiotic symbols: these are references to sexuality.

Love is contingent: alter's demands are higher the more alter individualizes herself/himself as a person; someone who loves must always fulfill these demands, but a higher degree of individualization endangers love because it can easily lead to conflict. The question is if ego's actions are really orientated to alter's world and not her/his own. This question cannot be answered because silence is also communication, as it is attributed to a person. Conflicts arise easily because everything is attributed to persons' behavior, and these attributions show if the orientation to intimacy is valid or has come under pressure from problems. The possibility of pursuing small, day-to-day disagreements in love thus avoids risk, because every behavior puts love to the test; however, any conflict can call love into question, because the conflict cannot relinquish an orientation to the person. Love loses value when alter's world is taken into account so strongly that it cannot be translated into ego's daily life ("if you could only be what you are not"). [C.B.]

Love as Passion (1986); Theory of Society (2012: 201; 206-207; 220-226, 231); Sozialsystem Familie, 1988.

Mass media (*Massenmedien*)

Mass media were differentiated as a subsystem of society after the diffusion of communication forms using technical tools for reproduction. Books, newspapers, photographic and electronic procedures are communications made through machines, which preclude face-to-face interaction between issuers and receivers. Both parties therefore have high degrees of freedom from the social pressure of communication. Receivers can see, read or listen to what they prefer, when they prefer, interpreting it according to their own interests. Issuers can produce more risky and unlikely communications, such as scientific or artistic communications.

Mass media do not focus on truth, but on informativeness, and are therefore constantly suspected of manipulation. The →*code* of mass media is the distinction between →*information* and non-information, where information is attributed to communication that produces a difference and generates further information within the system. Information as news cannot be repeated: once communicated, news become immediately old and lose their informational value. The system of mass media is constantly growing old and is forced to continuously produce new information. This produces a specific restlessness and irritability in the overall society: mass media keep society awake, opening up a self-produced horizon of uncertainty that must constantly be provided with new information.

The operations of mass media are guided by three distinct →*program* areas, which use the code information/non-information differently, in two cases realizing structural couplings with other functional systems [→*Interpenetration and Structural Coupling*]: news and in-depth reporting (realizing coupling with the political system), advertising (realizing coupling with the economic system), and entertainment (relying on the art system, rather than realizing coupling with it).

The choice of events that become news is driven by specific selectors, which privilege novelties, conflicts, quantity, local reference, violation of rules, moral evaluations, attribution to actors, individual cases, expressions of opinion, and compatibility with the organizational routines of media organizations.

Advertising is a form of communication that explicitly declares the intention to manipulate—i.e., to induce the purchase of advertised products—and is recognized as such by receivers. Therefore, it must find ways to circumvent the likelihood of rejection, so that the recipient, though aware that it is advertising, does not recognize how s/he is affected. Advertising uses obfuscation techniques, such as formal beauty, the paradoxical use of language, or withholding the object which is to be paid for. Alongside its manifest function, advertising has the latent function of providing taste to people who have no taste, i.e., to structure desires in a society that no longer attributes the privilege of taste to upper social strata, as in stratified orders.

Entertainment has the function of eliminating superfluous time, creating a second reality on the model of the game, which obeys different conditions than normal reality. With regard to this reality, as in the case of modern novels, the receiver does not answer to communication with communication, but moves to second-order observation: she observes the events, the behaviors and the ways of observing of the characters, knowing that they are not authentic, but drawing from the observation clues for building her own identity. The modern individual identifies herself as an individual through the distinction imitation/authenticity experienced in entertainment.

Mass media have a double relationship with reality. The reality of mass media lies on the one hand in their operations: in the fact that communications are printed, broadcasted and materially produced. In a second sense, the reality of mass media is also what appears as reality to them or through them: a sequence of observations with their own, often fictitious, objects. Overall, the social result of mass media is the production of a second reality without the obligation of consensus, requiring participants to communicate with each other on two levels simultaneously: what everyone knows that everyone knows, and the reality that each person builds with her own distinctions.

Mass media serve as the memory [→*Time*] of modern society, as they allow the making of the assumption that a range of themes are known and do not have to be explicitly introduced, while at the same time making a continuous discrimination between remembering and forgetting. Mass media constantly provide new communication themes that are immediately forgotten in the transition to more recent issues. *[E.E.]*

The Reality of the Mass Media (2000); Theory of Society (2012: Ch. 2.7); Theory of Society (2013: Ch. 5.20).

Meaning (*Sinn*)

Meaning is the universal medium of all psychic and social systems, i.e., the medium for all forms [→*Medium/Form*] that are generated in these systems. In the medium of meaning, any operation of the system refers to other possibilities of operation production, which remain in the background of what is produced.

Meaning is a medium as it generates loose connections between actual and possible selections, thus allowing any type of tight connection between selections in the system. Therefore, meaning is the basic medium of all forms produced in the system. This is because meaning has a form, too: the form of meaning is the distinction real/possible—or actual/potential. Meaning is the form of selection of social and psychic systems. It is an evolutionary achievement of social and psychic systems that gives form to their →*self-reference* and their structured →*complexity*. Systems selections, which are based on meaning, actualize something and leave the non-actualized possibilities in the background. Selection is the actualization of something through the →*negation* of everything else. Negation is not destruction but the fundamental way through which meaning operates.

The observation of the form of meaning as real/possible or actual/potential distinction comes from Edmund Husserl's phenomenology. Meaning is the premise for processing each experience: meaning reveals itself in the surplus of references to further possibilities of experience contained in each actual experience. Thus, meaning is the simultaneous presentation of the actual and the possible (the potential): every real datum is projected onto the horizon of further possibilities and each actualization potentializes further possibilities. Possibility and reality, the potential and the actual only ever appear together. Meaning is reproduced through an experience that actualizes the meaning and refers to further experiences that are not actualized.

This phenomenological definition of meaning is integrated in systems theory. Meaning is constituted in →*social systems* and in →*psychic systems*: The system operations of communication and thought are realized in the medium of meaning. These meaning-constituting systems are selectively open to other possibilities. In social and psychic systems, any operation is a selection of actual content among possible alternatives, and further operations can always select (actualise) other possibilities. Any operation is a specific decision of making something actual, while leaving any other option possible: meaning is made evident through the possibility to decide elsewhere. Paradoxically, meaning is the product of the operations that presuppose it, in that it can exist only in its reproduction through these operations. Psychic and social systems both presuppose and generate meaning in their operations. On the one hand, a communication (a thought) is constituted only in the reference to further communication (thought) possibilities. On the other hand, the actualization of a certain communication (thought) lays the foundation for opening further communication (thought) possibilities. Meaning facilitates the basic →*self-reference* of social and psychic systems: a communication can be connected to further communications (a thought to further thoughts) when it opens a surplus of communication (thought) possibilities. Meaning determines the connectivity of the elements, which secures the possibility for these systems to continue to operate.

For meaning-constituting systems, everything has meaning, because only on the basis of meaning can everything be communicated (or thought). The world can only be observed through the medium of meaning, which is only realized in systems. Meaning and system are therefore mutual requirements: they are only possible together. In social and psychic systems, meaning ensures present determinations, on the basis of the past history of selections, while opening future alternative possibilities.

Since meaning is the unity of the difference between the actual and the possible, everything (the totality of the real and the possible) has meaning. Meaning even includes its own negation: even the negation of meaning has meaning. The existence of non-meaning can be observed only through meaning. Any reference to non-meaning reproduces meaning; therefore, in system operations non-meaning must necessarily have a meaning. Every meaning content gains actual reality only in the reference to further meaning and the reference also includes the possibility of re-actualizing the same content. Meaning continuously refers to meaning; it is self-referential. On the one hand, meaning requires that only some of the possibilities produced are actualized, while everything else remains in the background. On the other hand, meaning refers to everything that is not actual—it allows the possible to be taken into account. Meaning makes the world accessible because it has not been actualized, and prevents the disappearance of the possible in the actualization of a datum. The →*world* emerges as the totality of meaning references: meaning determines the surplus of references for the social and psychic systems. This surplus constitutes the complexity of the world, and the world is the condition for the actualization of particular contents. By employing the concept of meaning, we shift from the postulate of unalterable ultimate principles to the possibility of observing everything as contingent.

The boundaries separating the system from the environment are also drawn in the medium of meaning [→*System/Environment*]. In the case of social and psychic systems, we therefore talk about meaning boundaries. These are not spatial or concrete boundaries. Meaning boundaries encompass the domain of possibilities within a system; thus, they make this system observable as a context of selection that produces its own operations. The boundaries show that, in the system, particular conditions of reduced complexity apply. Meaning allows the simultaneous reduction and maintenance of the world complexity within the system.

The concept of meaning allows the understanding of the specificity of social and psychic systems in contrast to living systems (organisms, brains). Meaning is an evolutionary achievement of social and psychic systems that does not permit analogy with living systems: meaning and biological life must be differentiated as different types of autopoietic organization. In order to refer to the evolutionary particularity of meaning systems, systemic concepts (e.g., autopoiesis, self-reference, observation) must be abstracted from their original bio-cybernetic contexts. A non-reductionist theory of social and psychic systems is thereby constructed on the assumption that these, like living systems, are autopoietic, but this assumption is specified by means of the concept of meaning. *[C.B.]*

Social Systems (1995: Ch. 2); Theory of Society (2012: Ch. 1.3); Meaning as Sociology's Basic Concept (1990).

Meaning Dimensions (*Sinndimensionen*)

→*Meaning* expresses the difference between the actual and the possible in three different dimensions. A meaning-constituting system can actualize or negate possibilities in a relatively autonomous way in each dimension, without necessarily needing to actualize or negate the corresponding possibilities in other dimensions. This is made possible by the fact that every determinations and negations refer to the horizon specific to each meaning dimension. The three dimensions are the fact dimension, the social dimension and the temporal dimension.

(a) In the fact dimension, the horizon of reference is structured according to the difference this/something else, where the determination of something requires the (implied) negation of the something else: a horse is not a cow, a number is not a game, speed is not color. In the case of social systems, the difference concerns the topic of communication; in the case of psychic systems, it refers to objects of conscious attention. For every topic and every object, the fact dimension expresses a difference between two horizons: the internal and the external of what is indicated by observation. The observer can indicate one side of the distinction and negate the other, whilst still keeping it available for further indications. In the fact dimension, we can select a system reference, for instance through the paradigmatic distinction system/environment. Thus the observer orients herself to a system and leaves everything else in the background as the environment of that system. The identity of the observed system is in this case the internal—to which the observation refers—and everything else constitutes the external of this form. In general, concerning the topic selected by the communication or the object that the consciousness is made aware of, we are dealing here with the reduction of environmental →*complexity*, which allows the finding of connections for further operations in the observing system. Complexity, for its part, is maintained in the form of other topics or other possible objects, i.e., as "something else" in relation to the topic or the intended object.

(b) The social dimension is constituted in the possibility horizon of the communication partners "ego" and "alter ego." Meaning, in this case, is not processed in relation to topics or objects, but rather is condensed in the difference between ego and alter's perspectives. The social dimension is based on the non-identity of both communication partners and treats this non-identity as the doubled reference horizon. Of relevance here is not simply the fact that ego indicates alter's internal horizon as a system observed in the fact dimension; rather it is of greater import that alter is also an observer operating contingently and unpredictably. Ego and alter observe one other reciprocally, and this reciprocal dependence of each on the other constitutes the social character of the difference ego/alter.

In the social dimension, a connection between perspectives is established that constitutes the world as a social world: here, different aspects, different selections, others' experiences, consensus and dissent can be observed. The social dimension reveals itself as →*double contingency*, the handling of which requires social systems: this double contingency leads to grasping the sociality of meaning as the plurality of perspectives of observation, and not only as a plurality of system references. Ego observes alter as an alter ego in that she duplicates the observable way in which meaning is determined. The horizons of references to the possible are therefore not limited to the fact dimension, but rather they must also be determined in the social dimension, in which the selectivity of meaning consists in the particularity of each perspective in reference to the others.

(c) The temporal dimension is expressed in the horizons of the past and the future, which can only ever be constituted in the present [→*Time*]. The possibility of grasping the passing of time is based on a particularly complex construction in the temporal dimension. This possibility requires two different ways of determining the present, which are only possible simultaneously. On the one hand, the present always occurs as an event—i.e., at a certain point in time—and indicates the moment in which changes become irreversible. On the other hand, this eventfulness can only be observed on the basis of a present that has duration and guarantees the possibility of reversibility. In the punctualized present, the future constantly becomes the past: this is the time measured by a clock and which passes continuously. The durative present, which holds access to the possible open, despite the irreversibility of events, is the present in which the beginning and end of periods can be determined, processes can be accelerated or decelerated, and permanent situations can be observed. The permanence of a situation is the background in front of which the irreversibility of events can be observed, whilst the punctuality of events makes it possible to observe a permanent situation. Only the distinction between punctuality and permanence allows the projection of a future and a past, since it would be impossible to construct a memory of past selections, or to project a time that has yet to occur, on the basis of simple irreversibility (or permanence). Thanks to the simultaneity of both presents, it is possible to distinguish →*structures* and →*processes*, depending on whether the duration of a temporal situation or the sequence of momentary events that occur in that situation is taken into account.

Every meaning-constituting system is based on the possibility of distinguishing between these three dimensions, in which meaning is expressed and differentiated. These three dimensions are differentiated in that the concrete actualization in one meaning-dimension does not determine what can be actualized in the others. The duration of an object (temporal dimension) is not determined by consensus (social dimension) about its existence, just as the choice of a period of time (temporal dimension) determines neither what can be observed (fact dimension), nor who will do the observing (social dimension).

That these three dimensions can be distinguished from one another does not mean, however, that they are entirely uncoordinated. Conversely, constituting what can be observed demands their interdependence, because what is actualized in one dimension limits (not determines) the possibility of determining meaning in the others. When, for instance, the perspectives on the future in a given situation change, consequences can arise both for the possibilities of consensus or dissent, and for the factual spectrum of the things that can be realized in the present. *[G.C.]*

Social Systems (1995: Ch. 2.6); Theory of Society (2012: Ch. 1.3); Meaning as Sociology's Basic Concept (1990).

Medical System (*Krankensystem*)

The medical system or the patient treatment system is one of the subsystems in the functionally differentiated society [→*Differentiation of Society*]. Communication in this system concerns the organic or mental conditions of human beings: it is oriented primarily towards the environment of society and the problems observed there. A doctor comes into play when someone can no longer serve unhindered as the organic or physical basis of communication. The goal of the medical system cannot be reached directly through communication. Communication with the patient certainly plays a role, but the function is fulfilled through the diagnosis and the treatment of the patient's physical or mental states.

The function of treating patients is based on the orientation towards the →*code* sickness/health. The sickness/health distinction structures the arena of communication between doctors and patients, fulfilling a function that is not fulfilled anywhere else in society (neither power nor money have the ability to heal). Thus, the terms "health" and "sickness" do not indicate particular physical or psychic states, but rather the values of a code: sickness is the positive value and health the negative.

Doctors are primarily oriented towards sickness, since, from their perspective, human life is only relevant in relation to sickness. Thus, communication about sickness finds connections within the system. Health provides no such impetus: it can only enhance reflection on what is not sickness. The medical system only functions when someone is sick. There are therefore many forms of sickness and only one of health: the descriptions of diseases differ, whilst the concept of health remains either problematic or empty. From a medical perspective, the healthy are only relevant as the non-sick (or no longer sick), or as people suffering from yet to be diagnosed conditions. The coding of the medical system is differentiated from the coding of other functional systems through a peculiarity: it is the only coding in which the socially preferred value (health) is not the one capable of connectivity in the system, but instead triggers reflection (negative value of the code).

The relevance of sickness follows from the relationship between the body and consciousness as two different autopoietic systems [→*Autopoiesis*]. The consciousness cannot directly observe the body; it can only reconstruct the physical, chemical and organic processes through imagination [→*Psychic Systems*]. Only through imagination can consciousness know that something external even exists; the body makes it conscious that there is simultaneity with the world. The body affects consciousness through pain, and this compensates the structural indifference of consciousness towards the body. Pain implements a reduction in complexity, focusing attention on the body. It highlights the fact that the body is the last thing that still has meaning when everything else has become meaningless. Diseases and wounds reveal themselves through pain and therefore take priority: when the body asks for help, the doctor has primacy.

The programs of the medical system refer to the health/sickness distinction and are, therefore, oriented towards sickness (curing diseases, courses of treatment). Since the function of the system is primarily oriented towards the environment of society and does not process the improbability of communication, the code does not define a →*symbolically generalized medium*; for the success of communication, the conditions of willingness to cooperate and special symbols (medicines with technical names, exact dosage instructions) suffice. Since sickness is the positive value, the medical system does not contribute to a theory of reflection [→*Self-Reference*]. Since medical treatment refers to the value of health, but health is not capable of connectivity in the system, there is nothing that can be reflected upon: medicine is merely about the treatment of patients. In place of reflection, the value of health (which is the maximal value in society) as being beyond question and the professional ethics of the doctor prevail.

Thanks to genetic technology, a secondary code has also arisen. The genetically perfect/genetically dubious distinction allows the definition of a secondary structural distinction, curable/incurable, in relation to a disease, since diseases are required on both sides of the distinction. This distinction can be defined as a secondary code because it allows the development of an internal dynamic within the system, which cannot be controlled due to pre-determined criteria (including ethical criteria). From a sociological perspective, the fundamental question concerning genetic technology is whether it entails a technicization of the code, or represents only one of many new interventions in the body.

The medical system requires the efforts of other functional systems: for instance, medical treatment requires political decisions, scientific knowledge, finance, and legal governance. The interdependencies do not, however, affect the autonomy of the medical system, since even if scientific publications, financial resources, parliamentary sessions, ethical commissions, priests, relatives, are involved, the construction of the disease (diagnosis and care, information and suggestions) remains in the domain of medicine.

Along with societal evolution, the area of relevance of the medical system has broadened and today includes the entirety of an individual lifestyle. This evolutionary change is also connected with an inflation of the demands on patient treatment: as long as a course of treatment is possible, it may not be ignored and inequalities in this regard are seen as scandalous. Rising demands also correlate with the introduction of expansionary politics and the related financial problems. The attempt to lower demands by lowering costs contravenes the autonomy of the medical system: an economic calculation is not simultaneously a calculation of suffering. Under these conditions, the regulation of requirements is left to individuals, who, in the end, are answered by doctors automatically with diagnosis, treatment and medicine prescriptions.

The fundamental question for the medical system is whether a functional surrogate for pain can be suggested. The problem would lie in removing consciousness functional indifference to the body in the case of environmental noises that are not pain, thus leading to generalized forms of prevention. Prevention broadens the area of interpenetration between the body and consciousness. In such a scenario, the need for a theory of reflection would become more urgent and the difference between curable and incurable diseases could be more clearly worked out. [C.B.]

Medizin und Gesellschaftstheorie (1983); Anspruchsinflation im Krankheitssystem (1983); Der medizinische Code (1990).

Medium/Form

The distinction medium/form comes from an idea originally expressed by Fritz Heider. Heider used the distinction to explain the individual perception of objects that are not directly in contact with the body, such as, for instance, optical or acoustic perception. According to Heider, such perception is made possible by a medium (light or air), which is itself not perceived, but conveys the properties of the object in question (i.e. its form) without changing them. Thus, under normal conditions, it is not light or air that are perceived, but the pictures or sounds they convey. The perceived objects take a form thanks to their higher "rigidity," as opposed to the "flexibility" of the medium, which can always accept forms.

The medium is characterized by a loose coupling between elements, which can be viewed as being dependent upon one another. Thus, the medium offers no internal resistance to forms impressing it from outside (for instance, from an object that vibrates or a reflecting surface). The forms "condense" the connections between the elements of the medium into tight couplings, which are thus perceived by a psychic system. The medium is formless: air makes no sound, and electromagnetic waves are not visible. For instance, a footprint in the sand establishes a tight coupling between the grains of sand, which cannot be resisted because the grains are not connected to one another strongly enough. The weaker the stable couplings between its elements, the better the medium is at accepting forms: for instance, stones or larger grains of sand already have their own form, thus conditioning the form of the footprint and making for a less suitable medium.

In this example, the totality of grains of sand is treated as a medium in which the footprint is established. Moreover, the distinction between form and medium is always relative: nothing is a form or medium in itself; everything may be either a medium in relation to a form that establishes itself, or a form that establishes itself in a medium at a lower level. For instance, the elements of →*language* (i.e., words) are established as forms on the continuum of sounds, thus condensing as stable configurations; however, at the same time they constitute a medium for conveying the content of communication. The distinction medium/form always operates as a distinction, each side referring to the other.

From the example of language, we are led to consider another sociologically interesting domain: communication media, which can make something probable that would otherwise have been improbable. Communication media connect the communications that would otherwise find no connections. The communication media are language, →*dissemination media* and the →*symbolically generalized media*. They perform the function of facilitating the constant coupling/uncoupling of the elements of the medium, i.e., the constant production of forms. Forms correspond, for instance, to words and sentences in language, written and printed texts, payments, scientific theories, legal norms. The communication media therefore provide a weak and formless substrate: language does not speak, the printing press does not determine what is printed, scientific truth as a medium creates no knowledge, and so on.

The distinction medium/form is applied in all cases in which the connections between previously loosely coupled elements are observed to condense and become tight: variety in the medium means that redundant configurations are established. At the level of society, we can observe an evolutionary differentiation of communication media (such as writing, printing, power, money), which enables communication to be connected to further communication, thereby creating forms that can be generalized and expected [→*Evolution*]. In this sense, communication media are social structures that facilitate the autopoiesis of communication. *[G. C., E. E.]*

Theory of Society (2012: Ch. 2.1); The Form of Writing, 1992; Sign as Form (1999); Art as a Social System (2000: Ch. 3).

Morality (*Moral*)

Moral communication differentiates primarily between what is good and what is bad, and relates this distinction directly to persons: morality is coded [→*Code*] in the possibility of attributing esteem or disesteem to persons. The code of esteem/disesteem refers not to someone's particular achievements, but rather to the person as a communication partner [→*Inclusion/exclusion*]. When we use morality, we communicate the conditions under which we are prepared to bestow esteem or disesteem, whilst taking as a starting point the implied condition that we bestow esteem upon ourselves. This schema makes morality polemical, the generator of conflict, and close to violence.

Morality is not a (differentiated) phenomenon localized in one particular subsystem, but rather can emerge in every area of society. For instance, we can advance moral motifs in order to contest particular scientific research projects such as genetic technology and genetic research. Political careers can be destroyed by moral questions, as demonstrated by the typical ease with which the political system generates scandals. Morality is not such an improbable phenomenon that a subsystem must be differentiated or symbolic sanctions introduced to provide moral motivation [→*Symbolically Generalized Media*]; it is sufficient that persons can orientate themselves to other persons as communication partners. This already occurs within the condition of →*double contingency*.

Due to the typical features of functional differentiation [→*Differentiation of Society*], societal subsystems are amoral; their codes are not congruent with morality. The true cannot necessarily be described as something good, and the not true as something bad: receiving moral sanction cannot and may not automatically mean being juridicallywrong. Conversely, morality has the effect of reducing communication to conflicts and polemics that hinder the normal reproduction of the operations of societal subsystems.

Morality is not synonymous with ethics; the latter arises when morality reflects upon itself. Ethics must therefore be understood in terms of reflection theory [→*Self-Reference*]. The most widespread ethical maxim assumes that it is good to differentiate between good and bad, and only rarely is the paradoxical structure of such a statement remarked upon: if it is good to differentiate good and bad, then bad is also good, since it would not exist without the distinction.

The stratified society of the Middle Ages had to deliver a unified moral description of the ranking order upon which it was based. The combination of morality and religion typical of the age allowed the existence of an integrated social order on the basis of a single morality, the alternative to which could only have been chaos and barbarism. Modern society can no longer be integrated, and this should discourage the use of morality. With the arrival of functional differentiation, society changed many of its characteristics. It became clear, for instance, that there is no hope of reaching total consensus, and that no norm of reciprocity can be expected because people are prepared to take their own risks, but not to endure dangers caused by others [→*Risk/Danger*]. Moreover, we know that selfish purposes provide the foundations for altruism, and that the best of intentions can have terrible consequences. In such circumstances, we are led to ask where we might find the moral conditions of morality. The answer can lie only in an invitation to observe reality at a level of an abstract amorality: ethics should stop defining morality as a good undertaking and instead warn against its use and consequences.

Whether ethics is still possible today is, however, a question that sociology is hardly able to answer. We can doubt whether it is possible to have an ethics that concerns itself with social relationships whilst at the same time holding that the ethics itself is good. We might imagine such an ethics, one that is capable of constituting morality as a distinction and not only as a positive (good) side, ignoring the negative. Such an ethics would concern itself with the questions of when it is good to differentiate between good and bad, and which positive conditions of the use of moral judgments exist. One of these conditions concerns one of the foundational requirements of morality: freedom of judgment. Whilst freedom in pre-modern society was a transcendental particularity of human action and, as such, functioned as a requirement of morality, this idea can no longer hold in the modern society. Freedom, as we might say from a sociological perspective, is a product of communication, which predominantly allows a yes or no answer to be given to every selective suggestion that is communicated—and these also count as suggestions for morality. The structure of modern society gives the possibility of rejecting the commandments of morality, and we may ask ourselves whether it is still appropriate to react to every possibility with moralization, allowing the paradox to arise of passing moral (and often negative) judgment on what is an absolutely necessarily condition for the judgment itself. *[G.C.]*

Die Moral der Gesellschaft (2008); The Morality of Risk and the Risk of Morality (1987); Paradigm lost: On the Ethical Reflection of Morality (1991).

Negation

In the conceptualization of system theory, negation has a functional primacy because it allows the world to be kept accessible despite the unavoidably selectivity of the operations of social and psychic systems. Negation takes the form of a reference to other possibilities than those that are actualized [→*Meaning*]. As such, it represents social and psychic systems' reference to the →*world* and allows the constitution of the meaning of each communication and each thought.

The concept of meaning indicates the possibility for meaning-constituting systems of reducing the world's →*complexity* without this reduction implying the destruction of non-actualized possibilities. A communicative context selects a topic, concentrates on this topic and temporarily leaves every other thematic alternative aside. These other possible alternatives are negated; however, they remain accessible for a potential further communication. That what is negated does not irreversibly disappear, but instead remains available, can be traced back to two different features of negation:

(a) Negation generalizes what the positive determination does not take into account. When communication selects a topic, it leaves the horizon of excluded topics undetermined. It is not necessary to determine all negations connected with every actualization.

(b) Negation requires a second feature, reflexivity, to make it possible to recover later what the generalization leaves undetermined, which does not disappear. Negation can be applied to itself, regaining what was temporarily excluded and positively determining it. Negating what was negated, the system can find the connections necessary to continue its operations.

Generalization and reflexivity are mutually necessary components of negation. Both are conditions for the operation of meaning-constituting systems: only when the unactualized is left undetermined and can possibly be recovered later without the world disappearing can communication and consciousness continue to operate.

Thanks to these features, negations are meaningful operations. They play a role in every social and psychic operation and therefore really exist in the real world. However, although it occurs in every social and conscious operation, negation does not have a correlate in the environment: there are no negative objects in the environment. This holds both for defined negations ("something is not") and undefined negations ("everything that something is not"). In this sense, negation must be understood as a positive operator because it is only used in operations that really (i.e., positively) take place. All negations are used to gain positive operative connections because, to be able to negate, one must be able to distinguish what one wants to negate: one can only negate within a distinction [→*Operation/Observation*]. For this reason, no system is able to terminate itself through its own operations; in any case, negation of oneself is yet another confirmation of autopoiesis. Negation thus seems to be a point of departure for analyzing the construction of reality in meaning-constituting systems [→*Constructivism*]. [G.C.]

Meaning as Sociology's Basic Concept (1990); Über die Funktion der Negation in sinnkonstituierenden Systemen (1975).

Operation/Observation (*Operation/Beobachtung*)

The distinction operation/observation is the basis for Luhmann's constructivist approach [→*Constructivism*] and for the extension of the concept of →*autopoiesis* from biological to meaning-constituting systems. Starting from this distinction, the absolute determination of autopoietic operations can be combined with the contingency of observation.

An operation is understood as the reproduction of an element in an autopoietic system by means of the elements in that system, i.e., the condition for the very existence of the system. There is no system without a system-specific mode of operation, but there is also no operation that does not belong to a system. According to the theory of autopoiesis, everything that exists must be traced back to the operations of a system. Every possible object only exists because a system constitutes it as an entity.

At the level of autopoiesis, the problem for the system is simply one of reproduction, which requires the ability to connect a new operation to every other operation in the same system and thereby maintain operative closure. Operations always run blind. Basic reproduction is not guided by either a teleological project or the orientation to a function, or by the need to adapt. Even →*time* does not exist for the operations because they are always, in their immediacy, bound to simultaneity with the world. Like the distinction earlier/later, these categories are introduced only by an observer observing the running of the operations (which basically reproduce themselves in an uncontrolled manner).

Hence, only an observer can speak of operations. It is therefore of great important to distinguish the level of operations from that of observations—even though observations are themselves operations. If observations were not themselves operations, it would be impossible to trace them back to a system, and thus impossible to take their existence into account.

Observation is a specific mode of operation that uses a distinction [→*Identity/Difference*] to indicate one side of the distinction or the other. Observations are always present when a system operates on the basis of distinctions and can obtain and process information. It is the system-specific mode of operation in →*meaning*-constituting systems, which allows their reference to further possibilities via the respective actualized datum.

This definition of observation is very abstract and is independent of references to people or vision. It refers to the logical calculus of George Spencer Brown, according to which each construction is based on an initial distinction. This separates the space into two sides (for instance the distinction system/environment, which splits the world into two separate areas) and, at the same time, indicates one of the two sides (the system or the environment). It is therefore impossible to draw a distinction without indicating something as distinct from something else (in the distinction between system and environment, the system is indicated as distinct from the environment). In this sense, the initial operation realizes the functions of both indication and distinction at the same time. Proceeding from the initial distinction, it is then possible to accomplish further operations, which can either repeat the earlier indication (in this case, there is a condensation that leads to the constitution of an identity [→*Identity/Difference*]) or refer to the other side (and thereby realize a crossing that "deletes" the earlier indication). The sequence of operations leads to the constitution of a complex system, which, however, always remains dependent on the first distinction.

Each observation uses a particular distinction (e.g., system/environment, whole/part, form/background) that allows its construction of a network of further distinctions and thereby the achievement of →*information* from what it observes. While an operation that realizes the self-reproduction of a system runs blind (and this also holds for observation as operation), it has more freedom as observation. This is because it is not subject to the condition of simultaneity with the world. It does not coincide instantaneously with its object. Observation is able to identify objects and can (when, for instance, it is oriented to the distinction system/environment) distinguish a system internal processes from those that do not belong to it; can determine causal relationships between inside and outside; can attribute a goal to the system.

The initial distinction is at the same time the condition both for being able to observe and for limiting the observation: without a distinction, we cannot observe, but each distinction allows us to observe only what it allows us to observe. The selection of the initial distinction determines everything that can (later) be observed. We see differently depending on how we observe. The distinction system/environment, for instance, leads to other information than that obtained through the distinction whole/part. It implies the inclusion of psychic systems in the environment of social systems: psychic systems are no more regarded as parts of society. Additionally, the distinction system-environment is incompatible with a concept of the individual as a unity of the psychic and organic systems. Organism and consciousness become autonomous and separate autopoietic systems.

However, observation is also an operation in a system and, as such, just as blind to its own reproduction. The initial distinction is its blind spot [→*Constructivism*], i.e., the point that it cannot observe. An observation oriented to the distinction true/untrue cannot observe whether this distinction is itself true or untrue. Thus, based on the distinction legal/illegal, we cannot determine whether it is on the side of legality or illegality. No distinction can be applied to itself in order to produce an unequivocal indication, because it is and remains an autopoietic operation. Besides observing something, it is produced as operation. This results in the form of the →*paradox* that always arises when applying a distinction to itself. We can say that the initial distinction is itself the observation as operation, which is distinguished from another distinction, i.e., the initial distinction for another observer. No operation of observation can observe itself: in order to see what an observer cannot see we need a "second-order observer" that observes this observation without coinciding with it [→*Constructivism*]. However, this always occurs based on a distinction that second-order observers themselves cannot observe, which a third-order observation can determine, and so on.

Observation does not represent a privileged from of knowledge (in the sense of access to an objective reality). It is itself the operation of a system that accomplishes its autopoiesis based on its specific limitations. Additionally, as an operation, it can always be observed and no final position exists from which "right" observations can be made. Besides, the distinction right/wrong is an observational schema with its own limitation and blind spot, and thus offers no particular guarantee of adequacy to the world.

Every entity we refer to is the construction of an observer and depends on the particular distinction that has been applied. Every distinction inevitably translates the world into its forms and as such grants no access to an objective world independent of the observer. The world can, therefore, never be observed from outside: the observation unavoidably changes the world with which it is confronted. In epistemology, the distinction operation/observation assumes the position of the classic distinction of subject and object. Radical constructivism elaborates the consequences of these considerations.

A special case is that of self-observation, which is when the observation is an operation of the system it is observing and takes part in the autopoiesis of that system. Self-observation, however, is not understood as an operation that observes itself as an ongoing observation (which is impossible), but as an operation that observes something to which it, too, belongs (another operation of the system in which it participates [→*Self-Reference*]). This operation of observation must be compatible with the ongoing process of reproducing the elements and is subject to specific conditions that regulate the autopoiesis of the system. Based on the condition of the operational closure of autopoietic systems [→*Autopoiesis*], an observation from outside can never know if and how it affects the running of the operations in the observed system. On the other hand, self-observation—since it directly contributes to autopoietic reproduction—inevitably influences the further development of operations and is a factor in their dynamics. Localization within the system, however, does not imply the ability to observe it as a whole. The dependence on a specific distinction cannot be overcome and self-observation, too, delivers only a selective picture of the observed system. It can observe only what its distinction allows it to observe and, in contrast with an observation from outside, is also limited by the necessity to find a connection within the system. Thus, self-observation cannot determine the reproduction of operations that always run blind.

Depending on which distinction it uses, self-observation takes on different forms. A rudimentary self-observation appertains to all operations in meaning-constituting systems: in order to connect themselves recursively to other operations in the system, they must distinguish the system from everything else that does not belong to it [→*Self-Reference*]. In terms of, for instance, a social system, each communication must simultaneously communicate that it is a communication, who is communicating and what is communicated. Only in this way can they produce other communications. Thus, every operation of communication must observe itself, using for this purpose the particular distinction between information and utterance. More complex forms of self-observation emerge when the system switches from observing its own operations to observing its own observations, and finally to observing the system itself (based on the distinction system/environment; i.e., the distinction between self-reference and other-reference). In this way, a →*re-entry* occurs and the system observes itself based on the distinction that constitutes it.

Self-observation serves to inform the system and obtain new knowledge from itself. However, self-observations as operations are always →*events* and remain bound to the respective situation. It is therefore useful to coordinate these observations with one another. Texts are produced accordingly, which allow observations to be repeated, commented upon and articulated: these texts are the self-description of the system. The form of the self-description of society changes with the evolution of society itself. In pre-modern society, there were forms of self-description that always assumed the separation of the description from its object: they made recourse to externalizations [→*Asymmetrization*]. Today, on the contrary, an appropriate self-description of society must always include an "autological" component: it must reflect that the attempt to describe society can only take place within society. The description itself falls within the scope of its object, which must be described as an object that describes itself. *[E.E.]*

Die Wissenschaft der Gesellschaft (1990: Ch. 1.VII, Ch. 2.VII); Art as a Social System (2000: Ch. 1.VII, Ch. 2.I).

Organization (*Organisation*)

Organization is a type of social system that, in contrast to →*interaction* and →*society*, is constituted through rules of admission. These are predominantly membership rules, which can be determined by recruiting personnel and specifying roles: there can only ever be a limited number of members of a formal organization. In this way, the social system of organization becomes identifiable, and it can specify its structures and differentiate its operational connections. "Organization" describes social systems such as companies, institutes, institutions, and so on.

The communications that serve as the organization's basic elements come in the form of decisions. Decisions are a special type of communication, the selectivity of which must always be attributed to a member of the organization. The fact that persons can be members does not mean that they are part of the organized system. Persons are members of the organization in that they contribute to determining the structures that make the system capable of operation; still, as psychic systems, they remain in the environment of the organization.

Membership of an organization is not in itself a criterion for decision-making: it does not yet specify who can decide what and when. The possibilities for decision-making are determined by decision premises, which limit the domain of alternatives to be chosen between. As such, the following decision premises can be distinguished based on the limited domain of alternatives:

(a) The organization specifies →*programs*, which provide a framework for evaluating the correctness of decisions. A program limits the possibilities of communication, for instance, by setting goals for the future (programming by goals) or providing at the outset the conditions that must be fulfilled should decisions be required (programming by conditioning).

(b) The domain of possible decisions is also limited through the creation of communication channels that give decisions a binding character. The hierarchical structure is the typical way in which organizations differentiate themselves internally: the selectivity of decisions is guided in such a way that they can take effect in the whole organization with no further requirements. It becomes clear through this structuring what kind of communicative success a decision can have: in this way, relatively reliable expectations can form.

(c) The third premise for decisions is linked to the persons who are members of the organization. Although the specific role already limits what each individual person can decide, personal characteristics can make these limitations more selective than intended. This may be seen, for instance, in the individual career, with its professional contacts and with the particular abilities or reputation that the individual has gained through personal experience and training.

Programs, channels of communication and persons constitute the structures of →*expectations* that allow the organization to operate. These three decision premises can be differentiated from one another because the variation in one of them does not necessarily need to correspond to a variation in another: we can, for instance, change the person in a particular role without needing to change the role itself (or the hierarchical structure) or the company's program, and vice versa.

The three premises condense into positions in the organization: every position is supplied with tasks (program), belongs to a certain department (communication channels) and is filled by one person. The contingency of the different forms of the decision premises can be handled by creating positions that maintain their identity as long as the three decision premises are not all changed at the same time. Contingency is used operatively in that every possibility for decision is bound regarding what can be changed and what must remain constant.

Contingency is also handled by the particular form assumed by communication when it is attributed as a decision. Before the decision is taken, a limited domain of possibilities is available, which present themselves as alternatives: once the decision has been taken, contingency is fixed in one form, which makes the decision itself contingent since a different decision could have been taken instead. This transformation of future contingency into past contingency allows the emergence of an internal temporality that is not coordinated with the outside. It happens in such a way that each decision constitutes the condition for other decisions whilst simultaneously requiring past decisions. This chaining of decisions allows the uncertainty found in every decision to be processed, and it is typical for organizations to develop targeted strategies in order to cope with the pressure of decision-making. Examples of these strategies are: the tendency, even which it no longer makes sense, to conform to expectations just to avoid appearing to be the decision-maker; the shifting of responsibility to another decision-maker; the tendency to decide contrary to certain expectations and thus to allow conflict to arise in the assumption that it will bring certain advantages or increase the decision-maker's reputation.

In the functionally differentiated society [→*Differentiation of Society*], formal organizations have become more relevant than ever before. This is not only true of the economic system, for which the importance of organizations is already well known and has long been the subject of research. In other subsystems, too, the capacity to operate is becoming more and more heavily based on organized systems, such as schools in education, churches in religion, research institutes in science, and so on. *[G.C.]*

Organisation und Entscheidung (2000); Organization (2003); Theory of Society (2013: Ch. 4.14).

Paradox (*Paradoxie*)

Paradoxes arise when the conditions for the possibility of an operation are at the same time the conditions for its impossibility. One of the most well-known examples of a paradox was given by Epimenides in the (slightly revised) statement: "this sentence is false." It is impossible to decide if the statement is true or false because the conditions of its falseness are simultaneously also the conditions for its truth (and vice versa): if the sentence is taken to be true, then it simultaneously contradicts what it expresses (the sentence is then false). If, however, the statement is taken to be untrue, we are forced to agree with its content (the sentence is then true). The paradox is not, therefore, of the form: "A = not A," which represents a contradictory but not a paradoxical statement. It is rather of the form: "A because not A," whereby the conditions of the statement are at the same time the conditions of its negation. For an observer, the undecidability lies in the fact that it is impossible to indicate one value without also indicating the other: the observer begins to oscillate between the two sides and it becomes impossible to continue the observation.

Paradoxes arise when observers making distinctions question the unity of the distinction they are currently applying [→*Operation/Observation*]. Every distinction is inherently paradoxical because both sides of it are always present simultaneously: one as the indicated side, the other as the intended, implied side to which the indication refers.

One example of this duality in every observation is the fundamental distinction between system and environment [→*System/Environment*]. Each system can only construct its identity as a system when it is able to distinguish itself from an environment, i.e., only when it negates that which it is not. The environment, however, can only be distinguished on the basis of internal operations, as the operation of negation can only be produced as a system-specific operation. The system must therefore observe the distinction between itself and its environment as a product of itself. This is paradoxical because the system must distinguish itself from an environment that does not belong to it, whilst simultaneously observing that this environment is nothing but an internal product of its own operations. This occurs whenever a self-referential system capable of observation—and therefore capable of negation—observes itself [→*Self-Reference*].

This self-observation becomes particularly problematic for today's society when it is undertaken in functional systems. One such case is the reflection of subsystems in modern society. In the case of science, the distinction of the scientific code can be applied to itself, landing it in Epimenides' paradox: the distinction true/untrue observes itself with the paradoxical result that the possibility for further observations is blocked in the way described above. This problem arises in all functionally differentiated subsystems. The legal system, which operates on the basis of the distinction between who is juridically right and who is wrong, finds itself confronted with a paradoxical situation when it questions whether it has the right to determine who is right and who is not. The question cannot be answered, since any answer (e.g., social contract, original act of violence that is justified by the actions that follow it) inevitably affects both sides of the distinction so that the problem becomes unsolvable. Similar examples can be given for all codes belonging to the subsystems and the →*symbolically generalized media*: when the observation is directed at the same binary schematization that the observation itself employs, the system must indicate the unity of the distinction that it is currently using—with paradoxical consequences. Every self-referential system capable of negation is therefore unable to establish exclusively self-observations, since self-observation can never be complete. In order to be complete, it should also be able to observe the distinction that it uses, and that is not possible [→*Operation/Observation*].

Paradoxes are a problem for the observer, but not necessarily for the operations of the observing system. That science operates paradoxically is a problem only for the observer of the system (which can be science itself). In this sense, paradoxes serve to separate operations and observations. They allow the occurrence of operations but block observations. Operations run blind without the ability to observe themselves: in order to observe an operation, a second operation is required that can observe the paradoxical constitution of the first, but also runs blind itself. Every observation can raise the question of how a system observes or how an operation is produced, but it cannot ask the question of itself: for every observation, the distinction it uses is a blind spot. In this way, paradoxes do not block the autopoiesis of the system, but represent a problem for its possibilities of observation.

In terms of structural aspects, every distinction exists only in the simultaneity of its two sides. In terms of operational aspects, the distinction can only be actualized as indication of one side (and not the other). For this reason, every system must unfold the paradox at the structural level; it must de-paradoxicalize itself in such a way that observations are not blocked.

This can happen when conditions are introduced that make the circularity of self-reference asymmetrical and avoid short-circuiting the references within the distinction used [→*Asymmetrization*]. These conditions can take on many different forms depending on the type of system and the form of differentiation in society as a whole [→*Differentiation of Society*]. In functionally differentiated subsystems, the de-paradoxicalizing function can be fulfilled by the way in which the system takes the relation between the two values of its code into account. Operations orient themselves to the binary schematization of the code in that they regard it as a self-contradictory difference and not as a unity. Thus, in the →*scientific system* an observation is true or untrue and one value excludes the other; the decision is facilitated by particular →*programs*, which in the case of the scientific system are theories and methods. These make the system capable of operation by determining the allocation criteria of the values, whilst only scientific reflection deals with the problem of the paradoxical constitution of scientific truth and the necessity of introducing specific asymmetries. The asymmetries, for their part, assume the form of contingency formulae, which allow the system's coherent description of itself without oscillating between the values of its own distinctions, unable to decide between them.

Whichever form the asymmetrization takes, it always allows the system to find anchor points for its operations. From this view point, paradoxes appear to fulfill a function of irritating observers, who, when confronted with a paradox and seeing themselves forced to make an impossible decision, either give up because their observation is blocked, or become creative by finding some form of asymmetrization. The recent tendency within different disciplines (e.g., cybernetics, systems theory, art, logic) to seek out paradoxes instead of avoiding them is probably undertaken with the goal of irritating observers (i.e., ourselves) searching for new forms of structuring their own operations.
[G.C.]

Tautology and Paradox in the Self-Descriptions of Modern Society (1988); Sthenography (1990); The Paradox of Form (1999).

Political System (*Politisches System*)

The political system is a subsystem within the functionally differentiated society [→*Differentiation of Society*], the function of which is to guarantee the capacity to make collectively binding decisions.

The political system is closely linked with the holding and use of →*power*. However, not all political communications are uses or threats of power: this is not true of, for instance, parliamentary debates and discussions within political parties. Yet a political system is only differentiated when power is able to motivate the acceptance of binding decisions. The code of power (inferior/superior) enables political communication to be reproduced.

The medium of power and the political system develop simultaneously: the political function needs the medium of power, and power needs a political system. The differentiation of the political system allows the concentration and generalization of resources of power, but the society as a whole is not dependent on a central political power. For instance, the economic system, the scientific system, the religious system are not based on the medium of power, but instead operate on the basis of other media and codes, such as money, truth, belief. Power is differentiated and fixed through state offices. The distinction inferior/superior corresponds with the distinction between holders of public office (the rulers) and the people addressing them (the ruled). Formally holding power through state institutions secures control over the use of power. Against this background, confusing person and office does not count as a deviation, but as corruption.

Since someone holding an office excludes others from holding the same office, the structure of state offices is given by the distinction between government and opposition: whoever holds the offices and the power governs, and whoever holds no offices or power is in the opposition. Thus, the distinction government/opposition is an additional code of the political system, which means that the →*code* of power can be technologized: thanks to this secondary coding, we can change directly from inferiority to superiority and vice versa. This secondary political code is a preferential code: for the system, the government and the opposition are equally relevant, but the government represents a positive value (connective value) and the opposition represents a negative value (reflective value). Through this code, the political system can observe itself and can reach a point at which it can attribute all decisions, to the government or to the opposition.

The distinction government/opposition is the basis of the form of the political system called democracy: democracy can be defined as the distinction between government and opposition, which divides the top of the political system. The top becomes the starting point for producing alternative possibilities, as the rulers can be replaced. Holding of public office is contingent; it is the result of a selection of persons and programs, and this selection is periodically revised. A lack of opposition means a lack of democracy because society becomes politically stratified (i.e. it becomes a dictatorship): lack of opposition limits differentiation in the political system because, with the loss of one of its values (the opposition), the political code disappears. The code is replaced with a reference to organization (the state, a single party).

In the political system, holding power must be legitimized. Legitimation is carried out through the processes permitted by the code government/opposition: elections are the most important of these processes. Political elections and a legitimate formation of government are the processes that the code and political programs coordinate together. There are government programs and opposition programs. The democratically elected government designs the program that has preference in the political system, in the sense that this program instructs communications that lead to collectively binding decisions.

Codes and programs are also linked through a further code: the code progressive/conservative. Through this distinction, points of view (values) can be determined for the selection of whatever can be bindingly decided for everyone. Its weakness, however, is that it cannot keep up with the dynamics of social change: conservatives suggest new programs of opposition and become progressive; progressives defend the decisions made whilst in government and become conservative. Thus, the connection between code and programs, in place of this confusing distinction, is provided by the distinction between expansionary state (or welfare state) and restrictive state.

The welfare state is characterized by the attempt to include [→*Inclusion/Exclusion*] everyone in the political system. The attempt to reach generalized political inclusion encounters numerous difficulties, however, since the political system is limited by two external codes: →*money* and law [→*Legal System*]. These codes cannot be used for generalized political inclusion, for instance for the treatment of people through therapy or education. Additionally, these codes impose strict limits on political intervention. Lack of legal means and, above all, economic difficulties have led to restrictive notions of generalized political inclusion. Thus, the distinction between expansionary and restrictive state becomes important as a new orientation for the selection of the political programs.

Even if the meaning of the state is obvious for the political system, political system and state are not a one-to-one match. The state is an organization within the political system that is defined by territorial boundaries. The political system of →*world society* is differentiated internally into territorial states. This segmentation into states makes fulfilling the political function easier: through state building, democracy can be realized locally and specific goals can be reached. This differentiation, however, also entails problems because the territorial boundaries can determine local, ethnic or religious conditions of political programs that do not correspond to the needs of a world society.

Aside from the state, there are other political organizations that do not directly produce any collectively binding decisions. Every territorial state differentiates itself into systems according to the pattern center/periphery. The organization of the state shoulders responsibility for the territory and is the point of orientation for all other political organizations (political parties, interest groups) that belong to the periphery. In the center, a hierarchy (inferior/superior) is constructed, whereas in the periphery higher complexity and higher sensitivity to irritations from the environment are reached. The periphery is differentiated by non-coordinated segments (like political parties) with the function of preparing, in a non-binding way, the collectively binding decisions.

However, the political system amounts to more than the mass of political organizations. In general, it can be observed as a unity of a three-dimensional distinction: politics, administration and public. This is not a differentiation into subsystems, but the result of a double distinction: on one side, political offices are differentiated from administrative offices and, on the other side, the unity of offices are differentiated from the public composed of citizens. The interdependence between politics, administration and public is circular—whereby no top and no center can be determined. The state is only the center in terms of the differentiation of political organizations. This makes the internal interdependencies of the political system extremely complex and they constantly demand second-order observation: politics cannot simply observe the public, but rather must also orient itself to the way in which the public observes politics. *[C.B.]*

> Die Politik der Gesellschaft (2000); Political Theory in the Welfare State (1990); Ecological Communication (1989: Ch. XIII).; Die Zukunft der Demokratie (1986).

Power (*Macht*)

Power is a →*symbolically generalized medium* that makes accepting alter's actions as the premises of ego's actions probable. Power is therefore not observed as held by someone; it is a communication medium for coordinating selections and producing the corresponding expectations.

In the functionally differentiated society [→*Differentiation of Society*], power is the specific medium of the →*political system*. It can potentially also be realized in other systems, but without being able to obtain the capacity to reproduce that it has in politics.

A particular constellation of attribution is associated with the medium of power: alter's action (the action of the power holder) triggers ego's action. The normal social condition is that actions performed by alter o and ego are related to one another. However, this relation becomes improbable when alter's action is a decision (a command) governing ego's action that must be obeyed. Alter acts and ego finds herself in the situation to accept or reject alter's action as the premise for her own action. Ego's acceptance is improbable because alter's command is specialized and there is no certainty of consensus or congruence of interests between alter and ego in the concrete situation. In this situation, the recourse to power allows ego's acceptance of alter's command to become probable. Power exists when alter's action motivates ego to act: therefore, power is not based on pre-defined motivations, but is itself the generator of the motivation. Power requires the freedom of alter (who could act in this way or a different way) and ego (who could reject alter's selection): only in this case is it evident that ego's acceptance of the premises of her action is linked to alter's power.

Power reproduces itself in the form of obedience to a command. It is realized when the action sequence command-obedience is combined with a sequence of threat of sanction (if you do not obey, I will punish you). Thus, the form of power is the difference between obedience and the alternative to be avoided (sanction).

Power threats negative sanctions based on physical violence, which must be usable in a generalized way and represents the symbiotic mechanism [→*Symbolically Generalized Media*] of power. It can occasionally use positive sanctions, but these are transformed into negatives (for instance, when dismissal is threatened). Neither alter nor ego want sanctions; however, they are more damaging for ego. For both actors, sanctions represent the alternatives to be avoided, but ego is more afraid of their realization.

On the one hand, the difference between obedience and sanction motivates ego to accept communication (it is better to be obedient than punished); power fails when ego prefers the alternative to be avoided and alter must give up or enforce sanctions (Iraq did not withdraw from Kuwait despite the UN ultimatum). On the other hand, alter's power is based on the avoidance of sanctions (the UN could only have had power if Iraq had obeyed): powers ends when the sanction is realized, as the use of physical force shows that no power is present. To maintain power, the use of physical force must remain an alternative to be avoided: the ability of power to assert itself is proven when it is not contradicted.

Power is symbolized: the symbols allow decisions to be determined and implemented (we must do this or that, for this or that reason), as well as making power visible (e.g., parades, flags). The symbolic side of power always plays a role—even when the use of physical force is threatened—because it always requires a decision. Even when physical force is employed, the effect of power does not lie in changing the physical state of the body, but rather in the consequences of such force for the acceptance of communication.

The code of power is the distinction inferior/superior. This is a preferential code, because it is positive to be superior and negative to be inferior. However, the code cannot motivate the acceptance of communication and, therefore, cannot motivate ego to accept her inferiority. Taking the difference inferior/superior alone can lead to fighting. A secondary coding it therefore necessary, which is provided by the law [→*Legal System*]: the code legal/illegal allows ego to distinguish between a legitimate and an illegitimate law, i.e., to motivate herself to accept legitimate communication. Without such secondary coding, the →*code* of power cannot be technicized. For this reason, the programs governing the correct attribution of the values of power are laws and legal decisions. Finally when power is political, a further code alongside that of the law provides technologization: the political code government/opposition.

Power is reflexive since it refers to other power and only develops when it can connect to other power. Power inflates when it is used in excess (alter demands conditions of ego's action that ego cannot fulfill) and deflates when implemented too narrowly, i.e., when not all the possibilities offered by power can be exploited (when alter either makes continual recourse to physical force or must give up). *[C.B.]*

Power (1979); Theory of Society (2012: 212-214, 223-228, 231); Die Politik der Gesellschaft (2000: Ch. 2).

Process (*Prozess*)

The term "process" describes a temporally irreversible sequence of →*events*. Processes have at their disposal a double selection of operative possibilities: the first selection begins by limiting the domain of the events that can follow each individual event in the course of the process. The second selection takes place in the concrete situation in which the process is realized, and this determines which event can be actualized in each case.

We should not conceive of "process" as a simple succession of one event after another. Instead, it is the organization of these events into sequences, so that selections that have already been realized and selections that are expected together provide the conditions for a selection realized in a particular moment. The form of the process establishes the limit of possibilities, which allows the determination of connections that are found by each event in each situation. In other words, this limitation forms a reference horizon for communication possibilities (in social systems) or thought possibilities (in psychic systems).

Processes can be observed as producing irreversibility only against the background of enduring →*structures*. The sequence of events elapses on the basis of structures, since it transforms the future into the past. [G.C.]

Temporalstrukturen des Handlungssystems (1980); Social Systems (1995: 44-45, 353-356).

Program (*Programm*)

Programs are generally defined as complexes of conditions of correctness. Programs provide criteria for the correct attribution of the →*code*'s values, so that a system oriented towards them [→*Differentiation of Society*] can reach structured complexity and control its own processes.

In an autopoietic system [→*Autopoiesis*] differentiated through a binary code, the code guides the unity of operations reproducing the system: it regulates the production of differences, through which it also regulates the system's information processing. Operations always run blind and, at the level of operations, the system has no control over its own processes. The code does not provide instructions for action; it provides only the orientation for operations, securing the connection to following operations. Self-regulation and self-control of the system happen at the level of programs, which guide the observation of the operations by the system itself (based on other distinctions than the ones orienting those operations). Programs determine the conditions necessary for the realizability of a certain operation. They determine, for instance, that attributing the positive value of the code is only correct under particular conditions. Hence the programs of the legal system (laws and procedures) determine which of the parties can be correctly claimed to be right and which to be wrong, and what must be taken into account in this decision. The programs of science (theories and methods) determine which conditions must be fulfilled in order to be able to claim that something is true. For instance, the programs of the education system determine the criteria for the selection of the pupils.

Programs compensate for the strict binarity of the code, which permits only two values to be considered, by introducing in the decision criteria that are foreign to the system. The programs of science can take into account political opportunity or research costs—even when the operations of the system are ultimately led only by the distinction true/untrue. One can therefore keep an eye on the available financial resources or on particular interests when programing research, but these influences cannot affect the truth of the results. This truth is not a political or economic fact, but is always dependent on the scientific code. As such, criteria external to the system, such as political opportunity or costs, in no way determine the production of knowledge: they can, however, limit research and influence the implementation of the programs.

Programs re-introduce the third value excluded by the binary code into the system that orients itself to the code. In this way, the rigidity of the code is mitigated. Even if the system orients itself only to its code (e.g., true/untrue, legal/illegal), at the level of programs it takes criteria into account that are valid in other systems. Even though, for instance, science never generates its truths in accordance with beauty or economic factors, it can attempt to make its truths compatible with these priorities. Based on the "foreign" criteria introduced by the programs, binary-coded systems can get enough distance from their operations to observe them and direct their own course. They are thus able to increase and structure their complexity.

As the self-observation of a system always requires the continuation of autopoiesis (of the operations) [→*Operation/Observation*], programming always requires orientation to a code. Through the code, the system differentiates itself as a unity from the environment, and none of the system operations can take place independently of the code. Only on the basis of the differentiation and functioning of the code can programming take criteria foreign to the system into account—and programs of course always refer to each system's respective code. If one is no longer able to distinguish between truth and property or between truth and beauty, one cannot set criteria for attributing truth. While the code can never be changed, programs can change on the basis of the operations of the system: in science, for instance, theories and methods can change, albeit always on the basis of the code true/untrue. Opening the system at the level of programs requires closure at the level of coding, whilst reaching a certain level of complexity in the system requires programming.

If we look at the correctness of behavior instead of the attribution of code values, programs are specific points of reference that serve to identify connections between expectations [→*Identity/Difference*]. For instance, a surgical intervention is a program that coordinates the behavior of various people and means that a particular behavior, exhibited by each person in each moment and coordinated with the others, can be expected. The program determines which behavior must be deemed correct and is therefore to be expected. The distinction between conditional programming and programming by goals regards the reference of the correctness of behaviors to the realization of particular conditions (when a specific state occurs, then a particular behavior must be realized) or to the desired consequences. *[E.E.]*

Social Systems (1995: 317-319); Codierung und Programmierung: Bildung und Selektion im Erziehungssystem (1986); Die Wissenschaft der Gesellschaft (1990: 197 ff., 401 ff.); Einführung in die Theorie der Gesellschaft (2005: Ch. 4.11).

Property/Money (*Eigentum/Geld*)

Money is a →*symbolically generalized medium* that corresponds to the constellation of →*attribution* in which alter's action is experienced by ego. As long as this action does not affect access to scare resources, the situation remains unproblematic. Ego's observation of the action of others does not provoke her own action: ego observes, for instance, that a neighbor cuts the grass. However, as soon as a situation of scarcity emerges (when, for instance, land is limited), alter's access (the fact that alter is cultivating a particular piece of land) limits ego's remaining opportunity for access. It is then unlikely that ego will be content not to intervene and to limit herself to experience.

The communication medium property, with the corresponding code ownership/non-ownership, has emerged in the context of this problem: in relation to every object that can be owned, everyone finds themselves with the alternative of being either owner or non-owner. The social designation of owner defines the freedom to dispose of one's own goods as one sees fit: everyone can do whatever they wish with the objects that belong to them and this right is guaranteed by society. In consequence, others are motivated to accept in their own experience the owner's very specific selections and not to intervene—even when these selections limit their opportunities to dispose of the objects. Property, which enables the exchange of goods, leads to the first form of economic differentiation [→*Economic System*].

The complete differentiation of the economic system requires, however, a secondary coding of property through money. Property is monetized when every object gets a monetary value. The positive value (ownership) is duplicated, generating the code payment/non-payment: ownership of money can be used to execute or not a payment. It becomes more likely that everyone but the owner accepts to be excluded from the enjoyment of a commodity and accepts the owner's selections, because every use of money is at the same time a transfer of that money to others, i.e., the circulation of property.

Monetization facilitates the accessibility of the medium and the degree to which it can be conditioned. Firstly, there is a duplication of scarcity: along with the scarcity of goods, there is now the scarcity of money. Goods are seen as assets, i.e., the equivalents of sums of money. Now, money is the primary subject of scarcity, rather than commodities (that could be bought with money). Money is not simply the sum of bank notes, but the sum of all property seen from the perspective of its ability to be transferred into liquid funds. This yields, among other things, the universalization of scarcity, in the sense that everyone always needs more money, while they do not necessarily need a particular commodity.

This development is possible because money is quantifiable. Whilst property is still bound to the natural indivisibility of things, money can be divided and multiplied at will: we can, therefore, compare any possible commodity with any other, because each has a price.

A money economy can be fully differentiated from other areas of society, because exchange takes place under purely economic criteria—without, for instance, being influenced by the social status of the parties involved. In addition, the economy is characterized by a very high degree of combinatory freedom, unhindered by external constraints or memory limitations. Payment in general, and prices in particular, are characterized by a high degree of information-loss: the payer does not provide information on the origin of the money, and the payee is not required to explain what will become of the money. That means that a price-oriented system can function almost without memory: we do not remember who executed the payment and why, and who could not execute payment. The payee is immediately free to use the money for any other combination.

Inflation of money as a medium occurs when money cannot be used at the expected value, while deflation occurs when its acceptance is refused. The bodily needs of human beings are the symbiotic symbol of money. The concept of needs is generalized in a money economy and widened beyond the area of basic survival. Today it includes everything that can be related to production. [E.E.]

Die Wirtschaft der Gesellschaft (1988).

Protest

Protest is a modern phenomenon that cannot be compared to either pre-modern reform movements or the political conflicts and riots of the nineteenth century. Themes, causes and goals have become so heterogeneous that protest movements can no longer be identified with specific contents.

In trying to understand which differences, or which forms, characterize the protest, we discover that we are dealing with a →*paradox*, with a protest by society against society. Protest movements communicate as though they were outside society, even though they are only able to communicate, and in so doing contribute to the reproduction of society. For this, they need themes that specify what it is that people are protesting against, and what they are engaging themselves for. Through specifying themes, a line can be drawn in society that allows protesters to be differentiated from the "the others."

Under the conditions of modern society, there is no shortage of themes, as demonstrated by the history of protest: gender equality, ecology, wars, ethnic minorities, the third world, large, predominantly transnational decision makers and, for far-right movements, uncontrolled immigration, xenophobia, and so on. Two aspects in particular seem to be especially important: social inequality within society, and imbalances in the relationship with the environment, which guarantee a practically inexhaustible reservoir of themes. As such, the themes function like the programming of the binary →*codes* of societal subsystems [→*Program*], since they clarify why someone is protesting. This tension between theme and protest gives the movements their unity and visibility, independently of defining a target (which often remains unspecified), or of success or failure. It is important only that a boundary can be drawn within society against society, and that the protest unreflectively takes itself to be something better, and takes on responsibility for society, but against it.

The system typology of protest presents a theoretical problem. Protest movements are not organizations: they do not consist of decisions and are not delineated by membership rules, since they differentiate only between followers and sympathizers. They are characterized by motives and engagement, not by hierarchy or control over decision premises. But these movements are not interactions either, since the meaning of protest does not reside only in individual encounters. We can therefore understand them as a particular type of autopoietic system that produces the protest, constructs the theme and generates controversy by itself.

Protest's main form of structural coupling is with mass media [→*Interpenetration and structural coupling*]. It is embodied above all in demonstrations and ad hoc organized events that can be reported in the media and fulfill an alarm function without taking into account the full scope of the arguments or the causal attribution: it is enough to self-identify as "alternative".

When we understand protest movements as autopoietic systems [→*Autopoiesis*], we are also confronted with the question of function. This can be described as the negation of society within society, i.e., the ability of society to observe itself within itself against itself. It does not concern who is right and who is wrong, but rather the assertion of the autonomy of the social system, which also includes communication against communication.

Precisely this function, however, is not reflected as a societal function. Unlike in societal subsystems, a reflection of the system within the system [→*Self-Reference*] is missing in protest movements, since that would mean conceiving itself as (part of) the society against which it directs its protest. The alternative proposed by movements cannot be understood as an alternative for functional differentiation: the alternatives are without alternative. It is only possible to be against, and for this only obligation is needed, without seeing that the other side of the protest—i.e., the one the protest is against—is a construction of the protest movement. [G.C.]

Theory of Society (2013: Ch. XV); Protest (1996)

Psychic Systems (*Psychische Systeme*)

Alongside →*social systems* and living systems, psychic systems, or conscious systems, are one of the three levels constituting autopoiesis. The operations [→*Operation/Observation*] of consciousness are thoughts, which are reproduced recursively in a closed network without any contact with the environment. Directly accessing the stream of thoughts within a consciousness is impossible; we can only observe thoughts from outside in the manner and form of the respective observer.

Consciousness as a closed system is also out of bounds to other autopoietic systems: neither organism nor communication can determine the stream of thoughts. They can only offer stimuli that the consciousness can freely process in its own form and according to its own structures. Social systems belong to the environment of psychic systems, and the relationships between the autopoiesis of different system types take the form of interpenetration [→*Interpenetration and Structural Coupling*]. The socialization of conscious systems is not carried out through outside intervention, but rather exclusively through "self-socialization": psychic systems use stimuli from the environment in order to re-specify their structures according to their own particular mode of operation. It is possible for society to refer to psychic systems, but only based on specific communicative structures: people's identities are constructed for this purpose [→*Inclusion/Exclusion*].

The operational closure of psychic systems also excludes any direct relationship between conscious systems. They can come into direct contact only through communication. Communication, however, always requires double contingency and the mutual opacity of the psychic systems taking part, which remain black boxes for each other.

As autopoietic operations, thoughts reproduce themselves blindly in simple succession: control of the autopoietic process can only be exercised at the level of observation [→*Operation/Observation*]. However, consciousness is a

→*meaning*-constituting system: a system whose operations are always accompanied by self-observation. Every thought contributes to the reproduction of the psychic system as a unity, because it is connected to an earlier thought (in the same system) through observation.

Observation always requires orientation to a distinction. The observation of thoughts through other thoughts uses the distinction →*self-reference*/other-reference. Consciousness constructs this distinction through identification with the body (*Körper*) it comes in, which it can observe both from the outside and the inside (for instance, as weight or as pain) and which it differentiates from other bodies and from other objects. Based on the distinction self-reference/other-reference, a thought is observed as representation-of-something (*Vorstellung-von-etwas*), and the next thought can decide, in a situation of "bi-stability," whether it orients itself to the self-reference (the representation) or to the other-reference (the represented "something") of the previous thought.

In this way, the system is also capable of exercising a type of control over itself, because it can differentiate the self-referential side of the previous thought and connect to it. The thought thinks other thoughts and develops into more complex and more abstract forms that are triggered by previous thoughts and not necessarily by events in the environment. →*Language* plays a central role in this process: when thoughts are expressed in language, they can be more easily observed, whilst linguistic forms and linguistic rules can support self-control.

On this basis, consciousness can develop advanced forms of self-reference such as reflexivity and reflection. Reflection arises when the psychic system observes itself as a unity ("all of my thoughts")—i.e., when it produces a representation of the identity of the consciousness within the consciousness itself. The system grasps itself as an identity, which can be recognized as distinct from the environment and can continue to be recognized in changing contexts.

The self-observation of consciousness through consciousness has, however, no privileged position compared to observation from outside. In both cases, a simplification based on a particular observational schema is involved, which has its own blind spot. Self-analysis does not lead to a complete self-description of the psychic system. [E.E.]

Social Systems (1995: Ch. 7); Die Autopoiesis des Bewußtseins (1985); Die Form "Person" (1991).

Rationality (*Rationalität*)

The concept of rationality refers to the form of self-observation [→*Operation/Observation*] that is the most improbable and is subject to the most conditions. We speak of rationality when a system capable of reflection—i.e., a system able to observe itself as distinct from its environment—can orient itself to the unity of this distinction. As such, the system is not only able to observe itself by using the distinction system/environment, but can also observe this distinction as different from others, posit it as contingent and thereby gather →*information*. A rational system would be capable of exposing its system/environment distinction to reality, of testing it and thus of observing what would change (in the system and in the environment) if the distinction were different. In other words: the system would be capable of distancing itself from itself and its own operations, and of correcting its position in relation to the environment based on criteria that are constructed and varied within the system itself.

A system would behave rationally if it could control the effects it has on the environment based on the repercussions these effects have for the system. In terms of the social system, this would mean that environmental problems generated for society by society are re-introduced and controlled in communication. Today's society demonstrates a rationality deficit, for example because it cannot predict how the change in the psychic environment caused by the dissemination of school education (which influences the motivations and behavior of huge numbers of people) rebounds on society as a whole. Ecological problems are another particularly incisive example.

Full rationality is unattainable, since it would require the system to be able to internally observe the differentiation between itself and its environment—and that always produces a paradox [→*Re-entry*]. In the case of a functionally differentiated social system [→*Differentiation of Society*], even a "bounded rationality" is hardly plausible: there is no social instance competent for grasping and representing as a unity the relationship between society and the environment. This is because the relationship to the environment is fragmented into a multiplicity of system/environment distinctions of individual functional systems (which can be related back neither to each other nor to a unified perspective). The urgent problems of modern society are related to the simultaneous necessity and impossibility of a global societal rationality.

Under these conditions, rationality judgments must be disconnected from external data and instead refer to how the differentiation between self-reference and other-reference is managed internally. We can thus formulate a concept of system rationality oriented to difference theory [→*Identity/Difference*]: a system is defined as rational if it takes as a basis of its observations the differentiation of itself from its environment as the difference between self-reference and other-reference. A system of this type therefore draws a distinction between itself and its environment at the level of its operations (in the sense that what is system is not environment, excluded from the system). At the level of observations, however, the system orients itself to this distinction as the distinction between internal reference and external reference (in this way it includes itself in the world at the level of observations). In its own operations, the system is indifferent to what happens in the environment and uses this indifference in order to build its own complexity. It grasps the environmental data only at the level of observations as irritations—only if they can be processed internally as information.

In this new formulation, the problem of rationality is transformed into the ability of the system to continue its autopoiesis on the basis of a more and more selective and improbable relationship with the environment. The system must be capable of maintaining and using differences in order to increase its irritability—even if it necessarily always operates self-referentially. [E.E.]

Social Systems (1995: Ch. 11.X); Modernity in Contemporary Society (1998); Theory of Society (2012: Ch. 1.11); European Rationality (1998).

Redundancy/Variety (Redundanz/Varietät)

The concept of redundancy is a classic one in systems theory, where it is contrasted with the concept of variety in order to describe two different ways to assess the complexity of a system.

Redundancy means the extent to which a certain level of knowledge about the other elements in the system is automatically acquired through knowledge of one element—in other words, the extent to which the knowledge of one element reduces the informativeness of the others. When elements are similar, the redundancy of the system grows; for instance, a message that communicates a known piece of news is very redundant. Communication can be understood as the dissemination of redundancy: if A communicates a certain piece of information to B, C can turn to either A or B when later seeking access to the same information. Redundancy is usually linked to a safety aspect: the same function can be fulfilled via various means. When difficulties arise, alternative possibilities are available.

Variety, on the other hand, is understood as the multitude and heterogeneity of the elements in a system, i.e., the improbability that an element can be predicted based on the knowledge of other elements. With increasing variety, the system is increasingly open to the environment.

Although variety and redundancy are usually held to be inversely proportional (in the sense that the increase of one entails the decrease of the other), Luhmann poses the hypothesis that forms can combine higher variety with an increase in redundancy. A scientific theory, for instance, can be more effective than earlier theories because it reorganizes their redundancies (i.e., determines new connections between concepts), reaching a higher level of generalizability and allowing different objects to be taken into consideration (more variety).

With the transition to functional differentiation [→Differentiation of Society] comes an eschewing of redundancy—in the sense that the different functions, once differentiated, can be fulfilled only at a single place within society. Multifunctionality, which characterizes, for instance, families, morality or religious cosmologies, is lost and each function can be fulfilled only in the competent system and nowhere else. *[E.E.]*

> Social Systems (1995: 172-174, 299); Ecological Communication (1989: Ch. XVI); Die Wissenschaft der Gesellschaft (1990: 436); Organization (2003).

Re-entry

The concept of re-entry describes the ability of autopoietic systems [→*Autopoiesis*]—which are differentiated on the basis of a distinction that allows the production of the unity of the system— to introduce this distinction into themselves and to use it to structure their operations. It is a re-entry if, for instance, a functional system differentiated on the basis of the particular distinction of its →*code* learns how to process this distinction internally: for instance, if the scientific system, whose operations are oriented to the code true/untrue, develops a scientific theory that observes the use of the code true/untrue using the code true/untrue. Epistemological reflection is the re-entry of the distinction true/untrue into the system established on the basis of this distinction: thus, there is a scientific operation in which the truth of scientific operations—i.e., the truth of the distinction true/untrue—is questioned. In this way, a situation arises in which the distinction is simultaneously the same (when it is the particular distinction of that system operations) and different (when it is the observed distinction). The problem that follows from this situation is how to handle this →*paradox* without being blocked by it. The problem of re-entry is the "otherness of the same": the necessity of processing the same distinction as if it were a different one.

Re-entry indicates the "re-introduction" of a distinction into a domain that is differentiated by the distinction itself. The term is derived from George Spencer Brown's logical calculus [→*Operation/Observation*], a feature of which is that it is based exclusively on the operation of indication/distinction. Systems theory interprets this operation as observation: something is indicated and at the same time distinguished from others things. The connections between operations within one and the same system lead to the construction of ever more complex forms, until the point at which the calculus has reached a sufficient level of complexity. Then the system includes an operation that, in place of an external object, again indicates the system-constituting operation of indication/distinction, i.e., the same operation that the operation itself realizes.

Through recourse to time, the system is able to process this operation within itself. It is then possible to produce an (observational) operation that distinguishes its own distinction from something else—i.e., an operation in which the distinction appears twice, both as a system-specific distinction and as a running distinction; as observing distinction and observed distinction. Here we have a re-entry.

The concept of re-entry is useful first and foremost in order to tackle the issue of the →*paradox*, because it shows how a system can neutralize paradoxes through recourse to the temporal sequence of its operations. It is also useful because it allows the possible binary distinctions [→*Code*] to be discriminated in terms of which of them are appropriate for guiding the autopoiesis of a system. Only distinctions capable of re-entry enable a minimal level of complexity to be overcome in the construction of a system. These distinctions are capable of processing the unity of the distinction on one of their sides. One such example is the distinction system/environment: once the system has reached a certain level of complexity, it is able to tackle the question of its own relationship to the environment. The capacity for re-entry sets this distinction apart from alternatives such as, for instance, the distinction whole/parts. If we only had the distinction between the whole and its parts, it would not be possible to take the surplus into account, which makes the whole more than the mere sum of its parts. In order to qualify this surplus, we would need a term defined independently of the opposition of parts and whole: we would need recourse to another distinction. [E.E.]

Die Wissenschaft der Gesellschaft (1990: 83 ff., 479 ff.); The Paradox of Observing Systems (1995); Observing Reentries (1993).

Religious System (*Religionssystem*)

The function of religion lies in using communication to process the distinction between what is observable and what is not observable. This function can only be fulfilled paradoxically [→*Paradox*]. In order to explain this definition, it is necessary to recognize that every form (i.e., every distinction [→*Identity/Difference*]) draws a boundary between what can be determined and something else that is excluded, implied—but not indicated. In every communication a reference is made to something unobservable. In this way, all communication implies religion, although this universalism is offset by the fact that religion can observe reality only on the basis of its own specific criterion. What is special about religion is how it processes the difference observable/unobservable, since it makes this difference its primary problem. Forms of communication are religious when their meaning refers to the unity of this difference. In the more developed religions of modern society, this difference is encoded [→*Code*] through the binary distinction of immanence and transcendence. For every immanent fact that can be communicated, there is always a transcendental correlate that is as such not observable.

Religion is permanently concerned with a double reality: on the one hand, there is the immanent, real reality and, on the other, the transcendental, imaginary reality. The distinction observable/unobservable is presented by religion as a unity such that a →*re-entry* occurs: the distinction observable/unobservable is observable; it re-enters on the observable side. Forms of meaning can then be experienced religiously if, as the unity of the difference, they are indicated as mysterious and paradoxical.

The reproduction of the distinction observable/unobservable and its social control constitute a problem shared by all religions that have developed throughout the history of society: how can they prevent the imaginary from being reduced to such a degree of arbitrariness that anyone can say something religiously relevant? The other side of the question constitutes the complementary problem: how can they permit and enable situations in which the religious experience, as the unity of the observable and the unobservable, is possible?

One of the first methods used to enable a religious imaginary reality to be projected is the secret: communication is limited to such an extent that it is possible to distinguish the sacred from everything else, for instance from its trivialization. The objects that religious communication refers to (e.g., bones, statues, animals, places) are rendered foreign compared to normality and yet remain perceivable. There is something there that we can touch, but we may not actually reach for it, since objects are always only objects and the events occur within utterly normal processes. This is precisely what secures the possibility of programming behavior in a religiously adequate way.

An evolutionary leap occurs when, alongside the old distinction between things and events, the true code of religion, the distinction between immanence and transcendence, is differentiated. This is advantageous because it allows the whole world to be observed and clearly and precisely duplicated: for everything that is immanently observable, there is a transcendental meaning correlate. Rather than sorting things or events according to sacred or profane, we must now turn to God as observer. In the case of the Jewish religion, for instance, God has no name; he eludes all knowledge and reveals himself to the world only as text that must be interpreted. The duty of tradition is thus to pass on the contradictory interpretations and, in turn, the resulting controversies benefit this passing on. God is therefore the transcendental observer and, at the same time, the unity of observer and observed: every form of holiness permitted in the immanent world is only ever a reflex of transcendence. The particularity of religious coding lies in the fact that the re-entry of the code is realized not on the positive, but on the negative side. While the other codes start out with the condition that it is positive to distinguish between positive and negative (e.g., it is a logical truth that true and untrue must be distinguished between; it is good to keep good and bad separate), religion makes every meaning determinable by referring to what in every meaning is indeterminable.

At least in the high forms of religion, the code is programmed in connection with →*morality*. The difference good/bad provides the orientation for communication, with the resulting problem that God also allows bad actions and thereby proves to be beyond all distinctions. The freedom of choice is thus seen as the pinnacle of creation; the only divine recommendation is to see transcendence in everything that happens.

The particularity of monotheistic religion lies in their specific formula for contingency: God. Transcendence exists as a person, presumably in order to refer to transcendence as an observational perspective on the immanent world. God is a person and as such an observer, but a very special observer, since he needs not make any distinction. Simply put, he can simultaneously realize every distinction schema as a difference and as a unity. People need not know how or what God is and nor may they try (unlike Lucifer), since this would mean distinguishing themselves from God, which means wanting to observe him. But if we assume that God observes everything and must therefore distinguish himself from everything else, then he cannot be observed in the world.

With the shift to functional differentiation [→*Differentiation of Society*], religion encounters a new situation and with it new problems. Its worldview can no longer be valid for society as a whole, and even morality does not function to integrate society. Though morality maintains its universalism, its programs cannot find any general consensus: societal integration is realized only through the relations between the different functional systems, and no longer in reference to commandments. The relationship between religion and other societal domains is no longer one of stratification. In today's theological discussion and reflection, the term secularization is generally used to indicate that a social environment exists which is external to religion, and that religion constitutes only one of society's many functional systems.

Unlike in certain subsystems, religion has no →*symbolically generalized media*. Although faith exhibits certain characteristics of such media, the aspect it primarily lacks is the typical tendency to distinguish between action and experience [→*Attribution*] as improbable selections that require motivation. Religious faith cannot encounter such a distinction, because life in its entirety must be subject to God's observation. Moreover, it would not make sense to be able to obtain holiness through an experience without the accompanying action or, conversely, through action carried out at the behest of an arbitrary will. Religion is too close to the unity of human beings to distinguish in this way.

A type of functional equivalence perhaps lies in the particular tendency of religion to undertake inclusion and exclusion. Religion is society's only subsystem that does not join in with integration and exclusion behaviors [→*Inclusion/Exclusion*]: even those excluded from other systems (such as beggars or homeless) can be included in religious communication. Conversely, exclusion from religion does not mean, as it did in the Middle Ages, exclusion from society.

How far religion is really able to include the excluded, who make up a large proportion of the world population, is a question that can only be answered empirically and it remains difficult to understand how far religion can reflect this function as its own. *[G.C.]*

Funktion der Religion, 1977; A Systems Theory of Religion (2013); Soziologische Aufklärung 4 (1987: Ch. IV); Die Sinnform Religion (1996).

Risk/Danger (*Risiko/Gefahr*)

The concept of risk refers to the possibility of future damages occurring as a consequence of our decisions (in the present). Decisions in the present condition what will happen in the future, but exactly how they will do so remains unknown. Decisions must therefore be made without having sufficient knowledge of the future. In other words: who makes a decision in the present can never be protected from possible future damages, and these damages may result from the person's own behavior. A situation of risk is signaled by the fact that, despite the potential for negative consequences, it can still make sense and be advantageous to take one decision over another.

Perceiving risk is dependent on attributing [→*Attribution*] the (possible or actual) damages of a decision to that exact decision. This requires second-order observation [→*Operation/Observation*], in which an observer observes another observer (which can also be the observer herself). The form of observation allows the differentiation of different situations of insecurity and danger: a general insecurity dependent on uncontrollable (e.g., natural) factors is not yet a risk, since the potential for damage is not self-generated. In this sense, it is pertinent to distinguish between risk and danger. We speak of risk only if the possible damages result from a decision made by the affected system (or attributed to it) and would not occur without this decision. Conversely, danger is understood as possible damages that cannot be attributed to its decision—although they may be due to the risky decisions of others. The danger of getting wet when it rains (as a uncontrollable environmental event) has transformed, with the invention of the umbrella, into the danger of getting wet as a consequence of the decision not to bring an umbrella.

On the other hand, each risk leads to the production of further risks; for instance, the risk of losing the umbrella should we decide not to run the risk of getting wet. With the distinction risk/danger, the illusion of safety disappears. Safety becomes an empty concept, since we can never be safe from future damages. Even the attempt to avoid risk (for instance, by driving slowly) is risky (because it can lead to late arrival, lack of time to accomplish other tasks, or being run over by others wanting to go faster). Even lost opportunities constitute a risk, which increases the burden of decision. The old recipe of *prudentia* is no longer of any use today. The concept of risk can be arbitrarily generalized in the fact dimension. Every decision and every behavior can prove to be risky, and vice versa: there is no safe (i.e., risk-free) behavior.

Risk is one of the forms of time binding: one of the forms through which society controls its changes by binding future states to present decisions. The increasing dissemination of an orientation towards risks, however, leads to other forms of time binding (norms and property) being questioned.

Norms, as counter-factual expectations [→*Legal System*], determine what we can expect in the future and remain valid even if the →*expectations* are disappointed. In risky situations, however, it is neither possible nor plausible to determine in the present how others will behave in the future. When debating ecological questions, for instance, the need to leave options open for future generations is always mentioned, because their decisions may be based on motivations that we cannot know today.

Property deals with the problem of scarcity [→*Economic System*] and of striving to secure the possibility of accessing scarce goods in the future. Property protects against access by others: only the owner can dispose of the goods. In a monetized economy, however, all goods have a monetary value and property, too, is subject to risk: if we do not invest our property, its value can decline—but every investment is inevitably risky.

From a sociological standpoint, the question becomes more complicated still, because evaluating risks and the willingness to accept damages both vary depending on whether we see them from the perspective of risk (the decision maker's perspective) or from the perspective of danger (the affected party's perspective). Someone may accept the high risk associated with his decision to smoke cigarettes, but react completely differently to the danger posed by injury to health caused by environmental pollution or other forms of contamination. Smokers accept the risks that come with smoking, but do not want to be subject to the dangers generated by the risky behavior of others, even when they know that smoking can be more damaging than breathing polluted air.

From a more general perspective, it is crucial for sociology to emphasize the fact that decisions (which require the willingness of the decision maker to take on the associated risks) pose a danger to everyone else, particularly the people affected by them. When we take this difference in attribution into account, the following is valid: no rational argument can convince the affected party that the risk (which for her is a danger) is negligible. For instance, residents of an area in which a new power plant should be built cannot be convinced that the resulting risks (however statistically unlikely they may be) are acceptable. The dissemination of the orientation towards risks therefore has grave consequences for the forms of solidarity that are still possible in modern society.

The ineffectiveness of rational explanation points to a further characteristic of risk: gleaning new information does not lead to a decrease in risk, but rather to an increase due to greater awareness of the circumstances that come into play. As such, even science is unable to offer support against the surprises that may arise in the future. [E.E.]

Risk: A Sociological Theory (1993); Risiko und Gefahr (1990).

Scientific System (*Wissenschaftssystem*)

Science is a functionally differentiated subsystem of modern society [→*Differentiation of Society*], which uses the communication medium →*truth* for its own reproduction. The function of the scientific system is to construct and obtain new knowledge. Scientific truth is not understood as the equivalent of the real world, but rather as a →*symbolically generalized medium*. To produce operations, truth refers to the coding of the difference between true and untrue: both values mark a communication as scientific, which becomes observable through these values. As such, scientifically untrue knowledge must also be treated as scientific.

The structures of the scientific system consist of →*expectations* of a cognitive type, which are changed in the case of disappointment. This means that scientific knowledge changes when research produces new, hitherto unknown results: new theories and concepts are formulated, following which scientific structures engender different expectations than they did before. Compared with how deviation is handled in other subsystems of society, science handles it the other way around: each scientific communication produces something new, and this new thing can be adopted as a condition for further communication, or abandoned if it is later shown to be untrue or has no connectivity for research. At any rate, it only makes sense to conduct research when we have something new to say.

The values of the code true/untrue [→*Truth*] indicate scientific communication by differentiating it from other communication that takes place in society. The code, however, provides no instructions for the topics or structures that scientific communication facilitates and steers. This is done by the scientific system's →*programs*. Theories and methods function as correctness conditions in the allocation of code values. As conditions, theories and methods limit and determine what is accepted in scientific operations. Both make observable whatever research refers to (e.g., organisms, psychic or social systems, machines, nature). In this way, science can condition its observations in a specific form, namely through limitationality: the determination of an element in a relationship contributes to the determination of the other elements in the relationship. When a hypothesis proves to be untrue, certain other hypotheses become more probable and attract research resources: in this way, new research opportunities are constantly being formed. Limitationality, in this sense, should be grasped not as the limitation of observable objects, but rather as the condition for scientific communication.When everything could be completely arbitrarily different, it would be impossible to produce new knowledge that could be used as if it were true. The negations that are constantly produced in the scientific system must be informative—in a theoretically and methodologically conditioned way— for instance, for what can still be done, for which hypothesis can be held as reliable. The choice of one distinction limits, for instance, what can be indicated by its exclusion of other possibilities; at the same time, this choice is contingent because it excludes something. Only in this way can science refer to objects and use certain distinctions in its observations, and it is only in this way that is it possible to train scientific knowledge.

Since reality is constructed on the basis of theoretically guided distinctions, the system favors making distinctions that take its contingency into account, i.e., it can exert a certain control over itself. This is possible when the distinction can indicate itself through a →*re-entry*. One example is the guiding distinction of systems theory between system and environment: a system can only observe itself when it can distinguish itself from its own environment—i.e., when it refers to the distinction system/environment. The observer making this distinction (in our case, systems theory in the scientific system) can observe the distinction in question without having to leave it, and it therefore has the chance to justify this distinction without having to reach for theory-external reasoning. The justification of the chosen distinction lies, in other words, in the ability to compare this distinction with other possible, alternative distinctions within the initial schema. The necessity of using distinctions that can be reapplied is primarily emphasized in the epistemological reflection of science. The description of scientific knowledge as an operation of a self-referential system is today accepted by theories of knowledge known under the heading of "→*constructivism*". The question that scientific reflection asks itself no longer concerns the correspondence between knowing system and known world, but rather the structures of a social system that itself constructs the reality that it observes, and can make this question the starting point of its own reflection. Constructivism phrases the problem in terms of how a theory of knowledge can be constructed that takes into account the fact that the observers in the world it wants to describe empirically exist. The epistemology to which constructivism refers is one that includes the designer of the knowledge: it is an epistemology that also describes itself and therefore requires self-observing distinctions. The same goes for the case of a theory of society, which can only be autological because it is found among its own objects and must therefore include itself in its objects.

For sociology, these arguments are particularly important because the theories offered by this discipline often base their validity on assumptions that are more moral or ideological than scientific. Indeed, there is often the implicit assumption that the critic of the criticized society does not belong to it. The system-theoretical approach takes the opposite course: however well or badly we can speak of this society, the sociologist's task is primarily to retain the fact that everything she writes and says about society is also true of the sociologist herself. [G.C.]

Die Wissenschaft der Gesellschaft (1990); The Differentiation of Advances in Knowledge (1984).

Self-description (*Selbstbeschreibung*)

Self-description is a particular type of self-observation [→*Operation/Observation*] which is produced as a description of a →*social system* within the system itself through the communicative production of texts. Self-description is a simplified construction of the unity of the system that makes it possible to communicate in the system about the system; therefore, the system becomes its own theme. Thus, self-description generates the system's identity as a selective observation of the unity of the system.

Self-descriptions are produced in →*communication*, as communication is the operation of social systems. In particular, self-descriptions may be reproduced in written or printed texts and in oral narratives. Self-descriptions develop as the result of recursive observations in the system through operations of communication. These operations first generate descriptions, then establish and stabilize these descriptions as texts or narratives. They stabilize a →*semantics* that allows the social system's self-reference. Thus, self-descriptions also change the system in which they are produced, because they are part of this system. Self-description is a retrospective operation of communication that requires the existence of something to describe, in particular it requires the construction of memory [→*Time*] within the system. Therefore, self-description may be defined as a historical form of semantics.

Self-descriptions are selective because it is not possible to describe everything is happening in the system as the identity of the system. Thus, self-descriptions lead social systems to reflect on what possibilities are excluded from the form that the identity takes (e.g., society describes itself as unstable and this leads society to reflect on the conditions of stability). The system's reflection [→*Self-Reference*] on other possibilities of identity construction determines the contingency of self-descriptions, which in their turn change over time according to the system's changes.

On the one hand, self-descriptions orient communication in social systems (e.g., focusing on the condition of instability), thereby influencing the level of societal complexity, which may require new social structures (to face instability). On the other hand, self-descriptions are influenced by structural changes and societal complexity, as new connections between communications lead to the introduction of new themes and the production of new narratives or texts (from instability to critical reflection on conditions of change).

Self-descriptions can be produced in all forms of society simply based on →*language*. However, their production is influenced, on the one hand, by →*dissemination media* and, on the other, by the form of societal differentiation [→*Differentiation of Society*]. Concerning dissemination media, the invention of writing has allowed the production of the first elaborated self-descriptions, which fix the topic of communication. Much later, the system of →*mass media* strongly influenced the production of self-descriptions, generating a great amount, and rapid change, of options.

Concerning the form of society, the functional differentiation of society has triggered a huge amount of new, more articulate, more differentiated and contingent forms of self-description. In the functionally differentiated society, self-descriptions are produced in functional systems. In the subsystems of this society, there is a strong increase in second-order observations, which become relevant as self-descriptions. Comparing prices, conditioning politics through public opinion, scientific publications, conversations on demonstrations of love, and mediated communication are all opportunities for self-descriptions. Each functional system can both produce self-descriptions concerning society (e.g., in the science system, sociology describes society) and stabilize its own self-descriptions (e.g., the political system can describe itself as State, the economic system as free market). Against this background, sociology becomes both a description of society and a self-description within society. It can provide a theory of society that contributes to the production of the object it analyzes; specifically, it can change this object because it is part of it. The production of a sociological theory changes society because it is an internal production, regardless of its specific effects for other functional systems (e.g., political effects).

In the functionally differentiated society, self-descriptions also become the subject of self-descriptions: society can describe itself as a self-describing system and each self-description is contingent, since it is one among many different possibilities. Against this background, self-descriptions also make it possible for a social system to generate resistance against itself by defining critical points in the system. The social system can open up several possible scenarios of change, which increases the potential for change and its sensitivity to new problems.

Self-description requires a particular self-referential form of a social system: reflection, which is the →*re-entry* of the distinction between system and environment into the system. The theories of reflection, which develop conceptualizations of reflection, are specific and demanding forms of self-description. Through a theory of reflection, a social system can observe and describe itself. Each subsystem of the functionally differentiated society develops theories of reflection; for instance, there are theories of knowledge in the scientific system, theologies in the religious system, theories of law, of the economy, of aesthetics in the system of art, and so on. In the functionally differentiated society, a centralized theory of reflection is not possible, therefore theories of reflection can be realized only in functional systems. This society generates a plurality of theories of reflection.

The concept of self-description replaces the concept of culture in the history of societal semantics. The concept of culture refers to the supply of possible themes made available in concrete communicative processes. This concept has been produced in the history of society as a set of concepts and ideas, and, in particular, it has been linked to the comparison of different memories and traditions, and thus to the introduction of cultural diversity within society. The concept of culture has been used in Europe for this purpose since the end of the eighteenth century, stressing the necessity for social memory and comparative analyses of different social memories. Thus, culture is a concept which belongs to the history of societal self-descriptions, and should be replaced by the concept of self-description itself.

The limit of self-descriptions is that they cannot describe the distinction between the operation of describing and what is described, since what is described is the system that describes itself (e.g., self-descriptions cannot describe the difference between the societal operation of describing instability and the resulting description of societal instability). Self-description introduces the distinction between describing and the described into the social system, generating a paradoxical condition, i.e., it negates the difference between the observer (the social system) and its object (what is described in the system). For instance, instability is described as a condition of society, rather than a communicative production in society. [C.B.]

Theory of Society (2013: Ch. 5); Art as a Social System (2000: Ch. 7.I)

Self-Reference (*Selbstreferenz*)

The concept of self-reference describes the fact that there are systems that refer to themselves through their operations [→*Operation/Observation*]. These are (organic, psychic, social) systems that can only observe reality because of this self-contact [→*System/Environment*].

Self-reference occurs when the operation of observation is included in what is referred to, i.e., when it refers to something that belongs to it. A social system, for instance, can only reproduce communication and can only take the world into account through communication; self-reference is implied in every →*communication* in the form of utterance. In the same way, a consciousness can only think and reality can only gain relevance to the consciousness as the external referent of thought.

The concept of self-reference is intended to be neither purely analytical, nor a characteristic of the transcendental subject. System theory observes neither the human being nor the subject. The self-referential constitution of the organic, psychic and social systems is recognized as an empirical finding: such systems exist in the real world and are really self-referential. This description attempts to overcome the conflict between nominalism and realism; self-reference does not describe a solipsistic or transcendental conception of the world. Systems constituted self-referentially must be able to distinguish between what belongs to the system (its own operations) and what is to be attributed to its environment. On the one hand, self-reference requires the possibility to reproduce the system's own operations [→*Autopoiesis*] in such a way that every distinction used for observation (i.e., for the description of something) must be construed by the operations within the system itself. On the other hand, the system cannot mingle with the external reality, i.e., with its environment; the condition for its operativity and for each form of cognition is the possibility to distinguish internally between self- and other-reference. This ability distinguishes self-referential systems from trivial machines (according to Heinz von Foerster): while the latter always transform inputs into outputs in the same way, for self-referential machines the output depends on the particular internal state of the system; thus, depending on the different states of the system, the same input can lead to completely different results.

The concept of self-reference is not interchangeable with that of tautology. It does not concern an operation that directly describes itself (for example A=A), but rather an operation that refers to something (the "self" of the reference) that belongs to it. This reference is only possible because a difference which allows something that refers to itself is differentiated from something else. A tautology would be a non-informative form of self-reference, which would be fatal for the operations of the system: excluding the reference to other things would block every operative connection [→*Asymmetrization*].

Depending on which difference is used to refer to the "self", self-reference can be specified differently:

(a) When what is referring to itself is an element of the system (a communication, a thought, a cell) we speak of basal self-reference. The concept of the element refers to a fundamental unit of the system which cannot be further decomposed. Firstly, every element is an element only in reference to a system, and no elements exist without the system within which the elements are elements. Secondly, elements exist only in relation to other elements; what constitutes them is the difference between element and relation, and their behavior. The element can refer to itself because of the differentiation of element and relation. This differentiation is the basis upon which the system operations make circular references to themselves within connections to other operations. Self-reference is the form of →*meaning*, since what is actualized returns to itself within the reference to the possible. In the case of social systems, there is basal self-reference insofar as communications have no other points of reference than other communications: only due to this reference do they allow the autopoiesis of the system. The relations permitted between the elements are selected by the →*structures* of the system. In this sense, the difference between element and relation cannot be observed at the level of structures, but only at the level of autopoiesis. Meaning-constituting systems produce their own elements as operations and they have thorough responsibility for this production: the identity and the quality of an element can only be constituted within the system for which the element is an element. Input from operations from outside and the external definition of the relations between them are both unconceivable, because that would mean the destruction of the system.

(b) When the "self" of the reference is a →*process*, we speak of reflexivity that can be observed on the basis of the difference between before and after. Reflexivity consists in strengthening the selectivity of the process through applying the process to itself, which takes priority over applying it to that which is processed. An example is the learning to learn: instead of referring to the object of learning directly, it refers to the process of learning itself, such that its ability and its selectivity will be strengthened.

(c) In the third case the system refers to itself through its own operations, and this demands that the system can be differentiated internally (itself) and externally (its environment). In this case, we speak of reflection. The difference, which in this case guides self-reference, is that of system and environment. In reflection, a →*re-entry* of the difference system/environment is realized within the system. This is done with the help of a further operation in the system itself, and in this sense reflection continues the autopoiesis, but at the same time makes it possible for the system to gain information about itself. This is conveyed by the system in the form of a difference (the difference system/environment), which it represents as a contingent entity and compares with alternative possibilities.

In all these types of self-reference, we are dealing with a closed circularity that nevertheless does not deny the existence of the environment; on the contrary, the environment is a prerequisite for the system's selections. Self-referential systems are autonomous systems that use this closure to maintain their own autopoiesis and make their own observations possible. For this reason, we should not understand autonomy as independence, but rather as self-referential closure: the environment can limit or increase the range of operative possibilities, but this does not change the fact that the operations can only be produced and linked with one another by and in the system.

For this reason, autonomy is always absolute and not relative, since it would not make sense to conceive of a system that is only partly autonomous, or only closed "a bit". External, observable influences on the system only affect its degree of irritability or the performance demands made by other systems, never its autonomy or closure. Thus autonomy should be understood as the relationship of dependence and independence between system and environment, where this difference can only be drawn within the system, i.e., self-referentially. For instance, scientific research surely depends on the financial resources (economic operations) available, but these resources cannot buy truth. The scientific system can increase its own complexity and structure itself accordingly if it becomes less and less susceptible to the influence of moral, religious or political demands. If, however, science has become a subsystem of the functionally differentiated society [→*Differentiation of Society*], it alone can make decisions regarding the production of knowledge, research and the difference between true and untrue. We can thus observe a system which reproduces itself at an autopoietic level through its own basal self-reference, and develops its own reflection in the form of the theory of knowledge. The relevance of the environment is not denied by the self-referential constitution of this system: we conceive of the environment as a complexity that can be determined only by the structures of the system. However, it is the →*complexity* of the environment that allows a system-internal complexity to be constructed [→*System/Environment*].

The concept of self-reference therefore rules out any continuity of system and environment. This implies that every description of the environment through the system (i.e., every other-reference and every opening) is only possible as a construction of the system. But self-reference is not to be equated with the observer, even if at first glance they look the same. The form of the observer does not lie in mere →*self-description*, but in the difference between self- and other-reference as a difference. The observer is the unity of this difference: the self can only be mentioned in contrast to the other, and in general the unity of the observer appears paradoxical, in that it is the unity of the difference, the simultaneity of self- and other-reference. *[G.C.]*

Social Systems (1995: 32-38; Ch. 11); The Autopoiesis of Social Systems (1986); Selbstreferentielle Systeme (1987).

Semantics (*Semantik*)

Semantics is the set of oral and written forms that can be repeatedly used, established and stabilized as guidelines to coordinate observations in society. Semantics therefore is not an autonomous system, but a set of forms produced in →*society* as a social system. The concept of semantics makes reference to the concepts of →*meaning* and →*communication*. In practice, semantics consists of concepts and ideas, in oral, written or perceptional [→*Art*] form, that can be used and constructed as a set of themes in communication: worldviews, scientific theories, opinions, essays, discussions.

Semantics is the set of forms that can be used for the selection of meaning contents in society: it establishes and stabilize the set of meaning premises worthy of preservation. This set of forms is used to select information in the medium of meaning, preserving the themes that can be potentially included in communication. Semantics includes the condensed and re-usable meaning contents that are available for communication. The concept of semantics substitutes the concept of culture intended as a set of concepts and ideas produced in the history of society.

While meaning exists only in the present as an event, in order to make the coordination of meaning selections possible, every meaning content in society must be expectable. As such, meaning must be processed, standardized and defined with regard to a set of forms. Processing and standardization of meaning entail the possibility of developing what is familiar, but also what is new, expectable and even ambiguous; even unusual or critical meaning contents must be able to connect to the current usage of familiar meaning contents. Semantics connects communications by making reference to the preserved forms of meaning. This enables both the re-use of existing observations [→*Operation/Observation*] in society and the opening up of new possibilities of observing, which can connect to existing observations. Semantics can thus generalise meaning, generating distinctions that orient observations in society.

Semantics consists of generalized meaning, which is selected from the emerging contents of communication. These contents are standardized and made available independently of the particular situation. Standardization of meaning corresponds with the necessity for connecting communications: the connection is made by selecting specific meaning contents according to a specific typology, which renders the connection between the new and the already known understandable. Through the standardization of meaning, semantics makes society sensitive to certain contents of communication and not others.

Two levels of production of semantics can be distinguished in society. The first level includes all texts and themes of communication (e.g., cursing, idioms). It orients familiar communication. The second level is a selection of the first level, i.e. it is refined (*gepflegt*) semantics, which is preserved and reproduced for →*self-descriptions*, which include historical-cultural materials and also theories of society.

The evolution of society correlates with the development of →*dissemination media* and with the change in its structure [→*Differentiation of Society*]. In non-literate societies with segmentary differentiation, semantics is only available orally and is dependent on the memory of participants. With the invention of writing (in hierarchical societies), it becomes possible to anchor semantics in written texts. These can anticipate or dissolve processes of social development, or even insist on outdated traditions. The selection of semantics is made according to the criteria of plausibility and evidence. It is stabilized as a set of dogmas. The invention of new dissemination media—from the printing press to the internet —and the functional differentiation of society trigger an important change: semantic forms develop and are differentiated, abandon earlier selection criteria, de-dogmatize, and connect to the reflection [→*Self-Reference*] of the functional systems. In modern society, the refined semantics is thus produced as descriptions in different functional systems (e.g. scientific system, economic system, legal system, religious system).

Changes in semantics correlate with the changes in social structure via the intervening variable of societal complexity. With the change in social structure, selectivity in the connections between communications change, too. This means a change in the level of societal complexity. Such changes demand a change in semantics, which function to orient communication. Semantics changes when the connections between communications change and it can no longer orient the reproduction of communication. The relationship between structure and semantics is thus circular: a change in semantics depends on structural changes, but at the same time determines the success of new forms of standardization of meaning and communication. Despite this circularity, semantics always evolves with a temporal lag compared with structural changes: therefore, the self-description of society is always more or less inappropriate for understanding new developments. [C.B.]

Gesellschaftsstruktur und Semantik I (1980: Ch. 1); Theory of Society (2013: 325-327); Ideenevolution (2008); The Self-Description of Society (1984).

Social System (*Soziales System*)

A social system is an autopoietic, self-referential system [→*Autopoiesis*; →*Self-Reference*] that is constituted as differentiated from its environment [→*System/Environment*]. It is a →*meaning*-constituting system. Its operations and final elements are →*communications*. There is not just one social system, but many. Through self-catalysis, social systems emerge from the problem of →*double contingency*, which is processed through communication.

The concept of a social system is related to general systems theory, which formulates the essentials of the description of each system. There are three analytic levels that allow the differentiation of social systems from other types of system, and the determination of connections between the different types.

The first level is the conceptualization of general systems theory. The paradigm shift in general systems theory has important consequences for a theory of social systems. This shift is from the system as a whole, made up of parts, to the distinction between system and environment, where the system is autopoietic and operationally closed [→*Autopoiesis*]. A system exists only if it can reproduce its operations through its operations, i.e. in the network of these operations. The autopoietic process of self-reproduction determines the operational closure of systems.

This general definition, however, does not suffice for the analysis of social systems. In order to observe social systems, we must first differentiate them from other types of system (living and psychic) and avoid any mixing of analytic levels. Above all, we may not assume that what is identical at one level is also identical at other levels.

At the second level in the schema, we find concepts that indicate the specificity of social systems and distinguish them from other types of system. Here, the central concepts are meaning and communication. The concept of meaning distinguishes social and psychic systems from living system such as cells, organisms and brains. Social and psychic systems are meaning-constituting systems. The specificity of social systems as autopoietic and meaning-constituting systems is that their operation is communication. They generate communication through communication, in a network of communications that is based on the medium of meaning. This distinguishes social systems from psychic systems based on the operation of thinking; thinking cannot be included in social systems through communication.

The formulations at the first two levels lead to an analysis of social systems that, contrary to sociological tradition, no longer takes the problem of stability as a starting point. Instead, the problem of social systems is the continuation of autopoiesis in relation to the environment. The initial problem of double contingency transforms into the question of how communications without duration (that disappear as soon as they emerge) can be continuously produced and connected to one another.

At the third level, three types of social system can be differentiated: →*interactions*, →*organizations* and →*society*. We can neither reduce one type into another, nor use models that presuppose the primacy of any one type. The theory of social systems explains the social reality with recourse to the three types, their autonomy and their interdependencies. For this reason, we can no longer speak, as Talcott Parsons did, of a theory of the social system in the singular, but must speak instead of social systems in the plural. *[C.B.]*

Social Systems (1995); The Autopoiesis of Social Systems (1986); Insistence on Systems Theory (1983).

Society (*Gesellschaft*)

Society is a particular type of →*social system*. Society is the social system that encompasses all social systems and incorporates all communications; hence, no communication exists outside of society. Society sets the boundaries of social complexity because it limits the possibilities that can be grasped and realized in communication. Every distinction of particular social systems occurs within society.

Unlike corresponding formulations in traditional sociology, it is not individuals, relationships between individuals, or social roles that are the elements of society, but communication. Nor are the boundaries of society territorial boundaries, but rather they are boundaries of communication. Individuals (as psychic and bodily systems) are in the environment of society and society relates to individuals as systems in the environment [→*Interpenetration and Structural Coupling*].

Society is only one type of social system alongside interaction and organization. Its uniqueness can be observed as a particular effect of complexity reduction: society is the social system that institutionalizes the final fundamental reductions in complexity and, in doing so, sets the premises for the operation of all other types of social systems (interactions and organizations). Society's selectivity facilitates the selectivity of all other social systems; society is the basis for every further →*differentiation* in the domain of communication.

The societal system serves as a point of reference for understanding social evolution. Society is always internally differentiated [→*Differentiation of Society*]. Over the course of society's evolution, the form of the primary differentiation varies. This form is the structure of society; hence, social evolution consists of changes in the structure of society.

Society differentiates itself primarily in subsystems that produce communications under conditions of strict limitations. These are not interactions or organizations, but specific systems that reproduce society as a whole from a particular perspective. These subsystems vary with the change in the structure of society: for instance, they are functional system, social strata, tribes. These systems are localized within society. Based on the first reduction of complexity undertaken by society, they can constitute specific forms of communication.

Theory of society is a specific theory within sociology, related to a particular case of the theory of social systems. This theory delivers a →*self-description* of society from the perspective of science; it is a perspective included in society that thematizes society itself. Since it results from the operation of an autopoietic subsystem, i.e. the scientific systems, theory of society does not reflect any objective reality, but offers one particular perspective among other observations of society. Due to its scientific nature, sociological observation is distinct from other observations, since it can include the observer: sociology knows that its description of society is an internal product of society itself. For this reason, sociology can reflect on the structural conditions of this description.

Sociological self-description thematizes the →*meaning dimensions* in which society's operations assume a form. It is realized as the theory of communication and the media that make communication probable (social dimension), as evolutionary theory (temporal dimension), and as the theory of differentiation (fact dimension). These specific theories together constitute the theory of society. [C.B.]

Theory of Society (2012: Ch. 1.1, 1.5); Social Systems (1995: Ch. 10.II); The Self-Description of Society, (1984); Gesellschaft (1970).

Sociological Enlightenment (*Soziologische Aufklärung*)

The concept of sociological enlightenment describes the general program of Luhmann's sociology. The enlightenment requires an observation [→*Operation/Observation*]. Every observation is based on a distinction. Operations of enlightenment use a specific distinction in the observation: the distinction conscious/unconscious in the observation of psychic systems, and the distinction manifest/latent in the observation of →*social systems*. The distinction manifest/latent indicates the sociological enlightenment.

The Enlightenment emerges historically in the eighteenth century as European society undergoes the transition from stratified differentiation to primarily functional differentiation [→*Differentiation of Society*]. In this historical period, the Enlightenment is understood as the unfolding of human reason, which led to rationality and justice taking hold in society. Unlike this first Enlightenment, the sociological enlightenment presupposes the capacity of reflection [→*Self-Reference*], which results from the development of the functionally differentiated society. The sociological enlightenment is understood as the broadening of the observational capacity of social systems—i.e., their ability to understand and reduce world →*complexity*. Thus, the means of this enlightenment are social systems capable of observation.

Sociological enlightenment arises upon producing the possibility to observe what is latent in society and to distinguish it from what is manifest. Latency lies in the possibilities that cannot be used in a system, although they are determined or determinable. There is latency in every social system: every social system withholds certain conditions of its own autopoiesis from observation in order to preserve, relatively unproblematically, its own unity. Hence, for a social system it can be useful to protect certain principles of its internal order and to exclude them from observation (thematization). The inappropriateness of the observation and the appropriateness of the protection are determined by the →*structure* of the system, which provides certain distinctions and excludes others, by making them latent. Latency is always contingent: some latencies can become manifest and others can take their place. The possibility of observing the distinctions varies with the variation in social structures.

The expansion of the capacity for observation—i.e., the ability to handle the problem of complexity in society—depends on the differentiation of the scientific system and, within it, of sociology. This differentiation allows the observation of latency and the setting of apparent self-evidence as contingent, but without giving up the protective function at the level of →*society* as a whole. Through systems theory, sociology can make manifest the complexity of what it observes, without society needing to give up the possibility of maintaining latency. Enlightenment also regards science and sociology because they are characterized by their own latency. They are not provided with greater observation capacity than other systems: their advantage lies in being able to observe that their observation is the result of their own operations.

Sociological enlightenment not only means making latent structures and functions in society evident, but also means comparing the different equivalents, which can be used as structures and functions, with one another [→*Functional Analysis*]. Since, when a system recognizes the function of latency, it also observes the equivalent alternatives that are available.

The enlightenment facilitates a consciousness (in →*psychic systems*) and a communicability (in social systems) of the contingency of the system. It also shows that, based on latency, society cannot see what it cannot see. Hence, it makes manifest that the function of latency requires that the function itself is kept latent. [C.B.]

Soziologische Aufklärung (1967); Social Systems (1995: Ch. 8.XVI).

Structure (*Struktur*)

Structures are conditions that limit the domain of connectivity of system operations: they are the conditions for the →*autopoiesis* of every system. The concept of structure describes the selection of the relations between elements that are accepted in the system. In →*meaning*-constituting systems, structures cannot merely consist of the relations between elements, since elements are events without duration [→*Event*]: with their disappearance, the relations also would disappear, and with them the system itself. The selections that become structurally relevant are those that limit the possibilities of recombining the elements (communications or thoughts).

This means, first, that structure and system are not coterminous. Although there can be no structureless systems, and structures can only ever be structures in a system, the two terms describe two completely different findings: whereas elements of a system are operations that, as such, must be constantly reproduced, structures condense only by repeating the identical in different combinations. Thus, the identity of the system can be maintained when its structures change. The same goes for objects, situations, periods of time, people, and so on: in all these cases, it is about meaningful combinations that become more significant as structures when it is possible to generalize their identity beyond each moment in which they take place.

Structures can also be described as selections of selections because they limit the connectivity (first selection), based on which the system produces its own elements (second selection). Without structures, the system could not determine whether its own further operations even occur: on the contrary, it would find itself confronted with the indeterminacy of the connections and therefore the impossibility of continuing its autopoiesis. The complexity of the system is made determinable by building structure, and the selectivity of the individual events is maintained and re-introduced in the next event as a range of possibilities from which the next selection can be obtained.

In this sense, structures guarantee the existence of the system not because of their stability, but for the sole reason that they can secure the transition from one operation to the next. The stability of the system must therefore be thought of as "dynamic stability," because the continuity of the system is only guaranteed by the discontinuity of its operations. Structures are maintained when they are repeated and condensed in various situations, otherwise they will be forgotten.

In the case of social systems, structures are the structures of →*expectations* that reveal possibilities of communication that the system can orient itself towards: by constructing expectations, a social system can determine connections and therefore also operative possibilities. Without structure, communication could decide neither which topics can be discussed, nor clarify who should begin to communicate when. Autopoiesis and structure of social systems, therefore, do not coincide: operations—i.e., system elements—are communications, whilst the structural elements are expectations.

From a temporal point of view, structures guarantee the reversibility of selections, although, as events, selections disappear irreversibly into the past. The structure admits duration against the background of the temporal punctuality of events and, therefore, also admits the re-actualization of situations in which new operations must be selected. Thanks to its structures, a system can recall past situations or imagine future ones by abstracting from the unceasing perpetuation of operations. In this sense, structures make the selectivity of communication visible, as well as revealing the possibility of different directions for selections.

Structures can change; the system is therefore capable of learning. We can only speak of learning in relation to structures, because events cannot be changed: they occur and then instantly disappear. Only their information value is surprising and introduces novelties compared to what the system expects on the basis of its structures. [G.C.]

Social Systems (1995: Ch. 8); Introduction to Systems Theory (2012: 239-247).

Symbolically Generalized Media (*Symbolisch generalisierte Kommunikationsmedien*)

Symbolically generalized media are specialized →*structures* that secure the probability of success of communication. They create expectations of acceptance when rejection is probable, although they cannot safeguard expectations from disappointment. Their function concerns the distinction between acceptance and rejection, which becomes evident after communication has been understood [→*Language*]. Such communication media are power (or power/law), scientific truth, money (or property/money), love, art and values. All these media are connected to the rise of the functionally differentiated society [→*Differentiation of Society*].

Language makes understanding probable. Thus, it makes also possible to reject a communication. Rejection of communication is probable when participants do not know each other (why should one accept proposals from an unknown person?), information is not immediately plausible (why should one accept knowledge that is not based on personal experience?), and attribution of selections is problematic (what is the reason for paying taxes?). In general terms, the success of communication is improbable because ego can reject the selection suggested by alter (a request, a proposal, an order) as premises of ego's own selectivity.

Symbolically generalized media deal with the improbability of ego's motivation to accept the selection suggested by alter. They can condition ego's motivation through alter's selection. The criteria for the coupling of selections function to motivate ego to accept alter's selection. Thus, symbolically generalized media combine selection and motivation, and thereby make it probable that alter's selection is accepted as the basis of ego's further selections. The concepts of "acceptance" and "motivation" do not refer to ego's psychic system. Acceptance and motivation are not observed as mental states, because the psychic conditions of acceptance and motivation are unknown. Rather, one can observe that a symbolically generalized medium enables the strict coupling of ego's and alter's selections through the specific form of the medium [→*Medium/Form*]. Both ego and alter know and accept that their selections are conditioned by the symbolically generalized medium. For instance, ego accepts alter's command to pay a fine because alter exercises power; ego accepts alter's claims that the earth orbits the sun because it concerns scientific truth; ego accepts alter's suggestion to spend the evening together because she loves alter.

Symbolically generalized media fulfill their function when the acceptance of the selection does not depend on the concrete situation: it is not the effect of the individual selection that counts, but rather the existence of generalized conditions of coordination of selections. Generalization means treating a plurality of references as a unity: the →*meaning* of a specific communication is not exhausted in the communication itself, but rather condenses into a unitary form that participants can refer to in other situations, at other points in time and with other communication partners. The generalization of the medium occurs through symbols that allow the formation of its unity from a plurality of references. Thanks to this symbolic generalization, the form of the medium can become universally applicable (love is love regardless of the identity of the partners, the circumstances of meeting, the history of the relationship) and regulate every specific situation, but without determining it (one can love differently, depending on the partner, circumstances or relationship history). The participants' selections are stably coupled, while the coupling is specified case by case.

The differentiation of symbolically generalized media is based on the differentiation of a reference problem, that is a particular problem of combination between selection and motivation. Not all communications need a symbolically generalized medium. In segmentary societies, in which all communication is oral, the possibility that a communication is accepted or rejected is settled on the basis of: a shared and unquestionable world experience; a shared memory; the pressure applied by those present to conform; a direct reference to those concerned. The differentiation of symbolically generalized media has developed during the evolution of society with the increase in the improbability of acceptance of communication, in the context of the diffusion of long-distance communication [→*Dissemination Media*]. Long-distance communication is addressed to those absent and is linked to unknown future developments. In these conditions, the combination between selection on the one hand, and motivation to accept the selection on the other, cannot be taken for granted.

The symbolically generalized media developed fully with the transition to the functionally differentiated society. In this transition, the symbolically generalized media worked as catalysts in the formation of some functional systems (the political system, the economic system, the scientific system, the system of families, the art system), in which the success of communication depended on the distinction between acceptance and rejection. The symbolically generalized media ensure operational closure and unity of these functional systems. They are absent in functional systems specialized in the communicative treatment of the environment (psychic systems, body, horizons of transcendental meaning), because these systems do not refer to the primary problem of improbable success of communication. In these conditions, either a code referring directly to the function [→*Religious System*] develops, or the interaction system plays an important function in ensuring the probability of acceptance [→*Education System*].

Starting from particular problems of combination between selection and motivation, the differentiation of the symbolically generalized media corresponds to the differentiation of ways of attributing coupled selections [→*Attribution*]. Selections can be attributed as actions (utterances) or as experiences (information): symbolically generalized media are differentiated according to whether ego and alter are observed in regard to their actions or experiences. The differentiation of symbolically generalized media is based on the coupling of alter's selections and ego's selections, which are attributed as action or experience. These forms of attribution allow the asymmetrization of →*double contingency* and the enhancement of communication, which can flow from alter to ego. They direct the conditioning of selection: when a selection is clearly attributed to the system (alter's action) or its environment (alter's experience), ego can be motivated to base her own action or experience on this selection.

Four constellations of attribution are possible, each of which correlates with particular symbolically generalized media:

(1) ego's action refers to the conditions set by alter's action. The corresponding medium is power (or **power**/law, because power must be legally regulated).
(2) ego's experience refers to the conditions set by alter's action. The corresponding media are **money** (or property/money, because money regulates the acquisition of property) and **art**.

(3) ego's action refers to the conditions set by alter's experience. The corresponding medium is **love**.
(4) ego's experience refers to the conditions set by alter's experience. The corresponding media are scientific **truth** and **values**.

Luhmann provides the schema below (see table 1) as a summary.

Table 1

	Ego's experience (Ee)	Ego's action (Ea)
Alter's experience (Ae)	Ae Ee Truth Values	Ae Ea Love
Alter's action (Aa)	Aa Ee Property/Money Art	Aa Ea Power/love

The most important structural characteristic of symbolically generalized media is a central →*code* based on a binary schematization. The code determines the form of the medium, which is thus not only symbolic, but also "diabolic" because it produces a difference between two values: for instance, between payment and non-payment (money) and true and untrue (truth). By differentiating the two values of the code, a symbolically generalized medium obtains information from every event and from every situation (e.g., something is true or untrue, someone pays or does not pay).

The code is characterized by a social preference for one of the two values (the "positive" value), which allows the self-localization of the code in this value (the truth in the true, the money in payments). The preference code does not remove the contingency of selections: one can always act against power or abuse power, or refuse to accept a scientific truth and produce an alternative. The preference code, however, is advantageous in that it binds this contingency to the orientation set by the medium: contingency refers to power, truth or money. This strengthens the possibilities for success of the coupling of selections.

Simplifying the transition from one value of the code to the other is called technologization. Technologization can be fostered by the development of a secondary code: money is the secondary code of property and law is the secondary code of power. It is also possible that a medium does not develop any technologization, using functional equivalents [→*Art*; →*Love*] in its place. However, since technologization allows for greater connectivity and capacity for interrupting interdependence, it is suited to the easier differentiation of societal subsystems. Technologization facilitates the formation of a functional system, as it facilitates the operational closure of the system. One exception is truth, which develops a subordinate code next to the main code. This subordinate code comes into play if the main code cannot secure the acceptance of communication. Since truth may not offer sufficient evaluative criteria in order to motivate the acceptance of the selection, one appeals to researchers' reputation. In the case of values, there is ultimately no unified code.

There are further important structural characteristics of symbolically generalized media. First, these media enhance processual reflexivity (e.g., love is triggered by love, money obtained through money, power acquired through power), which contributes to the differentiation of the medium because it makes the medium dependent upon itself. Second, these media differentiate between first and second order observation [→*Operation/Observation*] and condition selections at the second order. For instance, a lover observes if her lover still loves her; an investor observes how other investors invest their money; a political leader observes how other political leaders observe relevant interests and needs. Third, these media use →*programs* to allocate the code values (theories and methods allocate truth; investment programs allocate money). Fourth, these media are associated with symbiotic symbols or mechanisms, which determine how communication may let itself be irritated by the bodies of the participants (scientific communication is irritated by perception; money and property relate to needs, love to sexuality). Finally, these media can be inflated, when they are used too much because they are given too much trust (e.g., political decisions are promised but cannot be taken), or deflated, when they are used to little because their potential trust is not exploited (e.g., political decisions that are possible and supported are not taken).

The relationships between symbolically generalized media depend on the characteristics of the codes. Each medium has generalized validity in society, primarily because its code is only valid in a limited domain (e.g., money only has economic validity, but makes economic communication probable for society as a whole). Moreover, programs determine the concrete conditions for attributing value to a medium in the domain of another medium; for instance, economic investments (money) allow the realization of scientific research (truth). Between the media, however, there can be no transitive or hierarchical relationship: money cannot be transformed directly into truth or power; power cannot be translated into money, or love into truth. *[C.B.]*

> Power (1979); Generalized Media and the Problem of Contingency (1976); Theory of Society (2012: Ch. 2.8-2.12).

System/Environment (*System/Umwelt*)

The distinction system/environment is the starting point for Luhmann's systems theory. No system is independent of its environment, since a system is constituted drawing a boundary through its operations and thereby differentiating itself from what does not belong to it, i.e., its environment. No system can operate outside of its boundaries [→*Operation/Observation*]. Without an environment to distinguish it from, no system could be determined. A system is an autonomous domain in which particular conditions apply that escape one-to-one correspondence with the states in the environment [→*Autopoiesis*].

Defining a boundary does not mean isolating the system. Operations are always internals operations, but at the level of observation the boundary can be overcome and different forms of interdependence between system and environment can be identified. Every system needs a whole range of environmental conditions: a social system, for instance, requires the availability of psychic systems that participate in the communication, alongside a compatible physical environment (e.g., temperatures within a particular range, appropriate levels of gravity) and many other conditions. In addition, one and the same event can belong simultaneously to the system and to its environment. A particular event can, for instance, be an element of both a social system (as a communication) and a psychic system (as thought), even though these systems reciprocally belong to the environment of the other [→*Interpenetration and Structural Coupling*]. This →*event* is subject to conditions that are always different inside the system and in its environment.

The environment, for its part, is not environment in and of itself, but rather the environment of a system for which it is the outside ("everything else"). Concerning a system, everything that does not fall within the system belongs to the environment, which is thus different for every system. In fact, the environment is constituted by a system's operations as what is left out (as "negative correlate": it includes everything that does not belong to the system) and is itself not a system: it has neither its own operations, nor its own capacity for action. →*Attribution* to the environment is a system-internal strategy for managing its own complexity. Unlike the system, the environment is not defined by boundaries, but by horizons that cannot be overcome because they expand with the increase in the system complexity: the horizon moves further away the closer we get to it.

That the environment is relative to one system implies neither the devaluation of the environment nor the subordination of its role. The starting point of the theory is neither the system nor the environment, but rather their difference [→*Identity/Difference*], for which both sides are equally necessary. There can be no constitution of a system without a relationship to the environment, and also no environment without a system: they only ever exist together. On the one hand, the capacity for action is a characteristic of a system and forms an asymmetry in the system/environment relation—which is also expressed in the fact that only in the system a →*re-entry* of the distinction can take place. On the other hand, the environment is the side with higher complexity.

The distinction system/environment stabilizes a →*complexity* gap that forces the system to constantly make selections and imposes contingency on all operations: the environment always includes more possibilities than the system can actualize. Even if it is always relative to the respective system, the environment is not available for its needs passively and without resistance: it has its own forms and its own needs that the system must face. In a completely chaotic and entropic environment, however, it would not be possible to constitute a system. The environment must have at least enough order to allow the making and maintenance of distinctions [→*Constructivism*].

In order to understand the structuring and the autonomous dynamic of the environment, the distinction between the environment of a system and the systems in its environment must be taken into account. Each of these systems orient themselves to their own system/environment distinctions and include the first system in their environments. The environment of a communication system includes, for instance, a multiplicity of organisms, psychic systems and further social systems, each of which is characterized by a specific autopoiesis and is influenced only minimally by the operations of the social system itself. No system has access to the system/environment relation of other systems. For this reason, the environment of a system —which is constituted by the system itself—appears to the system as a complex network of mutually influencing system/environment distinctions, which the system cannot determine.

The environment is always much more complex than the system, and this asymmetry cannot be reversed. Every attempt that the system makes to control its environment means a change in the environments of other systems, which react making the environment of the first system yet more complex, and thereby reproduces the complexity gap.

This gap forces the system to undertake sharper selections concerning the environment than it does concerning itself. Environmental complexity is processed globally. The system reacts with higher sensitivity to internal events and processes than it does for events and processes in the environment (it could not take all of them into account anyway). It is relatively indifferent to environmental circumstances. Internal or external attribution is itself, however, an internal strategy for the orientation of the system operations: what is localized externally depends on internal structures, and in the orientation to the environment the system reacts to something that it constructed itself (but cannot necessarily control). The economic system can, for instance, attribute a stock market crash to itself as a consequence of its operations, or to the environment as a consequence of political events, emotional business people or other factors.

When the question of →*rationality* is posed, there is a re-entry of the system/environment distinction into the system, which processes its relation to the environment internally. Thus the economic system can ask itself, for instance, how its own processes affected the operation of politics, and whether the consequences triggered the events that caused the stock market crash.

No datum can be ultimately located in the system or in the environment, but rather belongs simultaneously to a system and to the environment of other systems, depending on the observation perspective. Every observation must specify its own system reference—i.e., the observer doing the observing—and cannot rely on the assumption of a given reality.

The distinction system/environment can be repeated within the system. The system itself represents an environment for the differentiation of subsystems, which constitute their own system/environment distinctions presupposing the overall complexity reduction by the system towards the undetermined environment [→*Differentiation*; →*Differentiation of Society*]. [E.E.]

Social Systems (1995: Ch. 1.II, Ch. 5); Theory of Society (2012: Ch. 1.4).

System of Families (*System der Familien*)

In functionally differentiated society [→*Differentiation of Society*], families are a subsystem that fulfills the function of including a participant in communication as a whole person [→*Inclusion/Exclusion*]. This function cannot be achieved by individual families: the system is therefore constituted of the multitude of families.

The meaning of the family in society has changed through the course of its evolution. In the segmentary society, the family serves as a fundamental form of differentiation. In the stratified society, the family is embedded within different social strata. In both forms of society, people are assigned to a subsystem according to the segmentation of families. This is no longer the case in the functionally differentiated society, in which families fulfill a specific function and no longer provide the organizational basis for other functional systems. Families are the only system in the functionally differentiated society in which people are treated exclusively as persons. This means that the function of families is to make sure that a participant in communication is included as a human being as a whole: everything to do with the participant—every action and experience, including those taking place outside the family—is potentially relevant for communication within the family. This function is fulfilled by a →*re-entry* of the system/environment difference by means of the person: the family is a form that, through the person, re-enters into itself. Everything relevant to the person (what happened at work, the quality of sleep, grades received, people met) is relevant to the family. The person provides a perspective to the family so that it can process what stretches beyond its boundaries without lifting them.

The fact that re-entry takes place through the person implies that every family has a special history: different families cannot cooperate because nothing holds them together and there is no common standard. Only the lack of unity among the various family systems ensures that the function of including persons is generalized. A single family could not fulfill this function for society as a whole.

In order to define the characteristics of communication within the family, it is not enough to observe that all participants know each other well personally. The relevant communication is intimate interpersonal communication. Intimacy occurs when a person's world becomes relevant for another person, and when this is reciprocated. Intimacy means that nothing personal may remain outside the communication. Secrets are not permitted: we cannot reject communication about ourselves with the argument "that doesn't concern you" (with problematic exceptions in the communication between parents and children). We have both the right to be heard and the obligation to speak about and justify everything which is defined as personal.

In the system of families, communication is irritated by anything regarding participants' psychic systems. The structural coupling [→*Interpenetration and Structural Coupling*] between the communication system and the psychic systems is noisy: communication thematizes what and how the participating psychic systems think, understand and listen. The psychic perturbation is observed ("what are you thinking about?") and reflected ("what are you thinking about when you notice that I'm trying to understand your thoughts?") in communication. The second-order observation [→*Operation/Observation*] is therefore relevant and takes place incessantly: every observation can easily become the topic of a further observation, because the interest in everything that happens is related to the observer. Therefore, the family is a historic system that is more sensitive to changes in expectations that the other functional systems. Sensitivity to the personal changes is particularly high.

→*Love* can be considered the code of the system of families because it determines the boundaries of an intimate communication as opposed to a non-intimate communication. Therefore, love also determines the boundaries of the autopoietic reproduction of a system of intimate interpersonal communication. However, within the family there are not only intimate communications, but also interactions connected with trivial daily activities. It is therefore difficult to decide whether familial communication is characterized solely by a semantics of love. Certainly, we cannot claim that all communication within the family is coded through love (unlike, for instance, legal communication, which is entirely coded through law, or economic communication through money).

Interaction becomes relevant due to the lack of a clear coupling between the medium love and the system of families. Moreover, love does not ensure any measure of stability for the family; its expectations are too high, which can lead to the disappointment of expectations and the possibility of dissolution.

Although interpersonal communication can be found in all social systems, it is a particular feature of the system of families since it is the basis of their differentiation as a social system. Differentiation makes it possible to assign to families—and families alone—the function of including the person. These characteristics apply not only to the legally institutionalized family, but also to all forms of intimate relationships, as systems in which the personal may not be removed from communication. [C.B.]

Sozialsystem Familie (1988); Glück und Unglück der Kommunikation in den Familien (1990).

Time (*Zeit*)

Time is defined as the observation of reality based on the difference between past and future. Each system only ever exists in the present and simultaneously (synchronically) with its own environment. In this sense, past is not a starting point and future is not a goal, but rather both cases concern horizons of possibilities [→*Meaning*].

Meaning-constituting systems construct reality as the difference between actuality and potentiality. This difference can be temporalized through the doubling of the distinction. On the potentiality side, we can continue to distinguish between past and future. The present is always secured by the fact that the system reproduces itself autopoietically [→*Autopoiesis*]: the temporal orientation leads to the distinction between actuality of self-reproduction and what is not actual, i.e. it is not contemporary to the system. In this way, a paradoxical situation is created, in which what is contemporary and what is not contemporary appear at the same time. The paradox is unfolded through particular temporal differences, such as, for instance, the difference between past and future.

For each observer [→*Operation/Observation*], time exists because each distinction has two sides and that, in order to change from one side to the other, operations, and therefore time, are required. Thus, a difference emerges between the observer herself, who is always actual, and the difference between before and after, which is generated
by the event that enabled the transition from one side to the other side of the distinction. The difference between synchronicity on one side, and the difference before/after on the other side, is time.

In the present, non-actual temporal horizons of the past and future are formed. This present moves through time, and with it the horizons move, too: in each moment, past and future are projected anew and there can be no move into the future or return to the past. As horizons, past and future are not quantities constituted from events, but rather selective performances of the system (of the observer). Not everything that happens is relevant to construct the past. This construction also depends on the system and cannot correspond with what "really" happened. The same goes for the future, because the projection of future possibility depends solely on the system.

The construction of the temporal dimension is based on the possibility to observe change and duration at the same time. Meaning-constituting systems can only observe events and changes in situations when they can hold something constant that serves as a background. Conversely, everything that remains constant only appears to do so against the background of events.

The present can be described in two mutually conditioning ways [→*Meaning Dimensions*]. First, the present is punctual and transforms the future into the past by moving: time passes irreversibly and inevitably. Under the second aspect, the present is observable as the duration that abstracts from the passing of events. The present makes it possible to remember past situations or to anticipate future situations. According to these two temporal points of view, meaning-constituting systems differentiate →*structures* and →*processes*, which in their interplay keep meaning accessible to social and psychic operations.

Since they are imaginary, the horizons of the past and the future are structurally determined constructions, which have no correspondences in the environment of the observing system [→*System/Environment*]: the system and its environment exist only in the present and only synchronically. However, the projection of temporal horizons means that the system can observe changes through constants in terminology without having to change itself. The system time is not in synch with what happens in its environment, because that would imply the dissolution of the system boundaries.

This complex construction of the temporal dimension reveals different characteristics depending on the societal structures: it corresponds to the type of primary societal differentiation [→*Differentiation of Society*]. Tradition sees time as movement, a concept that describes the unity of the difference between before and after. The temporal horizons of pre-modern societies refer to the distinction between time and eternity. Eternity indicates the divine position from which all times are given simultaneously: eternity guarantees that everything happens according to God's will. This is different from the finite time of creation, which has a beginning and an end whose meaning can only be interpreted in relation to eternity. In the functionally differentiated society, movement is replaced by the idea of the present: the primary temporal horizons become the completed past and the uncertain, open and contingent future into which the system can project numerous possible presents. Selections are guided by the fact that the past is only a premise of the future: it is "capitalized" as the history of already completed selections that can be recombined depending on future perspectives.

This modern conception of time has had consequences for the historical description of society. History is produced whenever the events relevant to society are observed on the basis of the distinction before/after: from antiquity until at least the seventeenth century, the difference before/after was considered as a unity against the background of the temporal horizon itself, and was reflected by distinguishing between passing time and divine eternity. In the modern era, from the eighteenth century onwards, history is grasped as self-referential—it must be continually written anew depending on the historical moment in which the historians find themselves. Also history is, in other words, something historical: history re-appears in history through a →*re-entry*. Writing history today means recombining data depending on the chosen theoretical approach. Now, the need for data no longer depends on the sources that can be discovered and taken into account, but rather from the theoretical approach itself. From a sociological perspective, it is therefore not so much the coherence of the events to be described historically that is interesting, but rather the consistency of the theoretical approach that the theory of society can deliver.

The distinction and connection between the past and the future is managed in the present by memory, which detects in the past the distinctions providing the frame in which the future can oscillate. Memory has the function of testing the consistency of system operations against its construction of reality, which it accomplishes through the double function of remembering and forgetting. Remembering recognizes repetitions as something already known, overcoming the need to learn the same thing over and over again. Forgetting prevents the system from blocking itself, and frees up processing capacity.

The forms of memory change with the evolution of society. In ancient societies memory was related to objects and rituals, while writing made it more mobile. Modern society, which is so complex that it has to remember and forget much more, has moved from forms oriented to identity (*Gleichheit*) to forms oriented to comparison (*Vergleichbarkeit*), realized as culture. The different functional systems have their own special memories, which are coordinated by the →*mass media*, but which cannot be integrated. The mass media operate as the overall memory of society, providing a reference reality that can be taken for granted. Everyone knows that the second reality without obligation of consensus that is built by the mass media is also known to everyone else, no matter what they think, and at the same time is constantly renewed (forgotten). *[G.C.]*

Social Systems (1995: Ch. 1.III, 5.III); Geheimnis, Zeit und Ewigkeit (1989); Gleichzeitigkeit und Synchronisation (1989); Theory of Society (2012: Ch. 3.13); The Reality of the Mass Media (2000: Ch. 11).

Truth (*Wahrheit*)

Truth is a →*symbolically generalized medium* that makes the acceptance of knowledge that is new, surprising, deviant and based on scientifically proven theories and methods [→*Science*] more probable.

This knowledge cannot be established simply by virtue of its own evidence or the reputation of the researcher who claims it. On the contrary, it often concerns knowledge and news that contradict the self-evidence of the facts and deviate widely from the normal course of daily life. The communication medium truth motivates the acceptance of such knowledge, without each further communication being forced to repeat the processes that first indicated a statement as scientifically true (or untrue).

Scientific truth is characterized by a constellation of attribution that refers to the experience of the communication partner: alter's experience conditions ego's experience. In other words, the content of scientific statements cannot be attributed as interest or will, but rather to the non-arbitrariness of the world that can be experienced as such.

The →*code* of the communication medium truth is the difference between true and untrue. The first value (true) allows the continuation of communication, searching for new connections, whilst the second value (untrue) forces communication to reflect on the conditions that have led to an error: this reflection, too, allows the continuation of autopoiesis of the scientific system.

The →*programs* of science are theories and methods. Theories are interrelated statements founded on concepts that constitute the other-reference of the communication, for instance to objects. They do not in any way guarantee an exact correspondence between scientific truth and the external reality [→*Constructivism*], but rather make it possible to compare different solutions to problems formulated through scientific communication. The methods, thus, determine the conditions under which statements can be labeled as true or untrue. Methods, obligated to use an appropriate logic, treat the two values of the code as equivalents and as equally probable, and impose criteria that are used to decide what is the case: a scientific statement can only be true or untrue. Here, it is not other-reference that interrupts the symmetry, as it does in the case of theories, but rather time: the methods describe a correct sequence of truth-finding independent of the respective cognitive content of the statements. The allocation of the values can be led by linear methods bound to causality, or through circular, functional methods [→Functionalism].

Methods and theories are differentiated from one another by referring to the difference between →self-reference and other-reference. Methods represent the self-reference of science because they have no external reference. Theories represent other-reference: they permit the asymmetrization of scientific observation and observed object. As observations, they are scientific constructions: it is not that theories are based on the identity or unity of the object that they refer to, but rather the object is constructed as unity and identity by the theory.

In this respect, we must emphasize the fact that scientific truth cannot mean successful adaptation to objects or the discovery of reality. Neither value of the truth code (true/untrue) corresponds in any way to reality: contrary to the assumption of classical Aristotelian logic, truth is not a feature of objects and error is not a special privilege of consciousness. An orthogonal relationship exists between the values of the code and the difference between inside and outside (i.e., between self- and other-reference): both the internal and the external can be observed and therefore both can provide themes for true or untrue statements. What, thus, should "objective" mean? Today, this question is answered by the radical constructivist approach. Scientific knowledge, and therefore everything constructed through the medium of truth, always requires a discontinuity between knowing system and external reality: knowledge is only produced through the operations of the system and through the connections of autopoietic operations [→Autopoiesis].

In this sense, the way in which knowledge is constructed is decisive (i.e., the way the system draws distinctions) because it is possible, depending on the distinction used, to see something in one way or in another [→Operation/Observation]. Scientific truth, therefore, cannot be founded on an ontological concept of objectivity, but it cannot reject the requirement to indicate reality, either. The positive value "true" simply indicates the state of affairs that communication can directly connect to a particular statement, and it is exactly this possibility of connection that makes every statement contingent; we can claim the same thing differently and we can find other connections, because there is no piece of reality behind a statement, but rather only, and over again, a piece of knowledge. The negative value, for its part, marks the point at which expectations are disappointed by reality presenting itself in the form of a surprise and a demand for reaction. The experiment fulfills, among other things, exactly this function: it confronts communication with the alternative true or untrue, and exposes scientific communication to the possibility of disappointment. *[G.C.]*

Die Wissenschaft der Gesellschaft (1990: Ch. 4); Theory of Society (2012: 203-207).

Values (*Werte*)

The function of values is to provide a shared basis for communication reproduced in society, despite conscious systems being inaccessible to one another and each social form only being able to constitute itself through →*double contingency*.

Values are valid beyond all contingencies and reproduce communication without there being motives for questioning a value orientation. Values emerge on the basis of the attribution constellation "ego's experience/alter's experience," as in the case of scientific →*truth* [→*Symbolically Generalized Media*]. In contrast, however, values are not introduced in communication through statements and also require no support from motivation. They are assumed, operating where they encounter no interference or doubt. Unlike scientific truth, communication based on values introduces only the strict alternative of accepting or rejecting the suggested selection. People assume that a certain value is common to everyone, and that it can be assumed in everything that is said: it is not necessary to constantly repeat that freedom is an uncontested value, even though ways to obtain it can differ widely. In this way, human rights can be violated, but not questioned.

This characteristic of indicating what is shared, however, comes at the cost of a very limited capacity to orient actions: the abstraction of values is itself a hindrance to forming operative criteria for action. Although values can be understood as symbolically generated communication media, they can offer only a very weak bond. Moreover, values lack many of the typical characteristics of such media: they have no binary code, and no subsystem can differentiate itself on the basis of values. As for their programs, these do not go beyond a very general value orientation: people can do virtually anything in the name of freedom, and the assumption that freedom is a universal value provides comfort to no-one. In this sense, values are a symbolically generalized medium that does not have the persuasive power of truth, power, money, or love. Although values combine selection and motivation and are symbolically generalized, values cannot steer communication decisively enough to be suitable for forming the fundamental structure of modern society.

Values meriting particular attention in modern society [→*Differentiation of Society*] are those that require a strong reference to the subject. One example here is what we call "human rights." In the current debate surrounding these values, the assumption is that the basic rights of the person are at stake, and that it is a matter of subjective rights. Freedom, equality, the recent addition of solidarity, and many others: such values cannot be questioned for the precise reason that they refer directly to the subject. One aspect that makes this type of value sociologically interesting is the discovery that being indispensable means escaping any kind of anthropological explanation: the subject cannot have subjective rights, but rather submits to them. In other words, there is a dark side of human rights and values in the fact that values in general are, as social dispositions, incapable of looking after the multitude of individual variants; on the contrary, they must be highly indifferent to subjective individuality. The price of the universality of the ideal is that it cannot be respecified for each individual case. [G.C.]

> Von der allmählichen Auszehrung der Werte (1985); Das Paradox der Menschenrechte und drei Formen seiner Entfaltung (1993); Theory of Society (2012: 204-206, 221-228); Theory of Society (2013: Ch. 4.10).

World (*Welt*)

From the point of view of an observer, the world is the unity of the difference between system and environment. The world is the unity of every distinction made by an observer; it can never be observed as a unity, thus the world is the blind spot for every observer.

In Old-European cosmology, the world was conceived as an aggregate consisting of the entirety of all visible and invisible things (*universitas rerum* or *aggregatio corporum*). In the functional differentiated society [→*Differentiation of Society*], this term loses its references to "things" and instead refers to the indeterminacy of meaning [→*Meaning Dimension*]. The temporal dimension represents an open and therefore uncertain future that makes every plan and prognosis contingent. The fact dimension is conceived as an unending (and therefore indeterminable) network of possible causal relations that does not determine in advance which relations should be taken into account. In the social dimension, individuals are conceived as equal subjects, so that social order can no longer be based on each individual nature—on the contrary, actions are generated by the indeterminacy of each individual. Against this background, the world can be grasped as the ultimate horizon that transcends all three meaning dimensions, as well as a formless correlate of the operations that take place within it. The world is the unity of past and future, of observer and observed, of ego and alter ego.

If we increase the degree of abstraction of the perspective taken here and refer to George Spencer Brown's calculus, we can grasp the world as an unmarked space divided into two parts by a distinction, which introduces the possibility to distinguish an internal and an external side [→*Operation/Observation*]. In other words, observers can only operate in a world in which they make distinctions. The chosen distinction indicated as form allows something to be made visible, but, in the same moment, the operation causes what cannot be indicated by the distinction to be hidden—namely, the distinction itself.

However, the world must remain distinguishable by its observations and descriptions, because the observations and descriptions themselves are only possible through the operations that take place in the world. Only in this way is it possible to see which distinctions can be used for observation and distinction and what their consequences are.

In this sense, the world is a paradoxical concept [→*Paradox*], since it conceives of itself always as a combination of determinacy and indeterminacy, of unity and difference. The world cannot be distinguished from the outside, but its unity can only be conceived as difference, for instance as the difference between the self and outside the self, or between a system and its environment: we cannot indicate without distinguishing. The paradox emerges in the idea of a world that includes itself [→*Re-entry*]. How can we distinguish something that is the unity of every distinction? How can observers indicate the unity of the distinction between themselves and their environments? We encounter the same paradoxical situation when we start out from the idea that a distinction attempts to indicate its unity—i.e., both of its sides—through only one of the two sides. This is the case, for instance, for the codes of →*symbolically generalized media*, which, when applied to themselves, must simultaneously use a difference (that of the code) and indicate its own unity. *[G.C.]*

Social Systems (1995: Ch. 5.VIII); Weltkunst (1990); Theory of Society (2012: Ch. 1.10).

World Society (*Weltgesellschaft*)

The expression world society means that there is only one →*society* in the entire world. The constitution of a world society is an effect of the →*evolution* of society. Until the sixteenth century there were very few systematic connections among different societies in the world. European colonization initiated the integration of these different societies by establishing regular communicative connections. The constitution of world society included all communication in one unique society, which in this way acquired unambiguous boundaries: the boundaries of communication in the world as a whole. The boundaries of society became independent of natural features, such as territorial conditions and physical presence. This happened with the birth and development of the functionally differentiated society [→*Differentiation of Society*] on the one hand, and, on the other, with the invention and systemization of new technologies that made communication simultaneously available in different places [→*Mass Media*].

With the constitution of functional differentiation, the unity of the societal system cannot be defined through territorial borders and the corresponding distinction between members and non-members. This form of society cannot be identified in terms of national political systems or regional territories, as the internally differentiated functional systems include all communications in the world. The world dimension of society is implied in every communication, regardless of its topic and the spatial distance between the participants. The world dimension of connections (and problems) is increased through →*organizations* that operate and cooperate worldwide (e.g., enterprises, universities, healthcare organizations). Functional systems and their organizations operate without regional boundaries.

World society stimulates the need for →*self-description*, which cannot be provided on the basis of individual experiences or specialized interactions (e.g., in the upper strata of society). In world society, self-descriptions reach a high level of abstraction, and this also enhances a theory of reflection in society about society, tentatively provided by sociology. Moreover, world society provides a new description of the →*world*, so that the description of the modern, acentric world is produced by the modern, acentric society.

Against this background, however, the segmentation of the →*political system*, based on the formation of nation states, determines a regional differentiation of world society. This regional differentiation is an effect of functional differentiation, in particular of the segmentary political system of states. The effect of this segmentation is to amplify the unequal distribution of functional differentiation in different regions of the world. This leads to the description of the world as more or less modernized (or developed), depending on the region being observed. The regional description of world society continues to be reproduced as it accounts for this different level of regional development of functional differentiation. However, regional differences depend on the involvement in and the reaction to the dominant structures of world society, as functional differentiation combines and reinforces its effects in the world. Functional differentiation can also inhibit the generalization of its effects, depending on the different conditions occurring in different regions, and this generates different regional patterns of functional differentiation. This regionalization of functional differentiation brings about different opportunities for inclusion in world society, leading to conditions of exclusion from wealth, rights, democracy, medical care, education, and so on [→*Inclusion/Exclusion*]. Exclusion determines impoverishment of the population, prevents the regional establishment of functional differentiation, and generates the description of differences between a center and a periphery of world society. This situation also enhances forms of local particularism, contrasting with the universalism of world society, in particular as religious or ethnic movements develop within nation states.

It is not possible to say if regional differences and their effects will decrease or disappear in the future of world society. What is clear is that their existence does not determine limitations in the development of a world society. On the contrary, the differences among regions, and the possibility of comparing different regions, depend on the world dimension of the functionally differentiated society. In other words, the possibility of observing regional differences is based on the unity of society. Thus, by comparing different regions, regional problems can be understood as problems that depend on functional differentiation (e.g., problems of democracy or political instability, economic deprivation or inequality, inadequate education, or lack of medical supplies).

Looking at the history of society, rather than simply at present regional differences, it is possible to observe an increasingly unified world society, highlighted by a large number of worldwide phenomena (e.g., dependence on technology, trends in education and scientific research, medical care needs, economic crises, international law, or pressure to democratize). Despite the production of regional differences, therefore, world society cannot be avoided or boycotted regionally, be it through political determination, autarchic attempts or ethnic and religious movements. Instead what happens is that different effects arise from the combination of the structures of world society on the one hand, and specific regional cultural conditions on the other. Looking at its future, rather than at its past or present, it seems evident that world society creates common problems everywhere, together with the need to face these problems. The temporal orientation [→*Time*] of society tends to shift from the past (societal identity) to the future (societal contingencies). It is evident that world society generates at the same time both the interest in cultural diversity, which depends on segmentation and unequal distribution, and the interest in common development, since describing the future of society means describing the necessity of dealing with problems which are common across the entire world. [C.B.]

Theory of Society (2012: Ch. 1.10).

List of Luhmann's works

The following list includes all the books published by Niklas Luhmann, all the works translated into English (in the first section, until 2020) and the articles in German which we refer to at the end of each entry. References at the end of each entry always indicate English translations, when they exist, and in square brackets the year of the first publication.

A complete list of Luhmann's works can be found on the Luhmann-Archiv website: http://www.uni-bielefeld.de/soz/luhmann-archiv/

English publications and translations

(1973). Society. In Kernig, C. D. (Ed.), Marxism, Communism and Western Society. A Comparative Encyclopedia, vol. VIII (22-29). New York: Herder & Herder [(1968). Gesellschaft. In Kernig, C.D. (Ed.), Sowjetsystem und demokratische Gesellschaft. Eine Enzyklopädie (959-972). Freiburg/Basel/Wien: Herder].

(1974). Institutionalized Religion in the Perspective of Functional Sociology. Concilium, 1, 45-55 [(1974). Institutionalisierte Religion gemäß funktionaler Soziologie. Concilium, 10, 17-22].

(1976). A General Theory of Organized Social Systems. In Hofstede, G., & Kassem, M. S. (Ed.), European Contributions to Organization Theory (96-113). Assen: Van Gorcum [(1975). Allgemeine Theorie organisierter Sozialsysteme. In Luhmann, N., Soziologische Aufklärung 2. Aufsätze zur Theorie der Gesellschaft (39-50). Opladen: Westdeutscher Verlag].

(1976). Generalized Media and the Problem of Contingency. In Loubser, J.J., Baum, R.C., Effrat, A., & Lidz V.M. (Ed.), Explorations in General Theory in Social Science. Essays in Honor of Talcott Parsons, Volume Two, New York/London: Free Press/Collier Macmillan (507-532).

(1978). Temporalization of Complexity. In Geyer, F., & van der Zouwen, J., Sociocybernetics. An actor-oriented social systems approach (95-111). Vol. 2. Leiden [(1980). Translation of a shortened version of Temporalisierung von Komplexität: Zur Semantik neuzeitlicher Zeitbegriffe (235-300). In Luhmann, N., Gesellschaftsstruktur und Semantik. Vol. I. Frankfurt: Suhrkamp].

(1979). Trust. In Luhmann, N., Trust and Power (1-103). Ed. by Burns, T., & Poggi, G. Chichester/New York/Brisbane/Toronto: Wiley [(1968). Vertrauen: Ein Mechanismus der Reduktion sozialer Komplexität. Stuttgart: Enke. 2nd extended ed. (1973)].

(1979). Power. In Luhmann, N., Trust and Power (104-208). Ed. by Burns, T., & Poggi, G. Chichester/New York/Brisbane/Toronto: Wiley [(1975). Macht. Stuttgart: Enke].

(1981). Communication about law in interaction systems. In Knorr-Cetina, K., & Cicourel, A.V. (Eds.), Advances in social theory and methodology. Toward an integration of micro- and macro-sociologies (234-256). Boston/London/Henley: Routledge & Kegan Paul [(1980). Kommunikation über Recht in Interaktionssystemen. In Blankenburg, E., Klausa, E., & Rottleuthner H. (Eds.), Alternative Rechtsformen und Alternativen zum Recht (99-112). Opladen: Westdeutscher Verlag].

(1982). The Differentiation of Society. New York: Columbia UP.

(1982). The Economy as a Social System. In Luhmann, N., The Differentiation of Society (190-225, 386-390) [(1970). Wirtschaft als soziales System. In Luhmann, N., Soziologische Aufklärung (204-231)].

(1983). Insistence on Systems Theory: Perspectives from Germany. An Essay. In Social Forces 61, 987-998.

(1984). Religious Dogmatics and the Evolution of Societies. New York/Toronto: Mellen [(1977). Religiöse Dogmatik und gesellschaftliche Evolution. In Luhmann, N., Funktion der Religion (72-181). Frankfurt: Suhrkamp].

(1984). The Differentiation of Advances in Knowledge. The Genesis of Science. In Stehr, N., & Meja V. (Eds.), Society and Knowledge. Contemporary Perspectives in the Sociology of Knowledge (103-148). New Brunswick, N.J./London: Transaction [(1981). Die Ausdifferenzierung von Erkenntnisgewinn. Zur Genese von Wissenschaft. In Stehr, N., & Meja V. (Eds.), Wissenssoziologie. Kölner Zeitschrift für Soziologie und Sozialpsychologie, Sonderheft, 22, 102-139. Opladen: Westdeutscher Verlag].

(1985). The Work of Art and the Self-Reproduction of Art. In Thesis Eleven 12, 4-27. Reprint (1990). In Luhmann, N., Essays on Self-Reference (191-214)

[(1984). Das Kunstwerk und die Selbstreproduktion der Kunst. In Delfin 2, 51-69. Reprint (2008). In Luhmann, N., Schriften zu Kunst und Literatur (139-188)].

(1985). A Sociological Theory of Law. London: Routledge [(1972). Rechtssoziologie, 2 vol. Reinbek: Rowohlt. 2nd extended ed. (1983). Opladen: Westdeutscher Verlag].

(1985). The Work of Art and the Self-Reproduction of Art. Thesis Eleven, 12, 4-27. Reprint (2003). In Harrison, C., & Wood, P. (Ed.), Art in theory 1900-2000. An anthology of changing ideas (1076-1080). Malden, Ma: Blackwell. Reprint (2009). In Herrero, H, & Inglis, D. (Eds.), Art and Aesthetics. Art as Social Institution and Collective Practice (191-211). London: Routledge.

(1986). Love as Passion. The codification of intimacy. Cambridge: Polity Press [(1982). Liebe als Passion: Zur Codierung von Intimität. Frankfurt: Suhrkamp].

(1986). The Theory of Social Systems and Its Epistemology. Reply to Danilo Zolo's Critical Comments. Philosophy of the social sciences 16, 129-134 [(1983). Risposta dell'autore all'introduzione di Danilo Zolo (Funzione, senso, complessità. Presupposti epistemologici del funzionalismo sistemico). In Schmitt, R. (Ed.), Illuminismo sociologico (XXXV-XLIV). Milano: Il Saggiatore].

(1986). Die Zukunft der Demokratie. In Kiwus, K., & Binder, K. (Eds.), Der Traum der Vernunft. Vom Elend der Aufklärung. Darmstadt/Neuwied: Luchterhand (207-217). Reprint (1987). In Luhmann, N., Soziologische Aufklärung 4 (126-132). Reprint (2005) (131-138).

(1987). The Evolutionary Differentiation between Society and Interaction. In Alexander, J.C., Giesen, B., Münch, R., & Smelser, N.J. (Eds.), The Micro-Macro Link. Berkeley/Los Angeles/London: University of California Press (112-131).

(1987). Modern Systems Theory and the Theory of Society. In Meja, V., Misgeld, D., & Stehr, N. (Eds.), Modern German Sociology (173-186). New York: Columbia UP [Moderne Systemtheorie als Form gesamtgesellschaftlicher Analyse. In Adorno, T. W. (Ed.), Spätkapitalismus oder Industriegesellschaft? Verhandlungen des 16. Deutschen Soziologentages vom 8. bis 11. April 1968 in Frankfurt/M. (253-266). Stuttgart: Enke, 1969].

(1988). The Unity of the Legal System. In Teubner, G. (Ed.), Autopoietic Law: A New Approach to Law and Society (12-35). Berlin/New York: de Gruyter [(1983). Die Einheit des Rechtssystems. Rechtstheorie 14, 129-154].

(1988). The Sociological Observation of the Theory and Practice of Law. European Yearbook in the Sociology of Law 1, 23-42 [(1985). El enfoque sociólogico de la teoría y práctica del derecho. Anales de la Cátedra Francisco Suárez 25, 87-103].

(1988). Basic Concepts on the Theory of Autopoietic Systems. Nine Questions to Niklas Luhmann and Humberto R. Maturana and Their Answers. In Hargens, J. (Ed.), Systemic Therapy: A European Perspective (79-104). Broadstairs (Kent): Borgmann [(1987). Grundkonzepte der Theorie autopoietischer Systeme. Neun Fragen an Niklas Luhmann und Humberto Maturana und ihre Antworten. Zeitschrift für systemische Therapie, 5, 4-25].

(1988). The Third Question. The Creative Use of Paradoxes in Law and Legal History. Journal of Law and Society 15, 153-165.

(1988). Tautology and Paradox in the Self-Descriptions of Modern Society. In Sociological Theory 6, 21-37. Reprint (1990). In Luhmann, N., Essays on Self-Reference (123-143) [1987). Tautologie und Paradoxie in den Selbstbeschreibungen der modernen Gesellschaft. In Zeitschrift für Soziologie 16. 161-174. Reprint (1996). In Luhmann, N., Protest (79-106)].

(1988) Familiarity, Confidence, Trust: Problems and Alternatives. In Gambetta, D. (ed.) Trust: Making and Breaking
Cooperative Relations (94-107). Department of Sociology, University of Oxford.

(1989). Ecological Communication. Cambridge, Engl.: Polity Press [(1986). Ökologische Kommunikation: Kann die moderne Gesellschaft sich auf ökologische Gefährdungen einstellen? Opladen: Westdeutscher Verlag].

(1990). Political Theory in the Welfare State. Berlin: de Gruyter (includes also chapters from (1987). Soziologische Aufklärung 4) [(1981). Politische Theorie im Wohlfahrtsstaat. Munich: Olzog].

(1990). Essays on Self-Reference. New York: Columbia UP.

(1991). Paradigm lost: On the Ethical Reflection of Morality. Thesis Eleven, 29, 82-94 [(1990). Paradigm lost: Über die ethische Reflexion der Moral. Frankfurt: Suhrkamp].

(1990). Sthenography. Stanford Literature Review, 7, 133-137 [(1987/88). Sthenographie. Delfin, 5, 4-12].

(1990). The Cognitive Program of Constructivism and a Reality that Remains Unknown. In Krohn, W., Küppers, G., Nowotny, H. (Eds.), Selforganization: Portrait of a Scientific Revolution (64-85). Dordrecht. Reprint (2002). In Luhmann, N., Theories of Distinction: Rediscriptions of the Descriptions of Modernity (128-152). Ed. by Rasch, W. Stanford UP, Reprint (2003). In Delanty, G., & Strydom, P. (Eds.), Philosophies of Social Science. The classic and contemporary readings (436-441). Maidenhead/Philadelphia: Open UP [(1990). Das Erkenntnisprogramm des Konstruktivismus und die unbekannt bleibende Realität. In Luhmann, N., Soziologische Aufklärung (31-58). Vol. 5. Westdeutscher Verlag: Opladen].

(1990). Meaning as Sociology's Basic Concept. In Luhmann, N., Essays on Self-Reference (21-79). New York: Columbia UP [(1971). Sinn als Grundbegriff der Soziologie. In Luhmann, N., Habermas, J. Theorie der Gesellschaft oder Sozialtechnologie (25-100)].

(1991). Paradigm Lost: On the Ethical Reflection of Morality. Speech on the Occasion of the Award of the Hegel Prize 1989. Thesis eleven, 29, 82-94 [Paradigm lost: Über die ethische Reflexion der Moral. Rede anläßlich der Verleihung des Hegel-Preises 1989. In Luhmann, N., Paradigm lost: Über die ethische Reflexion der Moral (7-48). Frankfurt: Suhrkamp, 1990].

(1991/92). Operational Closure and Structural Coupling. The Differentiation of the Legal System. Cardozo Law Review, 13, 1419-1441. Reprint (2001). In Cotterrell R. (Ed.), Sociological Perspectives on Law: Contemporary Debates (95-117). Vol. 2, Aldershot/Burlington: Ashgate/Dartmouth.

(1992). The Form of Writing. Stanford Literature Review, 9(1), 25-42.

(1992). Societal Complexity. In Széll, G. (Ed.), Concise Encyclopaedia of Participation and Co-Management (793-806). Berlin/New York: de Gruyter [(1992), Complessità sociale. In Enciclopedia delle Scienze Sociali (126-134). Vol. II. Roma: Istituto della Enciclopedia Italiana].

(1992). Perception and Communication through Artworks. In Lux, H., & Ursprung, P. (Eds.), STILLSTAND switches. Ein Gedankenaustausch zur Gegenwartskunst. An Exchange of Ideas on Contemporary Art. Symposium, Interviews. Shedhalle Zürich, 8.-24.6.1991 (75-84). Zürich: Shedhalle [(1992). Wahrnehmung und Kommunikation an Hand von Kunstwerken. Ibidem (65-74). Reprint (2008). In Luhmann, N., Schriften zu Kunst und Literatur (246-257). Frankfurt: Suhrkamp].

(1992). The Concept of Society. Thesis Eleven, 31, 67-80.

(1992). What is Communication? In Communication Theory, 2, 251-259. Reprint (2002). In Luhmann, N., Theories of Distinction (155-168) [slightly revised translation of (1987). Was ist Kommunikation? In Information Philosophie, 15, 4-16].

(1993). Observing Re-entries. Graduate Faculty Philosophy Journal, 16, 485-498.

(1993). Are There Still Indispensable Norms in Our Society? Soziale Systeme, 14, 18-37 [(1993). Gibt es in unserer Gesellschaft noch unverzichtbare Normen? Heidelberg: C.F. Müller].

(1993). Risk: A Sociological Theory. Berlin: de Gruyter. Reprint (2005). With a new introduction by Stehr,N., & Bechmann, G. New Brunswick: Aldine Transaction [(1991). Soziologie des Risikos. Berlin: de Gruyter].

(1994). How Can the Mind Participate in Communication? In Gumbrecht, H. U., & Pfeiffer, K. L. (Eds.), Materialities of Communication (371-387). Stanford UP [(1988). Wie ist Bewußtsein an Kommunikation beteiligt? In Gumbrecht, H. U., & Pfeiffer, K. L. (Eds.), Materialität der Kommunikation (884-905). Frankfurt: Suhrkamp].

(1994). Speaking and Silence. New German Critique, 61, 25-38 [(1989). Reden und Schweigen. In Luhmann, N., & Fuchs, P., Reden und Schweigen (7-20)].

(1994). Politicians, Honesty and the Higher Amorality of Politics. Theory, culture & society, 11, 25-36 [(1993). Die Ehrlichkeit der Politiker und die höhere Amoralität der Politik. In Kemper, P. (Ed.), Opfer der Macht. Müssen Politiker ehrlich sein? (27-41). Frankfurt/Leipzig: Insel. Reprint (2008). In Luhmann, N., Die Moral der Gesellschaft (163-174). Ed. by Horster, D. Frankfurt: Suhrkamp].

(1995) Social Systems. Stanford UP. [(1984). Soziale Systeme: Grundriß einer allgemeinen Theorie. Frankfurt: Suhrkamp].

(1995). Why 'Systems Theory'? Cybernetics & human knowing, 3, 3-10 [(1992). Hvorfor „Systemteorie"? In Jacobsen J. C. (Ed.), Autopoiesis. En introduktion til Niklas Luhmanns verden af systemer (10-20, 197-200). Copenhagen: Forlaget Politisk Revy].

(1995). The Two Sociologies and the Theory of Society. Thesis Eleven, 43, 28-47 [(1993). „Was ist der Fall?" und „Was steckt dahinter?". Die zwei Soziologien und die Gesellschaftstheorie. Zeitschrift für Soziologie, 22, 245-260].

(1995). The Challenge of Being New. In Salzburger Kunstverein (Ed.), Original. Symposium Salzburger Kunstverein (51-55). Ostfildern: Cantz [(1995). Neu-sein als Herausforderung. Ibidem (45-50)].

(1995). Society, Meaning, Religion—Based on Self-Reference. In Bruce S. (Ed.), The Sociology of Religion (245-260). Vol. 1. Aldershot Hants: Edward Elgar].

(1995). Theory of a Different Order. A Conversation with Katherine Hayles and Niklas Luhmann. In Knodt, E., Rasch W., & Wolfe, C. (Eds.), The Politics of Systems and Environments (7-36). Part II, Minneapolis: University of Minnesota Press. Reprint (2000). In Rasch, W. (Ed.), Niklas Luhmann's Modernity. The Paradoxes of Differentiation (171-194). Stanford UP. Reprint (2000). In Rasch, W., & Wolfe, C. (Eds.), Observing Complexity. Systems Theory and Postmodernity (111-136). Minneapolis: University of Minnesota Press.

(1995). Why Does Society Describe Itself as Postmodern? Cultural Critique, 30, 171-186. Reprint (2000). In Rasch, W. & Wolfe, C. (Eds.), Observing Complexity. Systems Theory and Postmodernity (35-50). Minneapolis: University of Minnesota Press.

(1995). The Paradox of Observing Systems. In Cultural Critique 31, 37-55. Reprint (2002). In Luhmann, N., Theories of Distinction (79-93).

(1995). Interview with Professor Niklas Luhmann, Oslo April, 2. Cybernetics & Human Knowing, 3, 23-26.

(1996). Complexity, Structural Contingencies and Value Conflicts. In Heelas, P., Lash, S., & Morris, P. (Eds.), Detraditionalization. Critical Reflections on Authority and Identity (59-71). Cambridge/Oxford: Blackwell.

(1996). The Sociology of the Moral and Ethics. International Sociology, 11, 27-36.

(1996). On the Scientific Context of the Concept of Communication. Social Science Information, 35, 257-267.

(1996). A Redescription of „Romantic Art". MLN, 111, 506-522 [(1996). Eine Redeskription „romantischer Kunst". In Fohrmann, J., & Müller H. (Eds.), Systemtheorie der Literatur (325-344). Munich: Fink. Reprint (2008). In Luhmann, N., Schriften zu Kunst und Literatur (353-372). Frankfurt: Suhrkamp].

(1996). Quod omnes tangit. Remarks on Jürgen Habermas's Legal Theory. Cardozo Law Review, 17, 883-899. Reprint (1998). In Rosenfeld, M., & Arato, A. (Eds.), Habermas on Law and Democracy. Critical Exchanges (157-172). Berkeley, Cal./Los Angeles/London: University of California Press [(1993). Quod omnes tangit. Anmerkungen zur Rechtstheorie von Jürgen Habermas. Aus Anlaß von Jürgen Habermas, Faktizität und Geltung: Beiträge zur Diskurstheorie des Rechts und des demokratischen Rechtsstaats, Frankfurt a. M.: Suhrkamp 1992. Rechtshistorisches Journal, 12, 36-56].

(1996). Modern Society Shocked by its Risks. Department of Sociology, The University of Hongkong, Occasional Papers 17. Hongkong.

(1997). Limits of Steering. Theory, culture & society, 4, 41-57 [(1988). Grenzen der Steuerung. In Luhmann, N., Die Wirtschaft der Gesellschaft (324-349). Frankfurt: Suhrkamp].

(1997). The Control of Intransparency. Systems Research and Behavioral Science, 14, 359-371 [(1997). Die Kontrolle von Intransparenz. in: Ahlemeyer, H. W., & Königswieser, R. (Eds.), Komplexität managen. Strategien, Konzepte und Fallbeispiele (51-76). Frankfurt/Wiesbaden: Frankfurter Allgemeine Zeitung/Gabler].

(1997). Globalization or World Society. How to Conceive of Modern Society? International Review of Sociology, 7, 67-79.

(1998). Politics and Economy. Thesis Eleven, 53, 1-9.

(1998). Observations on Modernity. Stanford UP [(1992). Beobachtungen der Moderne. Opladen: Westdeutscher Verlag].

(1998). Modernity in Contemporary Society. In Luhmann, N., Observations on Modernity (1-21).

(1998). European Rationality. In Luhmann, N., Observations on Modernity (22-43).

(1999). The Concept of Society. In Elliott, A. (Ed.), The Blackwell Reader in Contemporary Social Theory (143-155). London: Blackwell [(1991). Pojem družbe. In Teorija in praksa, 28, 1175-1185].

(1999). The Paradox of Form. In Baecker, D. (Ed.), Problems of Form (15-26). Stanford UP [(1993). Die Paradoxie der Form. In Baecker, D. (Ed.), Probleme der Form (197-212). Frankfurt: Suhrkamp].

(1999). Sign as Form. In Baecker, D. (Ed.), Problems of Form (46-63). Stanford UP [(1993). Zeichen als Form. In Baecker D. (Ed.), Probleme der Form (45-69). Frankfurt: Suhrkamp].

(2000). Problems of Reflection in the System of Education. Münster/New York: Waxmann [(1979). Reflexionsprobleme im Erziehungssystem. Stuttgart: Klett-Cotta (together with Karl Eberhard Schorr). Reprint (1988). With a „Nachwort 1988", Frankfurt: Suhrkamp].

(2000). Art as a Social System. Stanford UP [(1995). Die Kunst der Gesellschaft. Frankfurt: Suhrkamp].

(2000). The Reality of the Mass Media. Stanford UP [(1996). Die Realität der Massenmedien. Opladen: Westdeutscher Verlag].

(2001). Notes on the Project "Poetry and Social Theory". Theory, Culture & Society, 18, 15-27 [(1999). Notizen zum Projekt „Lyrik und Gesellschaftstheorie". Soziale Systeme, 5, 214-237].

(2002). Husserl, Science, Modernity, in Theories of Distinction: Redescriptions of the Descriptions of Modernity (33-60) [(1996). Die neuzeitlichen Wissenschaften und die Phänomenologie. Wien: Picus].

(2002). Theories of Distinction: Rediscriptions of the Descriptions of Modernity. Ed. by Rasch, W. Stanford UP.

(2002). Identity—What or How? In Luhmann, N., Theories of Distinction (113-127) [(1990). Identität—was oder wie? In Luhmann, N., Soziologische Aufklärung 5 (14-30)].

(2003). Organization. In Bakken, T., & Hernes, T. (Eds.), Autopoietic Organization Theory. Drawing on Niklas Luhmann's Social Systems Perspective (31-52). Herndon/Malmö/Oslo: Copenhagen Business School Press/Liber/Abstrakt [(1988). Organisation. In Küpper, W., & Ortmann, G. (Eds.), Mikropolitik. Rationalität, Macht und Spiele in Organisationen (165-185). Opladen: Westdeutscher Verlag].

(2004) Law as a Social System. Oxford/New York: Oxford UP [(1993). Das Recht der Gesellschaft. Frankfurt: Suhrkamp].

(2006). Communication Barriers in Management Consulting. In Seidl, D., & Becker, K. H. (Eds.), Niklas Luhmann and Organization Studies (351-364). Malmö: Liber & CBS Press [(1989). Kommunikationssperren in der Unternehmensberatung. In Luhmann, N., & Fuchs, P., Reden und Schweigen (209-227)].

(2006). The Paradox of Decision Making. In Seidl, D., & Becker, K. H. (Eds.), Niklas Luhmann and Organization Studies (85-106). Malmö: Liber & CBS Press [(1993). Die Paradoxie des Entscheidens. Verwaltungsarchiv, 84, 287-310].

(2006). The Autopoiesis of Social Systems. In Seidl, D., & Becker, K. H. (Eds.), Niklas Luhmann and Organization Studies (64-84). Malmö: Liber & CBS Press.

(2006). The Concept of Autopoiesis. In Seidl, D., & Becker, K. H. (Eds.), Niklas Luhmann and Organization Studies (54-63). Malmö: Liber & CBS Press [(2000). Translation of the chapter Organisation als autopoietisches System. In Luhmann, N., Organisation und Entscheidung (44-55). Westdeutscher Verlag: Opladen].

(2008). Are There Still Indispensable Norms in Our Society? Soziale Systeme, 14, 18-37 [(1993). Gibt es in unserer Gesellschaft noch unverzichtbare Normen? Heidelberg: C. F. Müller].

(2008). Beyond Barbarism. Soziale Systeme, 14, 38-46 [(1995). Jenseits von Barbarei. In Luhmann, N., Gesellschaftsstruktur und Semantik. Studien zur Wissenssoziologie der modernen Gesellschaft (138-150). Vol. 4. Frankfurt: Suhrkamp].

(2010). Love. A sketch. London: Polity Press [(2008). Liebe. Eine Übung. Ed. by Kieserling, A. Frankfurt: Suhrkamp].
(2012). Introduction to Systems Theory. Cambridge: Polity Press [(2002). Einführung in die Systemtheorie. Ed. by Baecker, D. Heidelberg: Carl-Auer-Systeme Verlag].
(2012/2013). Theory of Society. Vol. 1 and vol. 2. Stanford UP [(1997). Die Gesellschaft der Gesellschaft, 2 vol. Frankfurt: Suhrkamp].
(2013). A Systems Theory of Religion. Stanford UP [(2000). Die Religion der Gesellschaft. Ed. by Kieserling, A. Frankfurt: Suhrkamp].
(2018). The New Boss. Cambridge: Polity [(2016). Der neue Chef. Berlin: Suhrkamp]
(2018). Organization and Decision, Cambridge/New York: Cambridge UP [(2000). Organisation und Entscheidung. Ed. by Baecker, D. Opladen: Westdeutscher Verlag]

Publications in German (books and cited references)

(1963). Verwaltungsfehler und Vertrauensschutz: Möglichkeiten gesetzlicher Regelung der Rücknehmbarkeit von Verwaltungsakten. Berlin: Duncker & Humblot (together with Franz Becker).
(1964). Funktionen und Folgen formaler Organisation. Berlin: Duncker & Humblot. 4th ed. (1995). With an "Epilog 1994".
(1964) Funktionale Methode und Systemtheorie. In Soziale Welt 15, 1-25. Reprint (1970). In Luhmann, N., Soziologische Aufklärung (31-53).
(1965). Öffentlich-rechtliche Entschädigung rechtspolitisch betrachtet. Berlin: Duncker & Humblot.
(1965). Grundrechte als Institution: Ein Beitrag zur politischen Soziologie. Berlin: Duncker & Humblot.
(1966). Recht und Automation in der öffentlichen Verwaltung: Eine verwaltungswissenschaftliche Untersuchung. Berlin: Duncker & Humblot.
(1966). Theorie der Verwaltungswissenschaft: Bestandsaufnahme und Entwurf. Cologne/Berlin.
(1966). Automation in der öffentlichen Verwaltung. Hamburg: Verlag Deutsche Polizei (together with Wilhelm Wortmann).

(1967) Soziologische Aufklärung. In Soziale Welt 18, 97-123. Reprint (1970). In Luhmann, N., Soziologische Aufklärung (66-91). Reprint (2005). Wiesbaden: VS Verlag für Sozialwissenschaften (83-115).
(1968). Zweckbegriff und Systemrationalität: Über die Funktion von Zwecken in sozialen Systemen. Tübingen: J.C.B. Mohr, Paul Siebeck. Reprint (1973). Frankfurt: Suhrkamp.
(1969). Legitimation durch Verfahren. Neuwied/Berlin: Luchterhand. Reprint (1983). Frankfurt: Suhrkamp.
(1970). Soziologische Aufklärung: Aufsätze zur Theorie sozialer Systeme. Cologne/Opladen: Westdeutscher Verlag. 3rd ed. (1972). With the title Soziologische Aufklärung 1. Reprint (2005). Wiesbaden: VS Verlag für Sozialwissenschaften.
(1970). Gesellschaft. In Luhmann, N., Soziologische Aufklärung (137-153). Reprint (2005). Wiesbaden: VS Verlag für Sozialwissenschaften (173-193).
(1971). Theorie der Gesellschaft oder Sozialtechnologie—Was leistet die Systemforschung? Frankfurt: Suhrkamp (together with Jürgen Habermas).
(1971). Politische Planung: Aufsätze zur Soziologie von Politik und Verwaltung. Opladen: Westdeutscher Verlag.
(1972). Religion—System und Sozialisation. Darmstadt/Neuwied: Luchterhand (together with Karl-Wilhelm Dahm & Dieter Stoodt).
(1973). Personal im öffentlichen Dienst: Eintritt und Karrieren. Baden-Baden: Nomos (together with Renate Mayntz).
(1974). Rechtssystem und Rechtsdogmatik. Stuttgart: Kohlhammer.
(1975). Konfliktpotentiale in sozialen Systemen. In Landeszentrale für politische Bildung des Landes Nordrhein-Westfalen (Ed.), Der Mensch in den Konfliktfeldern der Gegenwart. Cologne: Verlag Wissenschaft & Politik (67-74).
(1975). Soziologische Aufklärung 2: Aufsätze zur Theorie der Gesellschaft. Opladen: Westdeutscher Verlag. Reprint (2005). Wiesbaden: VS Verlag für Sozialwissenschaften.
(1975). Über die Funktion der Negation in sinnkonstituierenden Systemen. In Weinrich, H. (Ed.), Positionen der Negativität. Munich: Fink (201-218). Reprint (1981). In Luhmann, N., Soziologische Aufklärung 3 (35-49). Reprint (2005). Wiesbaden: VS Verlag für Sozialwissenschaft (41-57).
(1977). Funktion der Religion. Frankfurt: Suhrkamp. Engl. transl. of pp. 72-181 (1984). Religious Dogmatics and the Evolution of Societies. New York/Toronto: Edwin Mellen Press.

(1977). Interpenetration. Zum Verhältnis personaler und sozialer Systeme. In Zeitschrift für Soziologie 6, 62-76. Reprint (1981). In Luhmann, N., Soziologische Aufklärung 3 (151-169). Reprint (2005). Wiesbaden: VS Verlag für Sozialwissenschaft (172-192).

(1978). Interpenetration bei Parsons. In Zeitschrift für Soziologie 7, 299-302.

(1979). Schematismen der Interaktion. In Kölner Zeitschrift für Soziologie und Sozialpsychologie 31 (237-255). Reprint (1981). In Luhmann, N., Soziologische Aufklärung 3. Soziales System, Gesellschaft, Organisation. Opladen: Westdeutscher Verlag, 1981 (81-100). Reprint (2005) Wiesbaden: VS Verlag für Sozialwissenschaft (93-114).

(1980). Gesellschaftsstruktur und Semantik: Studien zur Wissenssoziologie der modernen Gesellschaft I. Frankfurt: Suhrkamp.

(1980). Temporalstrukturen des Handlungssystems. Zum Zusammenhang von Handlungs- und Systemtheorie. In Schluchter, W. (Ed.), Verhalten, Handeln und System. Talcott Parsons' Beitrag zur Entwicklung der Sozialwissenschaften, Frankfurt a. M.: Suhrkamp, 32-67. Reprint (1981). In Luhmann, N., Soziologische Aufklärung 3 (126-150). Reprint (2005). Wiesbaden: VS Verlag für Sozialwissenschaft (143-171).

(1981). Gesellschaftsstruktur und Semantik: Studien zur Wissenssoziologie der modernen Gesellschaft II. Frankfurt: Suhrkamp.

(1981). Ausdifferenzierung des Rechts: Beiträge zur Rechtssoziologie und Rechtstheorie. Frankfurt, Suhrkamp.

(1981). Soziologische Aufklärung 3: Soziales System, Gesellschaft, Organisation. Opladen: Westdeutscher Verlag. Reprint (2005). Wiesbaden: VS Verlag für Sozialwissenschaft.

(1982). Zwischen Technologie und Selbstreferenz. Fragen an die Pädagogik. Frankfurt: Suhrkamp (together with Karl Eberhard Schorr, Eds.).

(1983). Medizin und Gesellschaftstheorie. I: Medizin, Mensch, Gesellschaft 8, 168-175.

(1983). Anspruchsinflation im Krankheitssystem. Eine Stellungnahme aus gesellschaftstheoretischer Sicht. In: Herder-Dorneich, P., & Schuller, A. (Eds.), Die Anspruchsspirale. Schicksal oder Systemdefekt? 3. Kölner Kolloquium. Stuttgart/Berlin/Köln/Mainz: Kohlhammer (28-49).

(1985). Die Autopoiesis des Bewußtseins. In Soziale Welt 36, 402-446. Reprint (1987). In Hahn, A., & Kapp V. (Eds.), Selbstthematisierung und Selbstzeugnis. Bekenntnis und Geständnis. Frankfurt: Suhrkamp (25-94). Reprint (1995). In Luhmann, N., Soziologische Aufklärung 6 (55-112). Reprint (2005). Wiesbaden: VS Verlag für Sozialwissenschaften (55-108).

(1985). Von der allmählichen Auszehrung der Werte. Sind die Zeiten gesellschaftlicher Utopien für immer vorbei? In Voswinkel, G., & von Baudissin, W. (Ed.), Zu neuen Ufern oder Aufbruch in die Sackgasse? Zum Problem des Fortschritts in unserer Zeit. Minden: Stadt Minden (69-76).
(1986). Die soziologische Beobachtung des Rechts. Frankfurt: Metzner.
(1986). Die Codierung des Rechtssystems. In Rechtstheorie 17, 171-203.
(1986). Zwischen Intransparenz und Verstehen. Fragen an die Pädagogik. Frankfurt: Suhrkamp (together with Karl Eberhard Schorr, Eds.).(1986). „Distinctions directrices": Über Codierung von Semantiken und Systemen. In Neidhardt, F., Lepsius, M. R., Weiß, J. (Eds.), Kultur und Gesellschaft. Special Issue n. 27 of Kölner Zeitschrift für Soziologie und Sozialpsychologie, 145-161. Reprint (1987). In Luhmann, N., Soziologische Aufklärung 4 (13-31). Westdeutscher Verlag: Opladen.
(1986). Codierung und Programmierung. Bildung und Selektion im Erziehungssystem. In Tenorth, H.-E. (Ed.), Allgemeine Bildung: Analysen zu ihrer Wirklichkeit, Versuche über ihre Zukunft. Weinheim/München: Juventa (154-182). Reprint (1987). In Luhmann, N., Soziologische Aufklärung 4 (182-201). Reprint (2005). Wiesbaden: VS Verlag für Sozialwissenschaften (193-213). Reprint (2004). In Luhmann,N., Schriften zur Pädagogik. Ed. By Lenzen, D. Frankfurt: Suhrkamp (23-47).
(1986). Die Zukunft der Demokratie. In Akademie der Künste Berlin (West) (Ed.), Der Traum der Vernunft. Vom Elend der Aufklärung. Eine Veranstaltungsreihe der Akademie der Künste Berlin. Zweite Folge. Darmstadt/Neuwied: Luchterhand (207-217).
(1988). Selbstreferentielle Systeme. In Simon, F. B. (Ed.), Lebende Systeme: Wirklichkeitskonstruktionen in der systemischen Therapie (47-53). Berlin.
(1988). Sozialsystem Familie. In System Familie 1, 75-91. Reprint (enlarged: 1990). In Luhmann, N., Soziologische Aufklärung 5 (196-217). Reprint (2005). Wiesbaden: VS Verlag für Sozialwissenschaften (189-209).
(1987). Soziologische Aufklärung 4: Beiträge zur funktionalen Differenzierung der Gesellschaft. Opladen: Westdeutscher Verlag. Reprint (2005). Wiesbaden: VS Verlag für Sozialwissenschaften.
(1987). Archimedes und wir: Interviews. Ed. by Baecker, D., & Stanitzek, G. Berlin: Merve Verlag.
(1987). Autopoiesis als soziologischer Begriff. In: Haferkamp, H., & Schmid, M. (Eds.), Sinn, Kommunikation und soziale Differenzierung. Beiträge zu Luhmanns Theorie sozialer Systeme. Frankfurt: Suhrkamp (307-324).
(1988). Die Wirtschaft der Gesellschaft. Frankfurt: Suhrkamp.

(1988). Erkenntnis als Konstruktion. Bern: Benteli.
(1989). Gesellschaftsstruktur und Semantik: Studien zur Wissenssoziologie der modernen Gesellschaft III. Frankfurt: Suhrkamp.
(1989). Individuum, Individualität, Individualismus. In Gesellschaftsstruktur und Semantik. Studien zur Wissenssoziologie der modernen Gesellschaft III (149-258).
(1989). Reden und Schweigen. Frankfurt: Suhrkamp (together with Peter Fuchs).
(1989). Geheimnis, Zeit und Ewigkeit. In Luhmann, N., & Fuchs, P., Reden und Schweigen (101-137).
(1989). Gleichzeitigkeit und Synchronisation. Grund- und Integrativwissenschaftliche Fakultät, Wien: Institut für Soziologie. Reprint (1990). In Luhmann, N., Soziologische Aufklärung 5 (95-130).
(1990). Beobachter: Konvergenz der Erkenntnistheorien? Munich: Fink (together with Humberto Maturana, Mikio Namiki, Volker Redder & Francisco Varela).
(1990). Soziologische Aufklärung 5: Konstruktivistische Perspektiven. Opladen: Westdeutscher Verlag. Reprint (2005). Wiesbaden: VS Verlag für Sozialwissenschaften.
(1990). Die Wissenschaft der Gesellschaft. Frankfurt: Suhrkamp. Engl. transl. of chapter 10 („Die Modernität der Wissenschaft") (1994). New German Critique, 61, 9-23. Reprint (2002). In Theories of Distinction: Rediscriptions of the Descriptions of Modernity (61-75).
(1990). Zwischen Anfang und Ende. Fragen an die Pädagogik. Frankfurt: Suhrkamp (together with Karl Eberhard Schorr, Eds.).(1990). Unbeobachtbare Welt. Über Kunst und Architektur. Bielefeld: Haux (together with Frederick D. Bunsen & Dirk Baecker).
(1990). Weltkunst. In Luhmann, N., et al. Unbeobachtbare Welt (7-45). Reprint (2008). In Luhmann, N., Schriften zu Kunst und Literatur (189-245).
(1990). Risiko und Gefahr. In Luhmann, N., Soziologische Aufklärung 5. Konstruktivistische Perspektiven. Opladen: Westdeutscher Verlag (131-169). Reprint (2005). Wiesbaden: VS Verlag für Sozialwissenschaften, (126-162).
(1990). Glück und Unglück der Kommunikation in Familien. Zur Genese von Pathologien. In Luhmann, N., Soziologische Aufklärung 5 (218-227). Reprint (revised: 1992). In Königswieser, R., Lutz Ch. (Ed.), Das systemisch evolutionäre Management. Der neue Horizont für Unternehmer. Wien: Orac (298-306).
(1990). Der medizinische Code. In Soziologische Aufklärung 5 (183-195).

(1991). Die Form „Person". In Soziale Welt 42, 166-175. Reprint (1995). In Luhmann, N., Soziologische Aufklärung 6 (142-154). Reprint (2005). Wiesbaden: VS Verlag für Sozialwissenschaften (137-148).
(1991). Selbstorganisation und Information im politischen System. In Niedersen, U., & Pohlmann, L. (Ed.), Der Mensch in Ordnung und Chaos, Selbstorganisation. Berlin: Duncker & Humblot (11-26).
(1992). Teoria della società. Milano: Franco Angeli (together with Raffaele De Giorgi).
(1992). Universität als Milieu. Ed. by Kieserling, A. Bielefeld: Haux.
(1992). Zwischen Absicht und Person. Fragen an die Pädagogik. Frankfurt: Suhrkamp (together with Karl Eberhard Schorr, Eds.).
(1992). System und Absicht der Erziehung. In Luhmann, N., & Schorr K.-E. (Eds.), Zwischen Absicht und Person. Fragen an die Pädagogik. Frankfurt: Suhrkamp, 102-124.
(1993). Das Paradox der Menschenrechte und drei Formen seiner Entfaltung. In Aarnio, A., Paulson, S.L., Weinberger, O., von Wright, G.H., & Wyduckel D. (Eds.), Rechtsnorm und Rechtswirklichkeit. Festschrift für Werner Krawietz zum 60. Geburtstag. Berlin: Duncker und Humblot (539-546). Reprint (1995). In Luhmann, N., Soziologische Aufklärung 6 (229-236).
(1994). Inklusion und Exklusion. In Berding, H. (Ed.), Nationales Bewußtsein und kollektive Identität. Frankfurt: Suhrkamp (15-45). Reprint in (1995). Luhmann, N., Soziologische Aufklärung 6 (237-264).
(1995). Soziologische Aufklärung 6: Die Soziologie und der Mensch. Opladen: Westdeutscher Verlag. Reprint (2005). Wiesbaden: VS Verlag für Sozialwissenschaften.
(1995). Gesellschaftsstruktur und Semantik: Studien zur Wissenssoziologie der modernen Gesellschaft IV. Frankfurt: Suhrkamp.
(1996). Protest: Systemtheorie und soziale Bewegungen. Ed. and introduced by Hellmann, K.-U. Frankfurt: Suhrkamp.
(1996). Zwischen System und Umwelt. Fragen an die Pädagogik. Frankfurt: Suhrkamp (together with Karl Eberhard Schorr, Eds.).
(1996). Die Sinnform Religion. In Soziale Systeme 2, 3-33.
(2000). Organisation und Entscheidung. Opladen: Westdeutscher Verlag.
(2000). Die Politik der Gesellschaft. Ed. by Kieserling, A. Frankfurt: Suhrkamp.
(2002). Das Erziehungssystem der Gesellschaft. Ed. by Lenzen, D. Frankfurt: Suhrkamp.

(2004). Schriften zur Pädagogik. Ed. and introduced by Lenzen, D. Frankfurt: Suhrkamp.
(2005). Einführung in die Theorie der Gesellschaft. Ed. by Baecker, D. Heidelberg: Carl-Auer-Systeme Verlag.
(2008). Ideenevolution. Ed. by Kieserling, A. Frankfurt: Suhrkamp.
(2008). Die Moral der Gesellschaft. Ed. by Horster, D. Frankfurt: Suhrkamp.
(2008). Schriften zu Kunst und Literatur. Ed. by Werber, N. Frankfurt: Suhrkamp.
(2013). Politische Soziologie. Frankfurt: Suhrkamp. Ed. by Kieserling, A. Reprint (2015).
(2013). Kontingenz und Recht. Rechtstheorie im interdisziplinären Zusammenhang. Ed. by Schmidt, J.F.K.. Berlin: Suhrkamp.
(2013). Macht im System. Ed. by Kieserling, A. Berlin: Suhrkamp.
(2014). Klaus Dammann (ed.), Wie halten Sie's mit Außerirdischen, Herr Luhmann? Nicht unmerkwürdige Gespräche mit Niklas Luhmann. Berlin: Kulturverlag Kadmos.
(2016). Der neue Chef. Ed. by and with an afterword of Kaube, J. Berlin: Suhrkamp.
(2017). Die Kontrolle von Intransparenz. Ed. by and with an afterword of Baecker, D. Berlin: Suhrkamp.
(2017). Systemtheorie der Gesellschaft. Ed. by Schmidt, J.F.K., & Kieserling, A. Berlin: Suhrkamp.
(2018). Schriften zur Organisation 1. Die Wirklichkeit der Organisation. Ed. by Lukas, E. & Tacke, V. Wiesbaden: Springer.
(2019). Schriften zur Organisation 2. Theorie organisierter Sozialsysteme. Ed. by Lukas, E. & Tacke, V. Wiesbaden: Springer.
(2019). Schriften zur Organisation 3. Gesellschaftliche Differenzierung. Ed. by Lukas, E. & Tacke, V. Wiesbaden: Springer.
(2020): Schriften zur Organisation 4. Reform und Beratung. Ed. by Lukas, E. & Tacke, V. Wiesbaden: Springer.

Bielefeld University Press

Haun Saussy
Are We Comparing Yet?
On Standards, Justice, and Incomparability

2019, 112 p., pb.
19,99 € (DE), 978-3-8376-4977-2
E-Book: available as free open access publication
PDF: ISBN 978-3-8394-4977-6

Angelika Epple, Walter Erhart, Johannes Grave (eds.)
Practices of Comparing
Towards a New Understanding of a Fundamental Human Practice

June 2020, 406 p., pb., col. ill.
39,00 € (DE), 978-3-8376-5166-9
E-Book: available as free open access publication
PDF: ISBN 978-3-8394-5166-3

Oliver Flügel-Martinsen, Franziska Martinsen, Stephen W. Sawyer, Daniel Schulz (eds.)
Pierre Rosanvallon's Political Thought
Interdisciplinary Approaches

2018, 248 p., pb.
39,99 € (DE), 978-3-8376-4652-8
E-Book: available as free open access publication
PDF: ISBN 978-3-8394-4652-2

Leseproben, weitere Informationen und Bestellmöglichkeiten finden Sie unter www.transcript-verlag.de